TABLE OF CONTENTS

SPRING 2022
VOLUME 2, NUMBER 3

EDITOR
LEON WIESELTIER

MANAGING EDITOR
CELESTE MARCUS

———

PUBLISHER
BILL REICHBLUM

———

JOURNAL DESIGN
WILLIAM VAN RODEN

WEB DESIGN
HOT BRAIN

Liberties is a publication of the Liberties Journal Foundation, a nonpartisan 501(c)(3) organization based in Washington, D.C. devoted to educating the general public about the history, current trends, and possibilities of culture and politics. The Foundation seeks to inform today's cultural and political leaders, deepen the understanding of citizens, and inspire the next generation to participate in the democratic process and public service.

———

Engage
To learn more please go to libertiesjournal.com

Subscribe
To subscribe or with any questions about your subscription, please go to libertiesjournal.com

ISBN 978-1-7357187-6-7
ISSN 2692-3904

———

EDITORIAL OFFICES
1604 New Hampshire Avenue NW
Washington, DC 20009

———

DIGITAL
@READLIBERTIES
LIBERTIESJOURNAL.COM

Liberties

LAURA KIPNIS

Gender: A Melee

The king was pregnant.
URSULA K. LE GUIN,
THE LEFT HAND OF DARKNESS

It turns out the supply-side cheerleader George Gilder was more correct than not when he forecast, in the poignantly titled *Sexual Suicide* in 1973, that women playing at being men would spell the collapse of Western civilization and probably the social order itself. What he meant by sexual suicide was "the abolition of biological differences between men and women" — in his day, feminists demanding paychecks and forcing men to do housework, and thereby selfishly violating the pact they were supposed to be upholding with nature. Nature had endowed humankind with different sorts of bodies, from which different social roles followed: motherhood for some, breadwinning for others. Nature did not intend men to clean toilets! Or women to go to work, needless to say. It wasn't just childbearing that society required from women; as the morally superior gender we were also meant to dragoon reluctant men into playing *patres familias,* according to Gilder, luring them into domestic cages like lion tamers at the circus, civilizing their beastly sex drives into socially productive ones. If we shirk the task, everything falls apart. Gay liberation was thus another sore spot in Gilder's catalogue of contemporary woe, a world where women's charms held no sway and male carnality thus ran amuck.

How vulnerable the "primacy of the biological realm" would turn out to be, how tenuous its hold on the species if each of us had to pledge fealty to the gender binary to keep civilization afloat. How confident can nature's defenders really be in the selling power of this story? After all, alarm bells aplenty have rung over the last half century yet have thus far failed to herd those renegade female factions back into their kitchens.

And look around now! Gender is more of a clusterfuck than ever, and yes, civilization's destruction indeed looms nearer: birthrates have dropped below replacement rates around the globe, down four percent in the United States in 2020 alone. Male breadwinner families are on the extinction watch list. And the damned liberationists still aren't happy. Today's gender vanguards — trans activists, the "genderqueer" — want to sever the link between biology and gender entirely, letting men become women and women men, surgically acquiring penises and cooches, rebranding important body parts with gender neutral language ("front hole" for vagina), not to mention poisoning innocent children with cross-sex hormones and puberty blockers. (Far more patriotic to mow them down with assault weapons, at least according to the child welfare experts of the GOP.) Some members of the younger generation want to abolish gender entirely, demanding the whole English language be revised to accommodate them and their impossible-to-remember pronoun preferences.

Where gender distinctions blur, monsters seem to lurk, like those snarling creatures at the edge of the world on sixteenth-century maps warning sailors away from the abyss. I was thinking about the monster problem recently while reading an interesting history tracing the relation between the invention of endocrinology and the growing demand for gender reassignment treatments. Called *Changing Sex: Transsexualism, Technology, and the Ides of Gender,* from 1995, it opens with the author, Bernice L. Hausman, a mostly lucid writer, confessing in the book's preface that she'd been pregnant while revising the manuscript, and was "perhaps one of few expectant mothers who worry they will give birth to a hermaphrodite." I was therefore not surprised when the book takes an anxious anti-trans swerve in its epilogue, though prior chapters provide fascinating facts about the discovery of glandular therapies in the late nineteenth century. This includes the story of a researcher named Charles-Édouard Brown-Séquard, who in 1889 found, by injecting himself with canine (or possibly monkey) testicular tissue, that what would later be called testosterone had sexually rejuvenating effects in men. Thousands of men were soon arranging to have themselves likewise injected, though whatever rejuvenation followed was later thought to be a placebo effect — the testes don't actually store testosterone, it turns out.

If commentators as disparate as Gilder and Hausman are, in their different ways, a little panicky about the gender system collapsing, if both envision nature-defying creatures (feminists, hermaphrodites) snapping at them from the abyss, then we're in the realm of what the fairy tale expert Marina Warner calls the monstrous imagination. Aroused by scenes of chaos and emergence, it mirrors our lack of understanding back to us in the form of menacing hybrids, typically depicted as scary inhabitants of dark underworlds. Among the chaotic emergent things no one much understands (especially these days) is gender, despite everyone supposedly having one. Yet what is it, where does it come from? Certainties abound, yet somehow they keep changing. With Western civilization itself a rickety boat navigating these tumultuous waters, perpetually about to sail over the edge into some posthuman future, no wonder the conversation gets a little shrill.

Revolutions are threatening, and what Hausman calls the "new forms of being human" that emerged in the twentieth century *were* revolutionary, especially once "hormones" — so named in 1905 — were extracted (from glands) and then synthesized, leading eventually to new possibilities in gender reassignment procedures. Oddly — though maybe this is just the usual blinkers of an academic with nose pressed to his own research subject (in this case, transsexualism) — Hausman fails to mention that the ability to synthetize hormones also led to the development of birth control pills, first marketed in the United States in 1960, which prevent ovulation in women. It strikes me as weird that Hausman doesn't see that far more widely implemented gender-altering technology as part of the same story, also ushering in new ways of "being human" for roughly a hundred million women worldwide. (Estrogen both figures in hormonal contraception and feminizes men who wish to change sex.) Maybe her pregnancy made her less attuned to this aspect of the narrative, but it's hard to think of anything more consequential for natal females than the ability

9

to effectively control fertility, which radically contested the existing gender regime, not to mention fundamentally transforming the experience of heterosexual sex. (See under: Sexual Revolution, The.)

But how did the old regime manage to uphold itself in the first place when it disadvantaged so many? Conservatives will tell you that gender comes from nature and sits firmly on top of biological sex; these sexual differences are imagined to be binary. But this binary was always rather imaginary — the incidence of intersex babies was always higher than was generally acknowledged. Doctors made capricious medical decisions and interventions to assign those babies to one sex or the other, precisely because gender ideology dictated that binary gender had to be preserved. (Apparently intersexed babies are as common as red hair.)

In other words, a certain bad faith seems to come with this territory, by which I mean a refusal to know what you know. Look at Gilder, famous for touting the very economic policies which crushed the single-paycheck family that *Sexual Suicide* was trying to corral America back into. The signature program of these guys (the *Bell Curve* author Charles Murray was another of the big guns) — suppressing wages and cutting taxes for the rich, shifting income shares from workers to capital — was a program so successful we're still living with the consequences. Everyone's seen the stats about upward redistribution of wealth in the last half century, and the gap keeps widening. As Gilder must know, it wasn't feminism that catapulted women into the labor market in the 1970s, it was stagnant male wages, post-industrialism, and the expansion of the service sector; and then came the economic hits of Reaganomics. When labor was winning, as it had been before 1973 (a bad year, between an oil crisis and a recession), a middle-class household *could* survive on

10

one income, not the two or more that are now the norm for vast swathes of the country, often sans benefits.

But why not finger-point at feminists, those sexual gargoyles, chewing up men and spitting them out, though between the union busting and the job exports, capitalists were doing a lot more chewing and spitting than women ever managed, not that we wouldn't have enjoyed it. Oh, and the declining birthrates? The majority of those recently surveyed in the United States cite childcare costs as the foremost reason not to procreate, along with climate change, another of free market capitalism's great accomplishments. (France, the EU country with the highest birthrate, also funds eighty percent of childcare.) Obviously blaming women, homosexuals, and pornographers for macroeconomic shifts is a better yarn. Behind the monstering process lies an appetite for thrilling perversity, Marina Warner observes, for "lurid scenes of other people's sins" — titillating even while they purport to condemn. (Speaking of titillation: along with feminists Gilder has a peculiar animus about sexologists, who come up frequently, though they can, admittedly, be creepy.)

What if we were to put it as a question instead of an answer: why *has* the traditional gender order lost so many adherents these days? A less hysterical version of Gilder's laments may be found in Francis Fukuyama's account in *The Great Disruption:* in his telling, late capitalism no longer required gender differentiation for the technology and knowledge-based jobs that a post-industrial economy needed to fill. Women didn't suddenly rise up and demand economic independence — Fukuyama goes so far as to call feminism an epiphenomenon of the information society, a symptom of social disruption and not its driver. The explosion of late twentieth-century liberation movements — the sexual revolution, second wave

11

feminism, gay liberation — that freed individuals from the tethers of traditional norms and morals were likewise sparked by the transition to a post-industrial society.

Capitalism smashes things while ushering into existence all sorts of new human freedoms. (Economic equality unfortunately not among them). If the male-female binary is losing its grip on the human psyche as a social organizing principle, and the premise that gender roles are rooted in nature has been crumbling for the last century, the causes are obviously multiple: an increasing focus on personal fulfillment, the decline of patriarchal authority that accompanied men's declining economic fortunes and women's economic independence, and resulting changes in the family structure. Or go back further: as Eli Zaretsky points out in *Capitalism, The Family, and Personal Life*, the gender order has been breaking down since Freud unwittingly hastened its demise by undoing the "knot that tied the sexual instincts to the difference between the sexes."

My point is that maybe feminism and transgenderism aren't separate stories. Maybe the rising reports of gender dysphoria and plummeting birth rates aren't separate stories either. There have always been people who did not fit easily into normative categories but were herded in by threat and force, and who are increasingly breaking loose. Because yes, the old structures are ever more enfeebled, unable to demand fealty. Conformity to their dictates is waning. For some that spells catastrophe, for others it's a circus of possibility. Paul B. Preciado, author of *Countersexual Manifesto* and *Testo Junkie*, billed by *Vice* as a "punk trans philosopher," says that "we're transitioning from being a society which is organized by sexual difference." We're moving from a binary gender and sexuality regime "to a new and different regime that has yet

12

to be named. "In other words: if endocrinology makes bodies malleable, and families instill (slightly) less repression this century than in previous ones, why not explore those possibilities instead of bemoaning the situation? Preciado suggests regarding gender disobedience as a model for social transformation. Why not start implementing "A Day Without Gender" in schools, hospitals, homes, museums and see what happens?

Gilder obviously wasn't wrong that paychecks and the sexual revolution gave women more access to what had traditionally been male prerogatives. (As to whether these were or are "freedoms" is a more complicated discussion.) But the question that Gilder and followers never get around to is this: if capitalism no longer requires gender differences (and soon will barely require workers at all, except for really shitty or "public-facing" jobs), why is it up to the rest of us to keep upholding these differences? What's in it for us?

That the snarling creatures at the edge of the gender abyss were once feminists now sounds quaint, since for today's gender liberationists (trans activists, "enbys," intersectionalists) the feminists are toothless and mainstream, also complicit in monstrous historical crimes. At least four books with "white feminism" in the title were published in 2021 alone; the term is not used with approbation. In the updated version of the story, white women are the ones responsible for electing Donald Trump — even those who voted or worked for Bernie — and will forever be saddled with the humiliating label "Karen" as payback.

In another twist, weirdly it's now feminists — well, a certain breed of feminist, mostly the dreaded white ones —

13

wielding the "nature" card, demanding that the old binaries be kowtowed to, otherwise monsters will get us. In Gilder's iconography of gender catastrophe, the monsters were women in pants; in the updated version they're wearing skirts, but disaster still beckons: J.K Rowling has been mounting alarms about the monsters in skirts — that is, trans women (assigned male at birth but who identify and live as women), who are supposedly haunting women's bathrooms and changing rooms, intent on sexually assaulting natal females. None of this has been great for her brand, but she seems undaunted. Among Rowling's fears are that if gender self-identification laws go into effect in the United Kingdom, trans people will be allowed to change the gender on their birth certificates without going through the previous gauntlet of psychiatric diagnosis and permission, and then any man who says he identifies as a woman would be able to get a Gender Recognition Certificate and state sanctioned access to gender-segregated facilities.

To inject a bit of reality into this anxious morass, the fact is that no one is stationed at the changing room entrances and public bathrooms checking birth or gender certificates now, so how would banning gender self-identification keep trans people out of non-state-run segregated spaces? There are, to be sure, no shortage of vigorous informal policing mechanisms not infrequently inflicted on trans people who don't sufficiently pass muster (are "clocked" as the wrong sex) in civic spaces, gender-segregated and not. Among the pernicious things about Rowling's statements is the likelihood of them empowering other women to make scenes when in proximity to anyone whose gender presentation is not to their standards, people who just needed somewhere to urinate when out for the day.

14

In a statement articulating these anxieties, Rowling revealed that she was herself a survivor of domestic abuse and sexual assault, citing this history as a reason for opposing gender reforms. She regards herself as a vulnerable party in the emerging gender order. Yet she doesn't appear to have been assaulted by a trans woman or a man masquerading as a woman. Then why shift responsibility for male violence against women onto trans people who, it is widely acknowledged, are disproportionately victims of violence and harassment themselves, especially when forced into facilities that don't align with their chosen gender? Rowling did acknowledge that the majority of trans-identified people pose no threat to anyone, yet the gender self-recognition movement was still "offering cover to predators like few before it."

Are there really legions of roving trans women predators out there attacking other women, aside from "problematic" Brian De Palma homages to Hitchcock? (*Dressed to Kill* is the *locus classicus* — spoiler alert: the psychiatrist did it.) Like Rowling, the feminist philosopher Kathleen Stock seems to think so. Until recently a professor at University of Sussex, Stock voluntarily resigned her post in 2021 saying that she had been subject to bullying and harassment because of her views on transgender identity, and indeed, there had been a student campaign calling for her dismissal. Even her receipt of an OBE — Officer of the Order of the British Empire — was protested by over six hundred fellow philosophers, though a counter petition signed by two hundred philosophers supported her, or at least supported her academic freedom to say what she wanted about gender.

Reading Stock's essay, "Ignoring Differences Between Men and Women is the Wrong Way to Address Gender Dysphoria," from 2019, it's easy to see why she is controversial. Things start out reasonably enough, with Stock delineating the difference between what she calls "sex eliminationists" — those who argue there's no difference between biological women and trans women because biological sex isn't a meaningful category — and "gender eliminationists," who hold that distinctions between men and women aren't meaningful, and we should treat all humans the same. From there things become, to my mind, exceedingly fuzzy. Stock argues that because "there will always be some social stereotypes about the sexes that remain programmed in our minds, if only because they correspond to statistically recurrent empirical truths about biological men and women," then the most we can reasonably hope for, when it comes to damaging social stereotypes, is to be "gender critical" — "consciously critical of the particularly damaging social stereotypes we collectively uphold, aiming to replace them over time with better and more socially useful ones."

This slides rather fast from social stereotypes to empirical truths. I find myself wondering how Stock, a lesbian active in LGB organizations, can speak so confidently about the empirical realities of gender, while mysteriously oblivious about how recently so-called experts defined a reality in which homosexuality was a pathology — psychological in origin and thus, notoriously, "fixable." Or one where women were unsuited to the professions. Nothing is less stable (or empirical) than social stereotypes about gender, as anyone who reads a work of history or anthropology knows. The traits associated with one or another gender bounce around and reverse over the centuries and between cultures: sometimes men are the more sentimental ones, elsewhere women; men are the lustier ones, no actually it's women (amoral and multi-orgasmic); and so on.

Where I have some sympathy for Rowling and Stock is that the political interests of sexual minorities (gay people),

16

gender minorities (trans people), and feminists (Stock and Rowling are both speaking as feminists) do not always align. While you might be a trans lesbian-feminist, some trans-identified people are also quite attached to the kinds of binary gender distinctions that some feminists would like to abolish. Natal women and trans women have different health and reproductive issues. I don't think natal women need to hold onto some proprietary definition of womanhood, but there are political reasons, in the current political climate and with abortion rights under threat, to acknowledge that biological womanhood disadvantages biological women in ways that will always defeat equality if not addressed. (Trans men, too, can get pregnant and require abortions.) In any case, no one has to be monstered. Nor does cisgender (not being trans) need to be a slur, or "cishet" a synonym for clueless, nor "older generation," though no doubt these disagreements are generationally inflected. But even lumping "cis" women (a term I don't love) into one pile overlooks a lot — for instance, pro- and anti-abortion cis women see their interests very differently. Race complicates things even more.

Trans men and trans women are also not always allies. In fact, the age-old war between the sexes has lately been transposed to intra-trans disputes, with trans women calling out trans men for transmisogyny on Twitter. A trans man I know recently accused certain trans women in our circle of being "hard core bros until like a year ago" and moving through the world expecting the same privileges while moaning about being victims of institutional sexism. The intra-trans tensions broke into public in 2020 in the academic journal *Transgender Studies Quarterly,* when trans theorist Jack Halberstam reviewed trans theorist Andrea Long Chu's book *Females: A Concern* (in a piece funnily titled "Nice Trannies") and accused her of being the Allan Bloom of trans studies, while having "a deep antipathy" to trans men and butches. (Chu was recently appointed book critic at *New York* magazine.)

Personally I'm more interested in political alliances than in gender- or identity-based ones. Clearly identity doesn't in itself predict anyone's political affiliations or savvy. A surprisingly high percentage of trans people surveyed — 36% — were Trump supporters in 2016, according to a peer-reviewed study a year later in the journal *Politics, Groups, and Identities,* to choose one of many available examples. Trying to make sense of this, the study's authors explain that one of the unifying themes in Trump support was anti-feminism; a big way that the GOP has attracted adherents is by signaling that rejecting feminist positions is part of what it means to be a Republican.

The trans versus feminist tensions are hardly new: open warfare was long ago declared between the brand of feminist some label TERFs ("trans exclusionary radical feminists") and the trans community. (Stock and others regard TERF as a slur and insist on "gender critical" as the correct label.) This often unpleasant standoff commenced with a vicious little tract published in 1979 by the radical feminist Janice Raymond titled *The Transsexual Empire: The Making of the She-Male,* which argued that trans women are closet patriarchs who want to colonize women's bodies by parading all the worst stereotypes about them. In the decades since, trans women were often excluded, in not particularly kind ways, from feminist spaces, because feminists such as Rowling declared themselves vulnerable parties, at risk of assault by trans women who came equipped with inborn male aggression despite presenting as women.

Natal men may indeed perpetrate the majority of the violence in the world (though it's been argued that female violence takes more hidden forms, for instance violence against children), but the majority of men are *not* violent. It's men, in fact, not women, who are far more often the victims of violence. The week that everyone was talking about the Gabby Petito murder case (the missing travel blogger who turned out to have been killed by her fiancée) and the grim prevalence of missing women, the FBI annual murder statistics for the previous year were released, according to which roughly seventy-five percent more men were murdered than women (14,146 men, 3,573 women, 35 gender unknown). Obviously women are subject to violence by men, frequently their husbands, boyfriends, and exes, but men are vulnerable to violence by men, too. (As are trans women, especially sex workers, assaulted by straight men who can't own up to attractions that might make them, in their minds, "gay.") Somehow we prefer telling stories about endangered cis women.

Stock, along with Rowling, also seems bent on shunting blame for male violence onto trans women. Stock offers the case of a pre-operative trans woman named Karen White who sexually assaulted two female inmates while housed in a British woman's prison. Described by her neighbors to *The Guardian* as "volatile and violent," White was also a convicted pedophile on remand for grievous bodily harm, burglary, multiple rapes, and other sexual offenses. Does Stock think White is a typical trans woman? Is this even typical cisgender male behavior? Stock seems to think yes. Arguing against those who say that excluding trans women from women-only spaces is analogous to excluding lesbians from women-only spaces, Stock counters that there's no "analogous pattern" of lesbian aggression comparable to patterns of male violence. In other words: trans women *are* men and must shoulder the blame for male violence. And one violent trans woman is a pattern.

19

Is this intellectually honest? I don't think so. As someone pithily tweeted about the sorts of fears circulated by Rowling and Stock, "The reason predatory men aren't becoming trans to prey on women? It's a lot easier to become a cop." In other words, we panic selectively. Reports not infrequently surface about mothers doing violence to, sometimes even murdering, their children. To date there are no attempts to ban motherhood. We see those episodes as anomalies, though non-anomalous enough that there are laws and (generally understaffed) child protection agencies, and of course a thriving memoir sub-genre devoted to abusive mothers. But motherhood is also supposed to be the "natural" condition of things, thus maternal abuse, no matter how many cases a year surface, is always an exception. Whereas an isolated case of a violent trans women is a pattern.

Let me press a little harder on the maternity analogy. Both Rowling and Stock worry that transness is contagious, and young girls will get the idea that changing genders is a good solution to the inherent problems of being female. But *all* our ideas about gender are contagious — that's how culture works — including deep seated ideas such as "maternal instinct." Except that it's not an instinct, it's a concept that arises at a particular point in history, circa the Industrial Revolution, just as the new industrial-era sexual division of labor was being negotiated, the one where men go to work and women stay home raising kids. (Before that everyone worked at home.) A new story arose to justify the new arrangements: that these roles were handed down by nature. As family historians tell us, it was only when children's actual economic value declined, because they were no longer necessary additions to the household labor force, that they became the priceless little treasures we know them as today. The romance of the child didn't get underway for the middle classes until the mid-nineteenth century (it was well into the twentieth that child labor laws went into effect). It also took a decline in infant-mortality rates for mothers to start regarding their offspring with much maternal affection. When infant deaths were high, maternal attachment ran low. It was only as families began getting smaller — birthrates declined steeply in the nineteenth century — that the emotional value of each child increased, which is where we find the origin of contemporary ideas about maternal instincts and fulfillments.

All I'm saying is that what we're calling a "biological" instinct is a historical artifact and a culturally specific development, not a fact of nature. An invented instinct can feel entirely real. I'm sure it can feel profound. As can the kinds of fears and vulnerabilities that Stock and Rowling are leveraging. But if we're getting empirical, let's acknowledge that childbirth has killed far more women than murderous trans women ever did, though I suppose the sentimental premise is that all those dead mothers died fulfilling their gender destiny, not defying it. The point is that a lot of behind-the-scenes conceptual labor goes into establishing the "naturalness" of gender, not to mention the vulnerability of gender critical feminists.

As far as nature goes, the reverence for it is pretty selective. We're happy to take cholesterol blockers, mood elevators, and erection enhancers as needed without worrying whether it's what nature intended. The other day a pig kidney was transplanted into a human. Technological possibilities on the horizon include uterine transplants for sterile women, which raises the possibility of uterine transplants for trans women — maybe eventually for cisgender men too. Why not? Humans have always made it their business to conquer, alter, and repurpose nature — and then to invent monsters lurking at the crossroads.

Gender: A Melee

Not surprisingly, Rowling's and Stock's brand of panic-mongering soon became fodder for the fringe right in America. In July 2021, QAnon followers staged two weekends of violent protests in Los Angeles after a customer at a Koreatown spa (Instagram handle: "Cubana Angel") filmed herself complaining vociferously to the manager about a trans woman supposedly using the jacuzzi in the woman's area of the spa. "He's a pervert," shouts Cubana, "waving his penis and testicles around!" The sight was traumatizing for her. "His dick is out!" says Cubana's friend, voice trembling. "His dick is swinging left and right!" She repeated the word "swinging" so many times it led me to wonder if these were rehearsed lines. "What about women's rights?" shrieks Cubana, as the manager patiently tries to explain that California's Civil Code prohibits businesses from discriminating against anyone on the basis of gender identity or expression. "We're concerned about women's safety," yells Cubana. "We're gonna take it worldwide!"

Which is exactly what happened: the video went viral. Tucker Carlson aired a segment about it, the first of seven on Fox over a week. Antifa showed up to protest the QAnon protesters, evangelicals and the Proud Boys showed up, a reporter was clubbed, protestors threw smoke bombs at cops and pepper sprayed each other, riot cops fired projectiles and beanbag rounds into the crowd. Amidst all this, reports appeared in *Slate, The Guardian,* the *L.A Times,* and other liberal outlets suggesting that the report about a trans woman in the spa was likely a hoax, and according to a spa employee there had been no trans patrons with appointments that day.

But the story turned out to be more complicated. According to the journalist Jason McGahan, who tried to

22

untangle it five months later in *Los Angeles Magazine*, there actually was a (possibly) trans person in the spa that day. Police issued a warrant for 52-year-old Darren Merager for indecent exposure; Merager does have a penis and is a convicted sex offender. But is Merager actually trans? It's unclear — he or she seems to have a female driver's license, though until recently was identifying as male, according to acquaintances, and McGahan isn't sure which pronouns he or she uses. Is Merager a predator? He/she has a criminal record for theft, but it appears that his/her previous sex crime arrests were for exhibitionism which, according to the psychoanalytic view, typically does entail wanting to be caught. (Robert Stoller calls these scenarios "scripts" in *Observing the Erotic Imagination*.) In this view, exhibitionism is a pathology of gender identity, not a sexual behavior. The motive is courting humiliation and punishment, not getting off sexually. It's a (not very successful) remedy for gender dysphoria, not predation.

Still, there it was, a penis in the woman's pool. Did this put natal women at risk? It is the case that many (or most, or lots of) cis women have been socialized in ways that can make the sight of an exposed penis in non-private settings feel alarming. Perhaps that will someday change, though I don't imagine such feelings are exactly voluntary — any more than gender dysphoria or compulsive exhibitionism is voluntary. But once again, to what extent is it possible to be intellectually honest about the distinction between an anomaly and a pattern? Perhaps it's not, especially when there are competing interests and clashing vulnerabilities at stake. Especially when titillating monsters hover — and Merager made a wonderfully convenient one — feeding the "appetite for thrilling perversity."

Why *is* gender such a melee? Can't it be a comedy instead of a tragedy, a playground and not a police state, with room

23

for experiments and transformations? You don't have to be some sort of pomo-structuralist to think that no one knows what gender is or where it comes from. Clearly all we have are stories about gender and sexual difference, which shift with the winds, the centuries, and political-economic contingencies. Why not see gender the way we do other human variables — personality for instance, capacious enough for thousands of permutations and infinite mutability?

"Smash the family!" feminists used to declare. Look around: it's smashed. As far as who done it, it's not that big a mystery — could Gilder and cohort not see its demise up ahead when they tanked wages and trashed the safety nets? They were so caught up in their deregulatory zeal that they couldn't imagine the S&L crisis, the housing bubble and evictions, Enron, and the opioid epidemic. No, the only thing they wanted to regulate was gender!

Yes, capitalism breaks things while ushering in all sorts of great new personal liberties — expressive individuality, your very own idiosyncratic unconscious, unisex clothes. It brings whatever you want right to your door at all hours (if you're among the lucky "haves"). Shopping for things, including identities, is the great modern consolation. Is having a gender identity — another recent development in the annals of modern selfhood — a trap or a freedom? Yes.

To those who fear trans women in the ladies room: make sure to pee before you leave the house. Those immutable laws of nature you're attempting to enforce today will be dust tomorrow, and soon enough so will you.

DORIAN ABBOT

Science and Politics: Three Principles, Three Fables

Science is a creative endeavor that requires the free and open exchange of ideas to thrive. Society has benefited immensely from scientific progress, and in order for science to continue to better the lives of individuals and nations scientific work must be evaluated on the basis of scientific merit alone. Over the past decade, however, scientific departments and organizations have become increasingly politicized, to the point that the development of science is now being significantly impeded. This time the assault originated from the radical left, but conservatives have done their share of meddling in science and are likely to meddle again in the future. Keeping politics out of science is something that all people of good will, both Democrats and Republicans, should be able to agree on. Or so, once upon a time, one would have thought.

How can we ensure political neutrality in science? I want to propose three critical principles for the protection of science from politics, and to illustrate them with three playful, slightly naughty fables about what has been happening when they are violated. The three principles are: (1) all scientists need to be able to say and argue whatever they want, even if it offends someone else; (2) universities and academic societies need to maintain strict neutrality on all social and political issues; and (3) hiring needs to be done on the basis of scientific merit alone. These principles have been lucidly outlined in three important documents at the University of Chicago, where I teach geophysical science: the Chicago Principles on Free Expression, which were issued by the university in 2014, and the Kalven Report "on the university's role in social and political action," from 1967, and the Shils Report on the "criteria for academic appointments," from 1970. All these reports assume, as the Kalven Report puts it, that "the mission of the university is the discovery, improvement, and dissemination of knowledge." This sounds prosaic, but the definition is important to emphasize because some people are now challenging it. They argue that faculty members should be activists who promote certain political positions and agendas, rather than pursue truth wherever it may lead. I should add that we are not perfect at the University of Chicago, and I sometimes fear that we honor these principles more in the breach than in the observance. And yet these principles are important goals for every scientific institution to at least aim for.

I started my own journey in this fraught environment simply by self-censoring — for no less than five years. I stayed away from campus whenever possible and avoided departmental gatherings. At first I thought that the problem was a few bad apples in my department yelling at everyone who disagreed with them and accusing people of being various types of witches. I slowly learned that I was observing just a small part of a national movement in favor of censorship and the suppression of alternative viewpoints. It is absolutely essential that we resist this movement and encourage students and faculty to speak freely about whatever they want on campus: we all lose when people self-censor.

Unfortunately, students and faculty are now self-censoring at alarming rates, in part as a result of the high-profile cancellations of academics who have been found guilty of wrongthink. The Foundation for Individual Rights in Education (FIRE) has documented 471 attempts to get professors fired or punished for their speech over the past six years, the vast majority of which resulted in an official sanction. In a recent report for the Center for the Study of Partisanship and Ideology, Eric Kauffman estimates that 3 in 10,000 faculty members experience such an attack each year, which corresponds to about one every three years at a large university with a faculty of a thousand. Since these cancellations are so public and potentially harmful to the victim's career, a small number can have an outsized impact on free expression. According to the same report, 70% of centrist and conservative faculty in American universities report a climate hostile to their beliefs and 91% of Trump-voting faculty say that a Trump voter would not express his or her views on campus or are unsure. Similarly, after a major academic freedom incident in the fall of 2021, MIT polled faculty at two faculty forums and found that approximately 80% are "worried given the current atmosphere in society that your voice or your colleagues' voices are increasingly in jeopardy" and more than 50% "feel on an everyday basis that your voice, or the voices of your colleagues are constrained at MIT." The problem extends to students, too: more than 80% of them self-censor on campus, according to a FIRE survey last year. To get a sense of the magnitude of the self-censorship problem at universities, contrast these numbers with the fact that, according to a recent paper in *Social Science Research Network* by James Gibson and Joseph Sutherland, only 13% of American respondents did not feel free to speak their mind in 1954, at the height of McCarthyism. The discovery and transmission of knowledge is severely hindered under these conditions.

Another factor encouraging self-censorship among students and faculty is a growing administrative apparatus that often has goals other than the pursuit of truth. One mechanism is the imposition of language games, which can seem silly but have the effect of establishing an orthodox way of viewing the world, discouraging dissent, and stifling creativity. This pernicious practice can extend to faculty's syllabi and even teaching. I was asked by an administrator not to use the term "blackbody radiation" in my class on global warming. Apparently "blackbody" — or more accurately, "black body" — is now exclusively a Critical Social Justice term. I refused. "Blackbody" is the scientific name for a hypothetical object that perfectly absorbs and emits electromagnetic radiation. "Blackbody radiation" is the correct physics term for what I was teaching, and there is no way that I will stop using it. Luckily for me, just standing up was all that was necessary in this case. But not everyone has the privilege of being a tenured professor at the University of Chicago.

It was my wife who inspired me to start making my views known. Her reason was that she was born in Ukraine at the tail end of the Soviet Union. When I told her what was happening on campus, she had a question: "If you speak out, will you have trouble?" I said, "Why?" And she replied: "It sounds like what my mother told me about Soviet times, and people who spoke out had serious trouble then." That was enough to convince me. Not in this country, not on my watch. My wife's mother is a teacher. In the aftermath of communism, she brought home the old propaganda books from school about Lenin and his pals. For fond memories? To teach her children about the old ways? Not at all. She brought them home to burn them to stay warm in the winter. Lenin's system failed so utterly that people had to burn the old propaganda just to stay warm. And no small part of this failure was due to the fact that they had allowed science to become politicized.

Now for the first story. Consider a situation at the Awesome Institute of Technology, or AIT. It involves two main characters. The first character is Dr. Centrist, a professor at AIT. Dr. Centrist has devoted the past thirty years of his life to developing his biomedical skills and is now at the top of his field. He is working in cancer research and is close to finding a cure. No one questions his ability in the lab, or his scientific honesty, or his devotion to science and his students. Moreover, Dr. Centrist has advised people of both sexes, all races, all sexual orientations, all religions, and all nationalities, and treated them all with equal respect. Dr. Centrist is a political centrist, smack in the middle of mainstream American viewpoints. Some of his views are center left — for example, he supports broad access to education and healthcare as well as protecting the environment for everyone. But some are center right, and these will

29

end up being considered "provocative" and "controversial" at AIT and cause him quite a bit of trouble.

The second character in my story is Mr. Woke (he/they), an undergraduate. Mr. Woke entered AIT as a physics major, but physics just "wasn't a good fit," so he switched to anthropology, which leaves him/them much more time for other interests, such as Twitter.

At some point it becomes publicly known that in his personal life Dr. Centrist "clings to his guns and Bible." Upon hearing this, Mr. Woke looks up in shock from his/their Macbook Pro with all the appropriate political decal stickers, spits out a mouthful of his/their venti soy chai latte, and declares that this is highly "problematic." According to Mr. Woke, supporting gun rights is a "dog whistle" or "coded language" for white supremacist vigilantism, and therefore minoritized people at AIT cannot feel safe and will be irreparably harmed if Dr. Centrist is allowed to continue his scientific research there. Moreover, Christianity is an exertion of power used by the cis-hetero-patriarchy to oppress gender and sexual minorities. The lgbtqia2s+ community at AIT will not tolerate this type of bigotry on campus, according to Mr. Woke, who has apparently appointed himself/themselves spokesfolx for the entire community.

But it gets worse. In a conversation at lunch about a recent Supreme Court case, Dr. Centrist lets it slip that he is pro-life. Mr. Woke declares that this is a blatant "war-on-women" position that cannot be tolerated. AIT needs to be a safe space where no gender minority ever has to hear, and thereby be harmed by, a viewpoint with which she disagrees. Mr. Woke says inclusivity dictates that this sort of violent hate speech must be restricted, and he/they takes to Twitter to demand a "Speech Code" and a "Code of Conduct" to ensure that the "climate" at AIT is made safe and inclusive for everyone — by inhibiting and silencing anyone who disagrees with him/them, of course.

I have saved the worst for last. Eventually it comes out that, horror of horrors, Dr. Centrist is a "deplorable" who actually voted for Donald Trump. Mr. Woke scrambles into action. He/they organizes a letter of denunciation of Dr. Centrist, demanding that he be fired in order to protect minoritized people on campus who have been threatened by Dr. Centrist's violent and aggressive racist hate vote. Mr. Woke has plenty of "allies" who sign, and then he/they threatens everyone else with a similar denunciation if they refuse to sign, declaring: "Silence is violence, and if you don't sign now you will be tarnished as a racist for the rest of your career. I will make sure of it!" Eventually most of the students at AIT sign.

AIT President Craven is interrupted from a busy schedule of meetings on inclusive pronoun usage, equitable landscaping, and bathroom diversity to deal with the latest campus controversy. President Craven is presented with a real conundrum: should he defend the fundamental purpose of AIT, which is the unfettered pursuit of truth, and risk being called a scary name by Mr. Woke, or should he panic and do whatever it takes to make his anxiety go away quickly so that he can return to attending his important meetings and enjoying his outrageous salary in peace? For President Craven, the choice is easy. He fires Dr. Centrist and returns to his pronoun and landscaping meetings.

An unfortunate result of his decision is that we never get the cure for cancer that Dr. Centrist was close to discovering — will another university or another laboratory hire such a disgraced individual? — but this was not high on President Craven's list of priorities. Afterwards Mr. Woke insists that Dr. Centrist was not "canceled." He was, rather, "held accountable" for his hateful, bigoted, and generally "problematic" views. Mr. Woke is fine with this result, because he/they believes that cancer is a social construct caused by systemic racism, and that Dr. Centrist's racist scientific method is useless compared to the medicinal benefits of other ways of knowing. But what does the public, who funded Dr. Centrist's research and pays for most of the tuition at AIT through federal grants, think about losing out on progress toward a cure for cancer because of someone's disapproval of Dr. Centrist's political views, which many people also hold?

What would it have taken to avoid this disaster at AIT? As annoying as Mr. Woke is, I think the real villain is President Craven. In order to prevent the terrible outcome that we have just described, President Craven doesn't exactly have to turn into Churchill, he just needs to turn into President Not-A-Complete-Dingleberry. He just needs a tiny bit of spine. All he has to do is say, "Sorry, Mr. Woke. That's not how we do things around here. You are free to express your opinions and Dr. Centrist is free to express his opinions. You don't get to silence people you disagree with at AIT." This idea is described in the Chicago Principles as follows:

> It is not the proper role of the University to attempt to shield individuals from ideas and opinions they find unwelcome, disagreeable, or even deeply offensive... Concerns about civility and mutual respect can never be used as a justification for closing off discussion of ideas, however offensive or disagreeable those ideas may be to some members of our community.

It is important to get the Chicago Principles adopted on your own campus before a crisis occurs. Even President

Craven might have been brave enough to stand up to Mr. Woke if he had an official policy to point to as an excuse. A standard part of the orientation for new students and faculty should be to explain the moral and intellectual foundations of these principles, and more generally of academic freedom: both why they are important and how they will be enforced. (There must be real penalties for violations.) This would help Mr. Woke understand that illiberal tactics will not work.

I should emphasize that the right of *everyone* to speak on campus needs to be defended. Let me give an example. I have a colleague who has tiled images of Karl Marx on his website and a Soviet flag in his office. He is actively introducing his Marxist-Communist views into campus settings in a way that Dr. Centrist did not introduce his own. This is deeply offensive, of course, to anyone who has taken ten minutes to study the history of the twentieth century, let alone actually suffered under communism. But the fact that my colleague openly advocates for what I consider to be an indefensible political position has absolutely no bearing on his scientific and mathematical ability. No matter how extreme, immoral, and offensive his or anyone else's political views may be, we need to defend his right to express them freely without letting them hinder his scientific career. Throughout history, many famous scientists have been highly eccentric and held weird and even repulsive social and political views. So what? Should we therefore renounce the fundamental and critical science that they produced?

Now a story in the Swiss Alps. Professor Right and Professor Left are attending the Global Economic Forum. They have been appearing at the Forum for decades and they agree on almost nothing. Whenever an economic issue arises, Professor Right argues for less government and Professor Left argues for more government. But they listen to each other's lectures seriously and they respond to each other's arguments. Sometimes Professor Left gets excited and makes a hasty a comment about Professor Right's lecture implying that she is stupid, but he never calls her evil. Even though Professor Right disagrees with Professor Left, she modifies her perspective when Professor Left shows data that contradicts a claim that she is making. In the end, after some back-and-forth, they tend to reach some sort of conclusion about the matter in question that both can agree is empirically justified. They do not like each other, but each understands that the other is necessary for the critical examination of his or her own views and can lead him or her to better economic research.

Enter a graduate student. Let us call her Ms. Oppressed. Ms. Oppressed doesn't think that Professor Right is merely wrong, she believes that she is morally corrupt. How else could someone argue for small government, when big government is clearly what is needed to fix the obvious systemic problems in our society that are oppressing women and marginalized people? Ms. Oppressed starts a Twitter campaign to force the Global Economic Forum to issue an official statement acknowledging that increasing the size of government is the only solution to all social and economic problems, as well as add a condition that in order to present a paper at the Forum, every participant must sign a pledge of agreement with this statement.

Professor Left finds himself in a bit of a bind. On the one hand, Ms. Oppressed seems to agree with him on most policy issues, and he has never been terribly fond of Professor Right.

On the other hand, banning speakers rather than contending with their arguments seems to go against the liberal tradition in which Professor Left usually locates himself. While he is considering this, Ms. Oppressed tells Professor Left that "silence is violence," and that he had better get on board with the program or she will turn to Twitter. Professor Left decides that the best course of action is to declare "no enemies to the left" and go along with Ms. Oppressed. The statement and the pledge are instituted, Professor Right refuses to sign, and she is henceforth banned from the Global Economic Forum.

Professor Left finds the next Forum meeting quite exhilarating. He can expound all his wildest ideas without the annoying Professor Right demanding evidence or logic. Yet he starts to get an uneasy feeling when he attends Ms. Oppressed's lecture, which is titled, "Data: Research or Oppression?" In it, Ms. Oppressed argues that data and the ideal of disinterested methodological rigor should no longer be used in economic research because "this idea of intellectual debate and rigor as the pinnacle of intellectualism comes from a world in which white men dominated." (These deathless words were actually uttered in October, 2021 by Phoebe Cohen, the chair of geosciences at Williams College.) In fact, at the end of her lecture, Ms. Oppressed attacks Professor Left because he refused to ban Professor Right for so many years. Silence is violence, after all, and by allowing that sort of hate think at the Global Economic Forum, Professor Left has actively participated in a horrible system of oppression.

After the Forum, Ms. Oppressed organizes a letter to have Professor Left and anyone else over the age of thirty-five banned from all future Forums for past collaboration with evil right-wingers, which, in addition to being essential for social justice, will have the added benefit of opening up lots of career opportunities for Ms. Oppressed and her allies. It works, naturally, and Professor Left soon finds himself banned from the most important meeting in the field, suffering the same fate that was visited upon Professor Right only a year before. Meanwhile, at the next meeting of the Global Economic Forum, all the presentations have titles such as "Indigenous Ways of Managing Global Economies," "Feminist Perspectives on Inflation," and "Intersectional Debt Management." No one dares to present data or make a rational argument, for fear of being labeled a white supremacist. Needless to say, the discussions of economics at the event quickly lose their previous influence upon business leaders and policymakers, whose job it is to make actual decisions in the actual world, but it becomes very popular with journalists at the prestigious journal of record, *The New York Spaces*, who write favorable pieces about the exciting new developments in a field that they used to treat with a mixture of confusion and disgust. It is not long before Ms. Oppressed is rewarded for speaking truth to power with a FitzArthur "Genius" Award.

The key error here was that Professor Left compromised on the principle that universities and societies should never take positions on social and political issues. He did this because he tended to agree with the political positions that were proposed. Doing so makes universities and societies into political entities rather than scientific ones, and has the effect of restricting free expression by members of the university community who disagree with the official position. It is particularly important right now that professors on the left do not fall for this trap. Aside from the principled reason for this, there is a practical reason: they will never be revolutionary enough, and the revolution is sure to eat them next if they fail to stop it now. In the words of the Kalven Report,

The instrument of dissent and criticism is the individual faculty member or the individual student. The university is the home and sponsor of critics; it is not itself the critic. To perform its mission in the society, a university must maintain an extraordinary environment of freedom of inquiry and maintain an independence from political fashions, passions, and pressures. A university, if it is to be true to its faith in intellectual inquiry, must embrace, be hospitable to, and encourage the widest diversity of views within its own community. It is a community, but only for the limited, albeit great, purposes of teaching and research. It is not a club, it is not a trade association, it is not a lobby.

Since the university is a community only for these limited and distinctive purposes, it is a community which cannot take collective action on the issues of the day without endangering the conditions for its existence and effectiveness. There is no mechanism by which it can reach a collective position without inhibiting the full freedom of dissent on which it thrives. It cannot insist that all members favor a given view on social policy; if it takes collective action, therefore, it does so at the price of censuring any minority who do not agree with the view adopted. In brief, it is a community which cannot resort to majority vote to reach positions on public issues.

The principle of political neutrality is extremely important for a university, though it is often neglected relative to the principle of free expression. But you cannot have the latter without the former. Free expression is not possible in practice at universities that release statements on social and political issues. Consider 2020 as an example of how this is *not* supposed to work: universities and societies across the country issued statements on social and political issues, and faculty members who disagreed with them publicly were attacked, silenced, and sometimes even fired. The attackers felt justified by the official statements.

Finally, there is the situation developing in the job search at the physics department at Winthrop University. Winthrop has had an aggressive DEI (Diversity, Equity, and Inclusion) program that has been in place for more than a decade, and it has already hired dozens of DEI deans and deanlets to implement and promote it. Yet Winthrop Physical Sciences Dean Shifty has recently received word from the President of the Henry Foundation that the Foundation is not happy with the numbers that Winthrop's DEI program has produced. In particular, the Foundation is expressing concern with the slow progress at appointing an appropriate number of underrepresented faculty in the physical sciences.

38

Given the Henry Foundation's deep pockets and cultural influence, Dean Shifty can see her dreams of a nice presidency at a liberal arts college with a fat paycheck slipping away, and so takes immediate action. Although the advertisement for the physics faculty search explicitly says that there will be no discrimination on the basis of race or sex, Dean Shifty slyly informs the chair of the physics department and the members of the search committee that she will not consider a nomination for the faculty position if it is an Asian or white man. She does this orally and through an intermediary, because she knows that it is a violation of Titles VI and IX of the Civil Rights Act. The members of the faculty search committee are uncomfortable, but they feel that they have no choice but to comply. They do not actually know what is in the Civil Rights Act — they are physicists, not lawyers; but they assume that Dean Shifty would not do anything illegal.

A fierce debate soon emerges on the hiring committee. It turns out that half of the committee thinks the department needs a woman and half of the committee thinks that the department needs an underrepresented minority. Instead of debating the scientific merit of the candidates, the committee spends its time debating which type of underrepresented person should be recruited. In the end they settle on hiring a woman, because there are more women than underrepresented minorities among the graduate students, and the students need more faculty members who "look like them." They hire a woman and both Dean Shifty and the President of the Henry Foundation are thrilled. Of course the entirety of the faculty are vaguely aware of what happened, which leads to a strange and uncomfortable situation for the new member of the department. Meanwhile similar hiring shenanigans have been implemented at universities across the country, so the male Asian and white candidates find it extremely difficult to get faculty jobs and many end up leaving the field.

Notice what happened when hiring criteria other than scientific merit were introduced: it immediately made the process political. Whether to hire a woman or an underrepresented minority is a political question, not a scientific question. In order to avoid the politicization of science, therefore, it is absolutely essential that all admission, hiring, promotion, and honors be awarded on the basis of scientific merit alone. Politics is automatically introduced when purely merit-based decisions are abandoned. Moreover, ideological purity tests called DEI statements are now often used as a gate-keeping mechanism to ensure political uniformity in faculty hiring, and this quite obviously violates the principle of political neutrality. Also, note that the purpose of the university and of science is being violated if criteria other than merit are used for hiring: in such cases we are no longer pursuing truth to the best of our ability. We have instead substituted some other goal.

These matters were presciently discussed in the Shils Report:

> The conception of the proper tasks of the University determines the criteria which should govern the appointment, retention, and promotion of members of the academic staff. The criteria which are to be applied in the case of appointments to the University of Chicago should, therefore, be criteria which give preference above all to actual and prospective scholarly and scientific accomplishment of the highest order, actual and prospective teaching accomplishment of the highest order, and actual and prospective contribution to the intellectual quality of the University through critical stimulation of others within the University to produce work of the highest quality.

Note that the last clause refers strictly to stimulating others "to produce work of the highest quality," and should not be interpreted as a way to sneak other criteria into consideration. And later:

> There must be no consideration of sex, ethnic or national characteristics, or political or religious beliefs

or affiliations, in any decision regarding appointment, promotion, or reappointment at any level of the academic staff.

The objective of this rule is simple: *fairness*.

The principles of academic freedom confer not only a right but also a duty. Some people think that the duty of academic freedom is to restrict your speech in certain cases, but this is incorrect. The duty of academic freedom is to use it. My obligation as a professor and a scientist is to say what I really think in public, while of course focusing my teaching on the particular subject I was hired to teach, not least because so many people in society cannot. That is the whole point of the professional protection known as tenure. Too often tenure is wasted on the timid. Anyway, they cannot cancel all of us.

BERNARD·HENRI LEVY

After Babel

I

How do you read?

In posing this question, I have in mind the Surrealists' question of 1919: "Why do you write?"

But this time around the question is about reading.

Weren't the Surrealists also great readers?

In André Breton's *Anthology of Black Humor*, didn't he turn his readings of Lautréamont, Roussel, Arthur Cravan, Leonora Carrington, and Alfred Jarry into full-fledged literary performances?

And what are we to make of Borges, the late-arriving Surrealist, so enamored of the fantastic and of artifice, seeking out the algebra of dreams and the key to cities, and maintaining thirty years later that the only history that counts is not that of literature but that of reading? Books are immobile, he said, compact, closed in on themselves, identical. And the only things that change over time, and thus make history, are the ways we read them. And what are we to think of his concocted "true confessions" in which he asserts that writers must be judged on the basis of the readings they have inspired, the enthusiasm they have generated, and that he, Borges, is no prouder of the books he wrote than of those he read well?

So, reading.

The practices and purposes of reading.

"How do you read?" asks another great reader, Italo Calvino. "Sitting, stretched out, head down, while eating, in a cafe, after getting up in the morning, before going to bed?"

Are there places, times, life circumstances, or historical moments that seem more suited to the unpunished vice that Valery Larbaud believed reading to be?

Is solitude required?

Silence?

Do you sometimes read out loud? If so, when?

And haven't we lent too much credence to Augustine's story of his astonishment at discovering Ambrose reading silently in the garden of the bishop's palace in Milan and declaring that this very place and time marked the passage from reading aloud to reading in a quiet, inward, concentrated, modern manner?

In the universities of our youth, we learned about Latins, such as Propertius and Martial, who, before Ambrose, already read silently. And if the contemporaries of Augustus were so given to oral recitations at the home of Maecenas, protector of poets, doesn't that mean that the usual practice was to read silently or in a low voice?

Conversely, Flaubert was not reluctant to put his books to the test of the *gueuloir*. He would bellow his prose, scream it as loudly as he could, until he thought it was right. Zola, in his remembrances of the Rue Murillo, said that Flaubert even required his readers to declaim what they were reading. Hugo did the same.

And the aging Louis Aragon who, in a bar on the Rue des Saints-Pères where he followed me one night, may have been speaking to the old man he was, to the former young man, to Antoine or Anthoine (his doppelgängers), to the person he called the performer, the narrator, or the third-party author, to Elsa, to his last readers, or in fact to me and to the young man I once was — in any event, there in the bar he is offering me a part in the film to be made from his novel *Aurelien*. He tries to persuade me by improvising, at 1:30 in the morning, amid the empty tables, a coruscant reading of several pages of the novel. How clearly I recall the stentorian delivery that he adopted to demonstrate that this was how he wanted to be read: in a very loud voice!

And of the many writers who recently did me the honor of participating in my inquiry into their habits of reading in my journal *La Règle du Jeu*, how many are of the same mind? How many would follow the example of Virgil, who could declaim the Georgics for four days straight? In Rome, it was said that he had no talent more enviable than his tone, his eloquence, his touch. Two thousand years later, don't authors write for ears as much as for eyes? And are we doing a text an injustice if we fail to recite it?

Frame the question any way you will.

There is an art of reading.

It is probably not as high an art as writing.

But among those who do it best, it is intimately tied to writing. And for fans of Borges, Aragon, or Virgil, it requires an aptitude no less rare.

Can that art be taught?

In principle, yes.

And on this point we must stand steadfast against the populist demagogy of innocent and protocol-free reading.

But if reading can be taught, how can we prevent the teachers of reading from becoming bogeymen like Monsieur Émile Faguet, the French professional critic, whom the Surrealists imagined slapping? He strove, in his mediocre art of reading, to reeducate the "pretty little reader" whose enthusiasm fades as fast as infatuation.

How to shield this "pretty little reader," who believes that a reading event is the same as an amorous one? "You don't learn to be in love," she says, "you fall in love! You don't learn to read, you read!" And she is right.

How to preserve the mixture of freedom and intelligence, of sensuality and culture, the bemused grace, the rapture that Roland Barthes called the pleasure of the text, which no initiation must be allowed to diminish?

That is yet another question.

And it is one of the puzzles that preoccupied the Surrealists as they worked, not only on automatic writing but also on automatic reading, with its free associations, its felicitous blunders, and its tendency, as they would say, to "slip on the roof of the winds."

An assortment of other questions.

Do we read better or worse (whether silently or aloud) when we know in advance (or do not know) the name of the author? At what point should we act on our knowledge of a

45

book's existence? Is it in the storm of its publication, when the weight of the reviews and misunderstandings that pile up so quickly wedges itself between the book and you? Or later? Is the wise reader the one who waits for the book to cool down, to disappear from the booksellers' shelves, and to move into the winter of the library?

Am I, the reader, in a state of peace or war with the writer?

Is the conversation with the book going to be a good one, or hand-to-hand combat?

What do we do when reading becomes difficult? Do we stall or do we push on? Do we stop? Do we try to resolve the problem? Do we put the book down and pick it up again a little later? Or do we jump to the next one (as Jarry said to the neighbor whose child he almost killed while shooting in her yard, "Don't worry, madam, we will make you a new one")? Do we do as Montaigne did when he decided that, if the book "vexes," one should simply pick another one and repeat the experiment?

What is the right tempo for reading? Should we follow Heidegger, who pretended that his texts had to be read at the speed they were written, at the same cadence, the same clip? A lifetime to write, a lifetime to read? Or Sartre, who read like a pirate, without rule or scruple, at his own pace, very slowly then suddenly very fast, adapting the text to his inner rhythm, his speed, his thinking needs, his mood?

What happens to a book when it is no longer read?

Does the dearth of readers condemn it to nothingness?

Do books lead their own lives in a parallel world devoid of living beings?

Are there books that exist only because a handful of readers, sometimes just one, light them up with their love?

Which comes first, the book or the reader? Am I the one

who goes for the book, uncovers it, chooses it? Or does the book fix me in its sights, target me like a homing device, a guided missile, the finger of God or the Devil? Does it locate me, torpedo me?

I have experience with such predestined books, those we refer to conventionally as having changed our life.

I could name some books that dropped down on me like meteors: *Le Vicomte de Bragelonne* in childhood; *Belle du Seigneur* in adolescence; André Maurois' biography of Disraeli; Malraux's novels; Baudelaire; Artaud; so many others. I spent my life reading, so it is impossible to cite them all. *The Gulag Archipelago* in 1976; Levinas a little later; my encounter with Romain Gary; the discovery of Lord Byron; reconnecting with Sartre; the Talmud with its square letters; a nineteenth-century Lithuanian rabbi; Curzio Malaparte.

Then there are those, parenthetically, that I avoided reading because I felt they were a threat, that they might shake me and I was not ready for it. Do I have to confess? The Kabbalah... Kierkegaard... Georges Bataille, whom I often cite but put off reading deeply for a very long time... Dostoevsky, yes, Dostoevsky...

And as for "bad books": Do I like some bad books? I have to admit that this may be the case. The failed attempts by the great writers. Or minor works by writers of the second rank who had a great life. Not to mention thrillers (detectives, spies, adventurers), of which I have always been a fan.

II

But there is another, related question: not how do you read, but why?

For pleasure or out of necessity?

To escape yourself or to find yourself?

Do we read, as Don Quixote and Madame Bovary did, to flee a painful present? Is reading an experience similar to the lightning bolt that seduced the "pretty little reader?" The start of a trip that pulls us out of our orderly life? A flight toward an exalted elsewhere? An inner exile? A conversion? Is it one of those adventures that I praised in *The Will to See*, the first virtue of which is to make us strangers to ourselves, to *estrange* us?

Or is it the other way around? Should we join Musil, Broch, and Kundera in believing that literature is a tool for knowing the world and, thus, our own soul? Do we read not to get out of ourselves, but to escape from melancholy, to feel what we feel more acutely, to live our lives in a better way, to become true subjects, to find each other and ourselves?

Here I must acknowledge something I heard from Marthe Robert, another great reader, a specialist on Kafka, who at the time had just fought like a lioness to convince the jury of a prestigious French book award to select my first novel, *Le Diable en tête*. We were at the end of the evening, in the deserted dining room of a restaurant on the Quai des Grands-Augustins, where Grasset, my publisher, celebrating the success of the book. And Robert confided to me, as if sharing a secret, in a slightly drunken voice and in pale makeup that made her look like the theosophist Madame Blavatsky: "Don't tell anyone... because the times are crazy with all the talk of the death of the author and the subject... but this novel, it's you... a hundred percent you... you're the author... you're the subject... what other virtue can a novel possess? It's the return of the subject... it's Artaud leaving Rodez, it's Kafka guilty and absolved, it's the bastard and the child reconciled... your Benjamin, it's you!"

A variant of the question: Is reading good for you? Does it bring reconciliation with the world and with oneself, liberation, freedom? Is it true that to open a book is to shut a prison? Is it the beautiful Enlightenment dream of a cure for packaged ideas, clichés, and religious or political obscurantism? Does it teach you to think for yourself? Or is it like any other vice which, when indulged to excess, becomes a poison? Consider Cervantes and his sorrowful knight, alienated in the "demon of analogy," as Foucault would go on to describe him. Consider Huysmans' Jean Des Esseintes, Don Quixote's successor, suffocating under his hallucinations, haunted by sleepwalking apparitions, sickened by the miasmas exuding from the overly tidy volumes in his Latin library and from the cut flowers he has placed in all the urns in his house, which, in wilting, have released their venoms. Consider the Sartre of *The Words*, seeing in the love of books a virus with which Poulou, the prodigal child, was infected by his grandfather. Consider Montaigne worrying about an "excess" of reading that, as he ages, will be "harmful" to his health.

Varying the question: "One of the greatest tragedies of my life is the death of Lucien de Rubempré." Who said that? Was it Oscar Wilde, around the time he was also claiming that before Turner fogs did not hang over the Thames? Was it, before Wilde, Thomas de Quincey declaring that "direct knowledge of *The Divine Comedy*" is "the most inexhaustible happiness" that life can offer? Whether Wilde or Quincey, this stance changes everything. Because the latter, a discerning eater of opium, knew what he was talking about when it came to venoms, poisons, and other narcotics. And I cannot help observing that the Maoist leaders of my youth showed more or less the same conviction in their discouragement of too much Homer, Juvenal, Aristophanes, or Artaud's *Voyage to the Land of the Tarahumara*. As did the radical leader Benny Lévy, who, despite having tempered his militancy, remained convinced that reading was a poison. And Byron deciding, in Missolonghi, to trade his library for a cargo of cannon, a shipment of Congreve rockets with inextinguishable fuses, and other arms for his Souliotes.

And today?

Today it's hard to say.

For my part, I swing between the two poles of this twin postulation.

I recall that the Latins were already distinguishing between two types of reading, depending on whether one let oneself be guided by *studium* or *otium*, by study or recreation, by involved, engaged, practical intelligence or by disengaged, theoretical, and gratuitous reflection.

Careful, though!

I also recall that Cicero's position on the subject was far from clear.

He rejected the first route, which seemed to him reserved for slaves and freedmen — but the second route, reading as leisure, reading for no particular purpose, found no greater favor in his eyes.

And this moralist so enamored of politics, this orator trying to be Caesar and Pompey and wanting to govern the republic, this philosopher and man of action, this rather successful prototype of what we might call today an intellectual in the city, gained clarity by separating the *otium* into two subcategories: the *otiosum otium*, literally sterile idleness (with which he wanted no more to do than with overly productive and contemptible *studium*) and *otium* coupled with *utilitas* (which was much better, as it equipped you to expose a conspiracy, destroy Catiline, and save the endangered republic!).

Is that the compromise solution?

And, for the writers and thinkers here and now who do

not reject the possibility of changing the world, or at least of repairing it, does it achieve the right combination of words and things, talking and doing, reading and dreaming?

For my part, it just about does.

I do not read for professional reasons or because I am involved in this or that (*studium*).

But neither (alas) do I read much for the pure pleasure of doing so (*otiosum otium*).

Occasionally, of course, that happens.

Last summer, for example, I yielded to the memory of long vacations and plunged into the ten volumes of an old-school French masterpiece, Romain Rolland's *Jean-Christophe*.

Another time, in a hotel library, I reconnected with the pleasures of my university days, when — thinking I knew all there was to know about *The Human Comedy* — I was amazed to discover this gem: *The Secrets of the Princesse de Cadignan*.

And then there are those nights when, hoping to quiet my insomniac fever, I grab a novel long ago read and forgotten, and *voilà*, as with Proust remembering who he was in the "closed room invaded by the scent of iris," a region of myself that I had walled up suddenly reopens, dilates, and releases a stream of sounds, smells, colors, and voices that works better than any effort of memory to bring back the me of the time. I see myself as I was at sixteen on each successive page of Gide's *The Counterfeiters*. I reexperience, as if preserved in the pages of a Hemingway novel, the emotion of the love-crazed suitor of the young actress out of an Eric Rohmer film for whom I was waiting secretly in Granville and passing the time by reading. Better archived than in any film, photo, diary, or memory is my precise recollection, upon rereading Thackeray's *Vanity Fair* recently, of the weather, the feeling of the air around me, the color of the garden and of the feathers of

51

the ibis that strutted about regally and came now and then to taunt me one day in a hotel in Cuernavaca decades ago when I was filming *Day and Night*. And a short while later, it happened again with *Ultramarine* by Malcolm Lowry, of whom I knew nothing at the time apart from *Under the Volcano*...

But most of the time everything moves too quickly.

For I read while writing.

Increasingly I read in order to write and to better understand the dramas, the specific situations, the challenges that punctuate my life and its political-philosophical work.

And everything combusts in the foundry, the factory, the flares of those engagements and the texts that accompany them. I burn words, consume them. I annotate, dismember, crumble, and cannibalize books that I might otherwise love. The real flavor of reading I savor from afar with a touch of envy and nostalgia, in the manner of Italo Calvino's "horrible worker" in *If on a Winter's Night a Traveler*. Calvino's character long ago stopped indulging in the innocent pleasure of reading. But before sitting down to work each morning, he watches through a telescope a young woman stretched out on a chaise longue reading a book that might be his. He sees her move her lips, lower the book, raise her eyes, resume reading, skip a page, dwell long on another, flip back, go to the end, come back, sigh, sometimes wipe away a tear — reading as he used to do.

III

But there is yet another question.

It is the most pressing, and I don't know any writer who doesn't face it with some degree of anxiety.

It is the question of what the internet, the giant that is Google, and the all powerful screens are doing to reading and its practices.

A part of me believes that everything has changed, and that this mutation in the way we read is as decisive (but for the worse) as the transition from the scroll to the parchment codex; or from the standing stones of the prytaneum, on which was engraved the calendar of sacrifices in Solon's time, to the first linden-wood tablets on which scribes wrote with sharpened reeds; or from hand-copied books to printed books; or from books in which, to save space, words and sentences were run together to those where the lines were separated by space and sentences by newly invented punctuation; or from reading out loud to reading silently, as with Ambrose and Augustine.

Surfing, we call it now, or browsing.

Plowing ahead at full steam.

Displaying several books simultaneously on a shared screen.

Or just one, but with access to the variations, glosses, corrections, notes, and guides that, in the pre-Internet world, appeared at the beginning or end of a volume.

Or with the aid of various applications, a dictionary, an encyclopedia, cross-references to other books, a translation site, a quasi-library, and soon, within "metaverses," an incorporated reading space.

Or even those indices, lexicons, and other research engines that can scan text at the speed of digital light, count the occurrences of a word, capture the avatars of a concept and pass that concept through a sieve.

Not to mention the flood of messages, alerts, flashes, beeps, intrusive notifications, security protocols, ads, cookies: they stream as I read; they sabotage my engagement with the author; they place between us that great impediment to reading that Proust called conversation but whose ultimate form has become the chatter of social networks.

How is it possible not to conclude that these mechanisms so central to online life have engendered new ways of reading?

Shouldn't a book proceed at its own pace, take the time to operate within me, sharpen my desire, disappoint it, resume the attack, hollow out a space for itself and come to dwell within me?

And doesn't the very word "navigation" suggest that we remain on the surface, above the water? When today we occasionally go fishing for meaning, do we still subject ourselves to the effort of sounding the depths? Wasn't this effort formerly an integral part of reading, just as it is with writing?

Hasn't our attention become distracted, constantly interrupted, tugged at, discouraged from dawdling, constantly uneasy, flitting, drifting in a permanent blue light that drives us crazy? Farewell concentration, reverie, contemplation!

Think of the impeachment of reading that so frightened Proust. Ponder the "art of not reading" in the context of the mannered frivolity, envy, and spite that La Bruyère described as widespread. Remember the "reading with a bird's eye view" for which Thomas de Quincey reproached Friedrich Schlegel and the German romantics. To all these bad practices, machines supply new and formidable weapons.

I loved the little acts that went with reading: the open book, fallen from your hands, underlined, highlighted; shifting your seat because the light has changed; losing your place, finding it again, dog-earing the page in anticipation of resuming where you left off; the page marker; untrimmed pages; the paper cutter used to separate those pages; the velum torn out of impatience; proofs.

I loved, in bookstores, book stalls, and friends' attics, the chances of happening upon an out-of-print book.

In public libraries, I loved the pleasure of requesting a

book, waiting for it expectantly, of hearing the librarian say sorrowfully that someone else was reading it, that it had been moved to a warehouse outside Paris, or that it was out for restoration — in short, unavailable. Tomorrow, perhaps; you have to wait, take your turn, come back, hope for the best...

And I loved the living past of libraries, with their narrow aisles, their stacks and shelves, their logical classifications, their inevitable random settling. How do you classify them, Georges Perec would ask about books that really matter? By author's name, by genre, by country? By color, language, binding, collection? Is the date of publication or the date of acquisition more significant? Does a personal library have an end? Is there a moment when, like Captain Nemo disappearing in his Nautilus, you say to yourself, "OK, look, I have more books than I could read in a thousand years, so let's act as if, from this day on, all publishing has ceased"? More important than an end, does your library have a beginning, a date of birth? And could you make out, in the stream of your rows of shelved books, those that came first, those with which the adventure began, the starters, the seeds and sprouts?

For me, the answer is yes. I can spot my first books from among a thousand. Eyes closed, by feel, as blind as Borges wandering the long, shelved galleries of his Babel, I will find them because they are the secret, living pillars of my library. They are my mother's books. Hidden among the multitude of books that I have since acquired in the course of my adventures in life, in writing, and in thought, there are the books that she had as a girl and that she presented to me as a gift when I was almost a man. I was fifteen. For a long time I would go to bed (late) and wake up (early) gazing at the shelves I had reserved for them. Over the years, they became diluted, separated, lost amid the rest of my books. But I can still pick them out of a

After Babel

thousand others because of their lovely yellowed paper, their stitching, their bindings with broken thread. And there on the flyleaf, in a hand elegant and firm, in pale ink or pencil, the first name of their beautiful first reader, the year she read them, and, occasionally, a word of commentary or criticism.

I cherish those books. Their number has dwindled in proportion to the mass of others. In the room where I keep them, they give off a light invisible to all but myself. But how many are left who think this way? What will the careful archaeology of libraries be worth once the era of the great connection has taken hold for good? Won't fidelity to a delicate stock of first books go the way of all the other rituals of the book age?

And yet...

I'm not sure things need to be as cut and dry as I've put them here.

First of all, is this revolution really so radical?

And have we really moved from the light of the old-fashioned book into the blinding shadow of text processing?

If I'm getting this right, reading on screen means three things. A zip through books, a hop over letter and image alike, a spray of works consumed in fragments with neither care nor deference.

But hasn't that been a pervasive modern trend for a long time now? The disregard for books, reading like a monkey, lifting out bits and slapping them together, misappropriating their contents — weren't those practices already customary among my beloved Surrealists, not to mention the Situationists? Didn't Guy Debord's reading logs, shown to me by his old friend, the collector Paul Destribats, classify the works that Debord was reading as either *"redeployable"* or not? Didn't that clear the way for books to become debris?

Electronic reading, which purports to be hyperconnected, loaded with meaning, and scholarly, is a stretching, a metastasizing, of the text, around which swirl constellations of metatexts that sometimes clarify it and sometimes cloud or obscure it. It is the door to the era of the "augmented book," just as the transhumanists, when musing about grafting implants, electrodes, into our brains, refer to the "augmented man." But wasn't that (except for the technology) the principle behind the "rhizomatic" (non-discursive) reading — in layers and plateaus, with constant interruptions, all bifurcations and bypasses — that Gilles Deleuze and Félix Guattari were preaching well before the arrival of the Internet?

Isn't electronic reading also akin to the "symptomatic reading" that was theorized by my professor, Louis Althusser? Althusser's conception consisted of finding the "undetected" part of the text, probing its "lacunae," "making its empty spaces speak," forcing out its "unsaid part." In order to achieve this, didn't we have to superimpose the text over another text that changed its context but was made to resonate within it?

Can't reading on a screen be seen as the generalization of an innovation of Jacques Derrida, who, in his writings in the second part of his life, proposed an art of page layout similar to what a philosopher version of Stéphane Mallarmé might have produced, inserting a commentary from *The Phenomenology of Spirit* here and bits of Jean Genet's fiction there, and pushing to the point of dazing the reader the art of scattering, of setting up spiraling columns, of transplanting pieces of text, of separating words in space, of hybrid writing with no end point, of cross-eyed reading in which the gaze pauses indiscriminately at the right or left of the page? In so doing, couldn't it be said that Derrida invented, when the Internet was still in diapers, the very notion of hypertext?

And Roland Barthes: wasn't he another precursor of this

mode of reading when, in *S/Z*, he pioneered the practice of taking hold of a great text (Balzac's *Sarrasine*) for the purpose of "sprinkling" it, making it "abound," cutting it into "lexies" (invented semantic units), dismembering and eviscerating it; listening to the "palimpsests" (or, as Ferdinand de Saussure might put it, the "paragrams") that made up its hidden matrix, and then, at the end of these serial "earthquakes," reducing it to a pile of broken blocks that form a landscape bearing only a distant resemblance to that intended by the original author?

And then there is the internet itself, which can be seen as an invitation to travel through a space that is limitless, endless, cosmic. It is the mad project of storing all of the knowledge published in every language of the world. Not all that different from the Babelian library of Borges, which was as vast as the universe, defying the imagination, whose nearly infinite number of rooms contained so many volumes that it was impossible, not only to view them all, but to embrace them in a single movement of thought. This unfathomable loop that is the Internet, this opening to the imaginary windows of the metaverse, can also be seen as the realization of the glittering utopia of the German mathematician and writer Kurd Lasswitz, who, in 1904, in a divine short story that Borges always said was the real source of inspiration for his "Library of Babel," described a "universal library" capable of containing all books, all words spoken and unspoken, all conversations between people whether they have met each other or not, all laws enacted or to be enacted in the future, all peace treaties between nations that have waged war on each other or that have no reason to do so, all encyclopedias, all the train schedules for the next century, all certificates of birth and death down the ages, all the possible combinations of all the letters of all the alphabets of the world?

But above all, is it really impossible for a scientist, an intellectual, or a writer to make virtuous use of these modern and postmodern protocols, this new relationship with books that the reign of the screens has brought about and that instills in me so much regret? Of course not.

I open my laptop.

I still write in longhand.

I have never been able to break myself of that other unpunished vice, writing with pen on paper.

But, like most people, I spend some time on my laptop verifying dates, checking references, documenting sources, or looking through a classic of which I have only a vague and reconstructed recollection.

And so begins a screen experience that aims, targets, destroys and punctures some of my fondest reading habits. Yet the incurable optimist in me can't help finding some merit in this. After all, isn't it true that certain poisons (most in fact) can also be used as remedies? And wasn't Achilles' spear thought to have the power to heal the wounds that it had inflicted?

Books come to me through the screen with a carefree air that I had not previously associated with them. They were noble, imposing, but also freighted with my earlier readings. Snowed in by the dust gathered on the shelves where I had left them. Domesticated by being arranged in the Perec-like order I had given them. Now here they are, galloping around. Here they flaunt their independence and escape from their little caskets. Here they catch fire, kiss, converse, agree and disagree, enrich each other, overlap, and, as Mallarmé says, light each other up through reciprocal reflections like a virtual swooping of fire across precious stones. The library regains its youth. It breathes deeply. It shakes itself off in a clatter of chains and thawed words.

In every librarian there sleeps a Birotteau who, like Balzac's character, is tempted to live inside his books as if on a frozen stage set. Or worse, an autodidact, the character in Sartre's *Nausea* who has resolved to read every book there is in order from A to Z. The organized disorder of Google has many faults, but it has the virtue of shaking all this up, breaking the ice, awakening books. It is a pipe organ gone wild. A keyboard playing itself like a virtuoso. And like Mallarmé's *Le Livre* — the ideal book in which, from multiple words, the poet formed composite terms unknown in the common language — it plays with words, combines them in infinite ways, and, to speak like another poet, makes of books a temple in which man passes through forests of symbols which watch him with suddenly foreign eyes.

I, reader, am gripped by a nearly equal drunkenness.

I am dispossessed, yes, of my page-to-page reading, sometimes dreamy, sometimes bored, and always consuming.

I am cut off from the delicious shiver of worry I felt when the librarian at Sainte-Geneviève would disappear with my slip and leave me uncertain about whether she would ever return with the book I had requested.

And I am deprived of the emotion that gripped me one day at the École Normale when, flipping through the cards neatly arranged in their long narrow drawers of polished wood and bearing the calligraphy of successive librarians at the school, I noticed, among many cards in the hand of the librarian Pierre Petitmengin, a very old one on which I detected the handwriting of Lucien Herr, his legendary predecessor, and a contemporary of Péguy, Jaurès, and Léon Blum...

But, as if in compensation, there is another emotion and another type of joy. In place of the concentration of long ago, a strange and gripping sense of immersion. In place of my nostalgia for books, a new energy that carries me away in a whirlwind of images and pages. I jump from link to link. I rush from node to node. I, too, gallop from site to site, without aid of landmarks or a compass. The virtual library is like Pascal's sphere, the center of which was everywhere and the circumference nowhere. Sometimes I read idiotic books in bad French and crater into a leaden ennui. Other times I come up with a rare pearl, tumble upon an old atlas or a brilliant PDF, get Aristotle and Thoreau to meet up, the umbrella and the sewing machine, the tinder and the spark, a monument and a document, the event, the unforeseen. An hour passes. Two. Day. Night. I don't pause to reflect — or to sleep. It's a form of hypnosis. It's one of those rare moments in life where time stands still. I have the impression of being in a haunted castle, moving from door to door, knocking, waking ghosts and bringing them back to life. I work breathlessly. I write. I move forward.

I have to say again, even if it is illusory, even if it seems blasphemous and irreverent, what a joy it is, for a devotee of texts and books, to be in contact with this underground library that is endless and, for the first time, entirely available. Before, when I scanned bibliographies at the end of books, I would suffer the same sort of dejection that Thomas de Quincey felt upon entering a library and realizing that he would not live long enough to read, or even to open, all the books waiting there. Here, too, I know that I won't read everything. But the everything is there. And the books, the sources, and the scholarly articles have relinquished their formal nonavailability and no longer oblige me to consult them in some archive in a faraway university. Presence. Plethora. The miracle of sudden profusion. The milk and honey of the digital land. A horn of plenty and a joust with a God who no longer plays with dice but plays now with the flow rate of the river. A new garden of the Hesperides with its golden fruits where I no longer forbid myself from playing the triumphant Heracles. It is Goethe's dream when he prophesied to Eckermann the advent of a world literature, or, better, a universal one that would succeed the era of national literatures and fulfill the plan of the Enlightenment. It is the world of Hegelian absolute knowledge, without origin or end; it is substance become subject, reason made world, the negation of the negation, History fully grasped. Yes, everything is there. Up to and including the works lost, destroyed, or burned, works that, according to the ancient sages, were supposed to live again only in the world of the future. I suspect, now, that if I searched diligently enough, if I clicked on the right links, I would find them! I am in this maze without a catalogue. I wander without a guide in a labyrinth of letters where everything and nothing is mystery. I get worked up, enthusiastic. I am a master of my books and of the universe, almost to the point of exulting, like Heidegger in his lecture "The Age of the World Picture," that "the researcher no longer needs a library at home."

At this point, I have only one fear. The last, but not the least troubling. There is no library without a hell. No labyrinth without a minotaur. Might the minotaur, in this case, have flown at dusk?

BRUCE D. JONES

Taiwan: Chronicle of a Crisis Postponed

I

The South China Sea, fabled and contested, stretches from the Taiwan Strait south to the Java Sea and the Singapore Strait, where the Horsburgh lighthouse, an active relic of Asia's violent encounter with Europe, now keeps watch over the world's most crucial chokepoint. North of Singapore, the sea is bounded to the east by the island of Borneo, to the west by the Malay peninsula. As each of these land formations slopes away, the sea opens to a wide expanse. Wide, but frequently shallow, and dotted with cays, atolls, reefs, sand bars, and small island formations. For the vast commercial ships that transit this shipping lane, they must hew closely to well-charted but narrow routes where the sea lane is deep enough to accommodate their giant hulls.

If you viewed the South China Sea simultaneously through satellite, radar, and sonar images, you would see a sea clogged with obstacles. There are the myriad islands and formations and shallows that constrain commercial passage. Across the remaining surface, every major shipping company in the world transits these waters, sailing mega-container ships, oil and natural gas tankers, grain ships and bulk carriers hauling copper, steel, and other industrial materials, and the "roll-on, roll-off" (or "ro-ro") ships that move the world's supply of cars and trucks from manufacturer to market. Several nations sail fishing fleets here, including two of the world's largest, from China and Taiwan; according to the Ocean Security Project at the Center for Strategic and International Studies in Washington, DC, fully half of the world's fishing fleet spends some of the year trailing in these waters. Six countries have made sovereign claims here and are seeking to profit from the economic rights that follow (under the UN Convention on the Law of the Sea), namely China, Taiwan, Malaysia, Vietnam, the Philippines, and Indonesia. In the shallow waters of the eastern and western reaches of the sea, dozens of nationally and internationally owned companies are part of their projects to drill into the huge estimated reserves of oil and gas captured beneath the sands. Along this sea floor lies the world's largest concentration of undersea cables, which carry more than ninety percent of all the data that powers the contemporary technological world. This is the busiest shipping lane in the world, the jugular of the world economy.

You would be blithely unaware of any of this, though, while sailing the main shipping lane, for that route runs far afield of most of these dangers. You can sometimes sail for hours without catching sight of another ship, even at the height of day. Perhaps you see the distant silhouette of a container vessel far ahead, or the outline of an oil tanker just at the horizon. Your radar shows you the position of these and other vessels too far away to be seen even with the binoculars that are still a standard part of sea-farers kit. On most modern vessels the Automated Information System (AIS) allows you, with a tap of the cursor, to glean the name, the speed, and the direction of these vessels, though you still need the binoculars because many small or mid-size Chinese fishing vessels do not carry AIS beacons or turn them off. But to the naked eye the sea is calm and can be all but empty.

That is, until you approach the Taiwan Strait. Here the sea narrows sharply, and the seabed rises dramatically, reaching no more than three hundred feet at its deepest. Shipping is squeezed into a narrow channel. And around you the world's most dangerous arms race comes into plain view.

To the west lies China, to the east the island of Taiwan. For a long period, it was known as Formosa—after *ilha formosa*, or "beautiful island," per a Portuguese account in 1542 — less fabled than the surrounding sea, but even more contested through contemporary history. Populated for the better part of six thousand years, it became a Dutch colony in the mid-1600s, then an independent kingdom. It was annexed to the Qing dynasty in 1683, then ceded to Japan in 1895, under the Treaty of Shimonoseki that ended the first Sino-Japan war. The short-lived Republic of China (which overthrew the Qing Dynasty in 1912) took over Taiwan in 1945, at the request of its World War II allies. When the Chinese civil war turned against them, in 1949, the Republic of China's government, having already been forced to move from Nanjing, relocated from Chengdu to Taipai. Thus was modern Taiwan born. It has been subject to threat and claim from China ever since.

It occupies a critical geography. It forms an essential part of what John Foster Dulles conceived of as "the first island chain" — an arc of islands from which the United States could project power in Asia by which to contain Soviet and Chinese military action in the Pacific. In our day, the greater focus is on Chinese naval expansion, for the arc collectively encloses the Yellow Sea, East China Sea, the Taiwan Strait, and the South China Sea — what China calls its "Near Seas," each of them bordering one of China's major economic hubs. North of this arc is the Japanese main island, where an American naval base homeports the USS Ronald Reagan and its supporting destroyer squadron, and the Korean peninsula, where the United States maintains a large concentration of armed forces. The island chain formation itself runs from the Japanese island of Kyushu, where the United States operates the diplomatically named Fleet Activities Sasebo, a naval base home to the Japan Maritime Self Defense Forces and to several American ships, including amphibious assault vessels (like a small aircraft carrier) and America's only forward-deployed expeditionary strike group. Southwest from Kyushu lies the Ryuku island arc, which encompasses Okinawa, home to not one but twenty-five American military installations, encompassing Marine and Air Force capacities, along with smaller Army and Navy units. The lower arc of the Ryukus wraps around the Senkaku Island group (described by Taiwan as the Tiaoyutai Islands and by China as the Diaoyu Islands), where China and Japan came nearly to blows in 2012-2013. The southernmost of the Ryuku islands is a mere twenty nautical miles from Taiwan's northeastern shore. Taiwan itself is the largest formation in the chain, spanning 245 miles from north to south, and pushing the waters of the East and South China Seas into a narrow strait, 97 nautical miles wide at its widest, separating Taiwan from the People's Republic of China.

Continuing down from Taiwan's southern tip, the 160 nautical miles of the Luzon Strait that separates Taiwan from the northern reaches of the Philippine archipelago constitute the largest gap in the chain — and the deepest channel. Then comes the Philippine archipelago, once home to the massive American base at Subic Bay, our largest overseas naval installation throughout the Cold War, rashly given away during the naïve and heady days of the early post-Cold War order. Now the United States maintains only basing rights, and collaborates with the modest Philippine navy and larger Coast Guard. Further south, the sea is enclosed by the island of Palawan, then Borneo, before abutting Sumatra; there is no exit to the wider oceans here. For that, you have to sail further south past Singapore and out through the Lombok or Malacca Strait, into the Indian Ocean. Oddly, Singapore is never counted among the first island chain though it abuts Malacca, through which flows almost eighty percent of the oil that fuels China's industry. American naval ships routinely dock at Singapore's Changi Naval Base, and there the United States also maintains the carefully named Logistics Group Western Pacific — actually a sub-unit of the Seventh Fleet, and the direct naval descendant of the powerful Asiatic Station fleet that operated out of Hong Kong and patrolled China's Yangtze river for nearly a century prior to World War II. (The Republic of Singapore Air Force, which maintains part of its fleet at bases in the United States, has also trained at launching its F-16 from both American and British aircraft carriers, adding to the potency of this ring of forces.)

These waters are home to the largest concentration of naval forces in the world. In the Yellow Sea, a coalition of western navies patrol to enforce UN-mandated sanctions against North Korea, also keeping a careful eye on Chinese and Russian ships operating nearby. China has the bulk of its fleet deployed in these seas, along with its growing submarine fleet; in terms of combat ready surface ships, it now deploys more seacraft than the United States Navy (though many of them are smaller and less powerful than their American equivalents.) The US Navy has two hundred ships — including five aircraft carrier strike groups, and the majority of its submarines — allocated to the Indo-Pacific Command, some forward deployed in Japan, others in nearby Guam, and still others in Hawaii, San Diego, and in bases surrounding Seattle, but all transiting frequently through these waters. (Indo-Pacific Command also patrols the Persian Gulf, but many of the ships that deploy there from Hawaii or the West Coast transit through the South China Sea on their route to and fro, thus doing double duty.)

Japan's Maritime Self Defense Forces sails upwards of 150 surface combat ships and 19 submarines, concentrating this substantial firepower along the Ryuku arc. At the northern end of this arc, North Korean surface ships and submarines are a major feature — Pyongyang has the world's largest naval fleet by sheer number of ships (though hardly that at all if measured in terms of fighting power.) Australia has a modest navy but an energetic one and frequently sails these waters, sometimes accompanying American exercises. The Russian Navy — either the second or third most powerful navy in the world, depending on how you measure — is a frequent visitor, and increasingly exercises with China's PLA Navy (PLAN). India, too, has begun to mount more frequent sorties off China's eastern coast, to Beijing's great irritation. And these waters are heavily trafficked by submarines — as many as two hundred at any given time, according to the US Navy. Even Germany has sailed a frigate into these waters, in a rather tepid effort to show that it, too, matters in geopolitical Asia. More important, France maintains several thousand troops in the wider region, and regularly patrols its mid-size navy, including from its overseas possessions in French Polynesia (roughly the same distance from the Taiwan Strait as Hawaii). Britain has recently rejoined this new maritime version of the old imperial "Great Game," after launching two new aircraft carriers sailing them and their supporting destroyer squadrons through the Luzon Strait.

The Luzon Strait: if a great power war breaks out in Asia's waters, this will be a decisive battle zone. As the Fulda Gap in Germany was to the Cold War, so the Luzon Strait will be to the world order unfolding now. It is the principal waterway through which the United States and allied navies flow their ships and submarines when seeking to reinforce their presence inside the South China Sea, or the Taiwan Strait itself. American submariners are familiar with it, at least from their studies, from frequent submarine hunting raids against Japan in World War II: Formosa and the Luzon islands were a key staging ground for the Imperial Japanese Navy's campaign in southeast Asia. If a major power war breaks out, keeping the Luzon Strait open will be a critical objective for Western forces. It is also a key objective of China's "counter-insurgency" doctrine — its focus on stopping the allies from reinforcing their position inside the "Near Seas."

It was not for nothing that the Royal Navy, which long dominated these waters (for purposes at once imperial, liberal, and brutal) chose this strait through which to sail the HMS *Elizabeth* and HMS *Prince of Wales* on their maiden

69

voyages to Asia, in October 2021. Indeed, for the several weeks surrounding that voyage, it seemed that the Luzon and Taiwan flashpoints might be triggered sooner rather than later.

II

In truth, tensions had been mounting for years prior. In the early 2000s, China began its rapid expansion of its navy and missile force, and, in repudiation of a promise to the United States, began to militarize some of the land features that it had claimed in the South China Seas (illegally, according to a 2016 ruling by the Permanent Court of Arbitration, ruling under Article VII of UN Convention on the Law of the Sea.) Moreover, Xi Jinping began something of a drumbeat of statements that indicated that he viewed the incorporation of Taiwan into the sovereign fold of China as a personal and national priority. In November 2013, China's Ministry of Defense announced that it had established an "air defense interdiction zone," or ADIZ, over the East China Sea, north of Taiwan. The move generated a striking response from President Obama, who ordered two nuclear-capable B-52s flown through that airspace; but China's naval build up on both ends of the Strait continued, as did sustained political and disinformation campaigns in Taiwan. President Trump then dialed up the American response, first by the symbolic (or in the Chinese rendering, provocative) act of taking a phone call from the Taiwanese leader during his transition to the presidency. More determined action followed, especially in the passage of the Taiwan Travel Act of 2018, which encouraged the United States government to elevate its engagement with Taiwan authorities, and a marked uptick in the rhetoric accompanying the transit of US Seventh Fleet destroyers and aircraft carriers through the Taiwan Strait. These sorties occurred both under the framework of

Freedom of Navigation Operations (FONOPs), by which the US Navy enforces the terms of open commerce and the Law of the Sea (somewhat ironically, as the United States is still a non-signatory to that Convention) — and as a show of deterrent strength. China continued and intensified its political and informational campaign in Taiwan, which, like Russia's disinformation tactics in Europe, was designed to stoke resistance to pro-western or pro-independence candidates in Taiwan's closely contested parliamentary and in Presidential elections. What's more, in a major speech in 2019, Xi Jinping, rather than simply repeating the long-standing formula of emphasizing "peaceful reunification," explicitly invoked the option of military force: "We make no promise to abandon the use of force, and retain the option of taking all necessary measures…" What's more, he said that the Taiwan problem should not be passed down to future generations — the first Chinese leader to say this.

And then things escalated further.

Sometimes assessments matter as much as events. They certainly did on March 9, 2021, when Admiral Philip Davidson, the four-star in charge of the Indo-Pacific Command, gave testimony to the Senate Foreign Relations Committee during which he warned that China could move to try to take control of Taiwan: "…they've long said that they want to do that by 2050. I'm worried about them moving that target closer. Taiwan is clearly one of their ambitions before then. And I think the threat is manifest during this decade, *in fact in the next six years*." Several China scholars reinforced Davidson's argument, noting that a crucial factor in determining whether Xi Jinping ultimately decides to use force to compel Taiwan is whether he would be confident of victory, and highlighting with concern mounting evidence that the PLA leadership itself is confident of the results of a potential action. Whether or not the PLA's confidence is warranted matters less for the onset of a crisis than the confidence itself.

Other China and Taiwan specialists pushed back, criticizing Davidson for scaremongering, and underestimating both the political and military costs to China of using force. The critics argued — with some merit — that excess alarmism has the pernicious effect of undermining Taiwanese confidence, thus actually making it more likely that the Taiwanese leadership would ultimately cede political ground to Beijing. Then history intervened in the discussion, and events appeared to reinforce Davidson's alarm.

On June 15, the United States sent its Tokyo-based aircraft carrier, the USS *Ronald Reagan*, and the guided-missile destroyers USS *Shiloh* and USS *Halsey*, into the South China Sea, transiting the Luzon Strait. This was neither unprecedented nor unwarranted, but it was muscular. Then, on July 27, a British warship entered the South China Sea and docked in Singapore, to Beijing's fury; the first of several British transits that year. The next day, the guided-missile destroyer USS *Benfold* made a foray through the Strait, the seventh of the year — a record pace. In previous iterations, the Chinese response to such transits has been primarily rhetorical. But now, China sent twenty-eight military aircraft into Taiwanese airspace, a sharp break from previous pattern.

The debate among Washington's deep bench of Taiwan experts continued. Several argued that the risk of war with China, specifically over Taiwan, was growing, and laid out strategies for response. Others continued to argue that Beijing preferred political strategies to military ones for dealing with Taiwan, and could not be confident of victory in a cross-Straits attack. *Foreign Affairs* published a collection of expert commentary on the "Strait of Emergency," but the bulk of analysis suggested that the alarm about imminent invasion was exaggerated. And yet the tension in the Strait continued to mount.

What we know now, though it was not leaked to the *Financial Times* until October, was that in late July China test-fired a long-range missile that entered space, circled the globe, and then released a hypersonic glide missile — a nuclear-capable one. According to a detailed report by International Institute for Strategic Studies in London, the missile incorporated high-speed glide technology into what is known as a Fractional Orbital Bombardment System. This combination of technologies would allow China to place a missile into low-earth orbit, then fire a warhead into the atmosphere, and additionally to maneuver the warhead as it approaches its target. Leave aside the engineering: it is a missile system that would allow China to evade most of America's existing missile defense systems; and it is a suite of technologies that the United States has not yet mastered.

China also made a major "lawfare" move, announcing that it had passed a new maritime law that would come into effect on September 1. The law as passed would require a wide range of vessels to declare their presence to Chinese authorities upon entry into Chinese territorial waters. Now, every state has the right to require ships to provide a range of types of information as they enter territorial waters. The problem here is that China's claim of territorial waters are vast, contested, and illegal (in the view of the UN tribunal.) So China was in effect claiming a right of information (and ultimately inspection) on shipping passing through what the rest of the world treats as international waters.

The United States and its allies moved swiftly to clarify that they would in no way comply with the new Chinese regulations. In early September, the aircraft carrier strike group accompanying the USS *Reagan* entered the Taiwan Strait again, while a second aircraft carrier strike group led by the USS *Carl Vinson* conducted exercises nearby in the Western Pacific, and a guided-missile destroyer separately conducted "freedom of navigation operations" within the twelve-mile nautical zone surrounding the aptly named Mischief Reef (one of China's claimed "territories" in the South China Sea and site of one of its largest military installations in the waters.) On September 17 the US Navy conducted its ninth passage of the Strait. In late September the USS *Reagan* strike group returned to the South China Sea, accompanied by Destroyer Squadron 15. On September 28 the British sent a warship, the HMS *Richmond*, into the Taiwan Strait, the first time in a decade that it had done so.

And then things really began to heat up. In early October, British and Vietnamese warships conducted joint exercises, their first ever. A second UK carrier group conducted training operations in the nearby Philippine Sea. Then the British carrier group led by the HMS *Queen Elizabeth* transited the Luzon Strait and entered the South China Sea. It was joined by Dutch and Singaporean frigates, with whom it conducted joint exercises. On October 3, the USS *Ronald Reagan*, the USS *Carl Vinson* (and each of their supporting strike groups) joined the HMS *Queen Elizabeth* strike group and the Japanese helicopter carrier Ise and its strike group, as well as frigates from Canada and New Zealand. Together they conducted the largest multinational naval exercise since the end of the Cold War.

China did not sit calmly by. On October 4, it began a series of air sorties into Taiwanese airspace, and over the course of three days flew at least 150 aircrafts through that area — by far and away the largest Chinese show of force in four decades. Beijing also issued a public and inflammatory warning to close American allies, notably Australia, that they would become "cannon fodder" if they chose to join Taiwan in defense against a Chinese incursion.

At which point both the Taiwanese and American government ratcheted up the diplomatic pressure. Taipei's leadership issued a stark warning that China would be able to successfully invade Taiwan by 2025. And Washington took the dramatic step of leaking to the press a reasonably well-kept secret: the United States already had special forces deployed in Taiwan, as part of a training operation. China had surely been aware of that, but the broad American public was not, and the decision to publicize the fact of the American military presence on the ground was designed to signal to China that we would treat those forces as a tripwire for a wider American response, should China choose to attack.

The commentators noticed the changing weather. Writing in the *Washington Post* in the same week, Ishaan Tharoor captured the gloomier end of the spectrum of analysis, arguing that while some had reasoned that an invasion of Taiwan was both unneeded and too costly from Beijing's perspective, the dynamic was shifting in the wrong direction. The deterioration of the US-China relationship, begun before Trump and accelerated by him, state-stoked nationalism, PLA confidence, and political-legacy dynamics all created incentives for Xi Jinping, Tharoor argued. What's more, "the Chinese military's capabilities are inexorably expanding and may have already reached a stage where

America's long-standing presence in the Asia-Pacific is an insufficient deterrent. Military planners in both countries treat a potential showdown over Taiwan as only a matter of time."

China has indeed been engaging in an intensive military build-up. It is now easily the number two defense spender in the world. It is rapidly expanding its nuclear stockpile, and it is building its navy at a fast pace. In the last fifteen years, the PLA Navy has gone from a fleet of 216 combat-capable ships to one with 348, many of them technologically sophisticated, including three aircraft carriers. (By contrast: in the last fifteen years, the US Navy went from 318 — down from a Reagan-era high of 590 — down to 275 combat ships, before ticking back up to around 290 recently.) Moreover, Chinese innovations in anti-ship missile technology are outpacing the United States. Anti-ship missiles have been a factor in war-planning since the Falklands War, when Argentina used a single air-fired Exocet missile to cripple a British destroyer (which later sank as it was being towed away). But China has greatly expanded the range of such missiles, and it has developed anti-ship missiles mounted both in land silos deep inside Chinese territory and on mobile units. Some of these have a range of up to 3000 miles, thus capable of targeting American ships at great distance — so-called "aircraft carrier killers."

It is true that these Chinese missiles have never been tested in combat conditions, and some forward installations of these missile batteries — especially those on reclaimed land formations in the South China Sea — could fairly readily be demolished by American airpower in a war scenario. Moreover, hitting an aircraft carrier at long range is harder than it sounds — the United States has substantial cyber counter measures, electronic warfare tools, and sophisticated missile defenses. But still — and this should really make us sit up and take notice — most military planners estimate that in a determined campaign China would ultimately succeed in using its large quiver of missiles to damage, cripple, or even sink American aircraft carriers and other surface ships. That is, unless the United States responded by launching large scale air, naval, and space-based attacks on those missile facilities, and on China's "eyes and ears" — that is, what the Pentagon calls C4ISR, for command, control, communications, computers, intelligence, surveillance, and reconnaissance. That would involve not only multi-faceted cyber operations, but also — under a range of highly plausible circumstances — American airstrikes on facilities on the Chinese mainland. What might start as a limited naval engagement could quickly escalate to large-scale "system war" between the world's two largest and most powerful militaries, both nuclear powers.

A series of articles in *The New York Times*, the *Financial Times*, *The Economist*, and other leading newspapers all warned of a possible, even imminent war. David Ignatius argued that the tide was turning in Beijing's favor, and Elbridge Colby, who oversaw Taiwan defense in Trump's Pentagon, argued that a Chinese attack on Taiwan could come within two years. Oriana Skylar Mastro, a close observer of the PLA, warned that even moderate voices in Beijing were abandoning a prior focus on 'peaceful reunification': "I think the military option is the option now." Taiwan's President Tsai said publicly that the threat from China was increasing "every day." (Later its Defense Ministry would clarify that it also believed that a naval invasion of Taiwan would be very difficult for China to

pull off, in part because it lacked adequate transport ships —
"ro-ro" ships used to transport heavy equipment like tanks and
armored personnel carriers. Commentators thus took note
when China shortly thereafter released to the press images
of large conventional ferries being retro-fitted to carry a high
volume of military materiel.)

Yet no attack occurred. And amid the drumbeat and the
escalating tensions, several of Washington's most knowledge-
able Taiwan experts argued that the crisis was not in fact
imminent. Ryan Hass pointed out that, among other factors,
the Beijing Olympics were scheduled for February 2022, and
even though those games were overshadowed by Covid and
a diplomatic boycott by the United States and a few other
nations, it was highly unlikely that China would launch a
military action prior to or during the games. The games would
be closely followed by the 20th People's Congress, a crucial
event in the political calendar in Beijing, where Xi would have
to secure a further five-year term (highly likely) and consoli-
date his control over the Central Committee and the Party as
a whole (also likely, but not without its challenges.) Which
brings the calendar to mid-2022; a mere two years away from
Taiwanese elections in 2024, when, as Richard Bush has noted,
Beijing would have another shot at using political, informa-
tional, and other lower-risk tactics to produce a political
rather than military outcome to its favor in Taiwan.

And while PLA generals might be growing in confidence,
others noted that from Xi's vantage point confidence is not
certainty, and so long as political options remained viable, the
risks to Xi of an uncertain military campaign were dissuasive.
The flip side of the point that the Taiwan issue is of higher
priority for Beijing than Washington (arguably) is this: Xi
cannot afford to lose. If the United States mounts a defense of

Taiwan and fails, it would be seriously damaging to America's role in Asia and in the world, but it would not pose a threat to the stability of the American regime. Whereas if Xi Jinping, who has made "reunification" with Taiwan a major part of his legacy, mounts an attack on Taiwan and fails, it will be not only very costly, it also potentially threatens his continued tenure as party leader.

In time, as the week-to-week tempo of escalation cooled, and the more sanguine specialists appeared to have called events more correctly. Notwithstanding the rhetoric, no Chinese military attack on Taiwan occurred, or from what we know now, was planned. (And for those who would say that the response forestalled the crisis: this misses the point that at no stage was there an actually observed Chinese military buildup, of the kind eminently visible in the case of Russian forces around Ukraine.) Still, even the most careful and all but the most sanguine Taiwan scholars acknowledge that while this crisis was not an emergency in the end, and that a crisis is far from guaranteed, it certainly remains possible. What's more, the odds grow as Chinese confidence mounts, and as the military balance in Asia continues to tilt in their direction — as it will absent substantial American re-investment in its navy and missile technologies and a range of additional moderniza-tions. The risks will grow absent effective strategy from both Taiwan and the United States. The calmer assessment should be a cause for focused preparations, not for relaxation.

The months from June to November 2021 proved to be a kind of dry run, a real-world tabletop exercise to test the free world's readiness to respond to a crisis in the Taiwan Strait. And it exposed critical weaknesses: in Taiwan's defense strategy; in America's current military options; and in our allies' and partners' readiness to reinforce Taiwanese and American action, if need be. The rattling conclusion from the recent turbulence is this: if China does resort to military action in Taiwan, and the United States responds, there is no guarantee that we would win. We are not ready for a Taiwan emergency.

The imbroglio in East Asia was not the only challenge confronting the United States or its close partners. Simultaneous with the mounting Taiwan tensions, Russia deployed several tens of thousands of troops to scheduled maneuvers on Ukraine's northeastern border, then ominously didn't bring them back. Moscow began a steady buildup of troops and equipment along the northeastern, southeastern, and maritime borders of Ukraine. Against American warnings of severe economic consequences for military action, Russia published a list of demands with which the United States and NATO would have to comply to forestall Russian military action — a set of demands that amounted to a rollback of NATO's expansion and consolidation in Eastern Europe since the end of the Cold War. With its forces surrounding Ukraine, Putin hoped to blackmail the West into reversing the terms of its victory in 1989–1991 and repealing Russia's defeat. We know what happened next.

The two crises are different but they have essential similarities. Neither Taiwan nor Ukraine are American treaty allies, but they are both "alliance-adjacent": in Taiwan's case, by virtue of longstanding defense partnership arrangements with the United States, in Ukraine's case, by NATO's decision in 2008 to open a pathway for Ukrainian membership. Both immediately border a power that seeks a global rivalry with the United States, and which has putative claims on the territory in question. Both are democracies, though Taiwan's is a fuller

80

democracy than Ukraine's. And both occupy geographies that crucially change the dynamics of "hard power projection" in their respective neighborhoods — a point frequently missed by American commentators who argue that America has no vital interests in either country. And so both raise delicate and significant questions about how far the United States is willing to go to defend a liberal or democratic concept of world order; about how much the United States is prepared to risk to retain primacy in the two major industrial, commercial, and technological regions outside the United States; and what strategy the United States is prepared to adopt to blunt the ambitions of two powers now seemingly bent, in some degree of coordination, on dulling American hegemony at least and supplanting it at most. Or will we in fact carry through on our present mood of withdrawalism and self-shrinkage, and proceed on the false but widespread notion that being a strong democratic power with global responsibilities is nothing other than hubris?

One critical difference between the two contexts, so far, is the nature of American policy toward our respective endangered friends. From 2008 onwards, US/NATO policy on Ukraine was a paradigmatic case of "talk loudly and carry a small stick." A decision to open a pathway for Ukraine to NATO membership and then not actually bring them in, or deploy some Western troops on Ukrainian soil, was surely a worst-of-all-possible-worlds move. It put a huge Russian target on Kyiv while doing little or nothing to buttress Ukraine's defenses. The modest American and European response (and the anemic global response) when Russia moved in 2014 to reverse its loses, by invading Eastern Ukraine and then annexing Crimea, made the situation worse. Even the relatively effective train-and-equip operation that followed, improving the defensive capability of the Ukrainian armed forces, did not bring — could not have brought — those forces to a level where they could single-handedly deter further Russian aggression. Russian energy sales to Europe not only continued, they increased; and the building of the NordStream 2 pipeline — which would still further increase European dependency on Russian gas exports — continued unabated. Far from satisfying Putin and forestalling a new crisis, all our half-hearted and strategically confused actions laid the groundwork for the deeper crisis of 2022.

By contrast, at least so far, American policy on Taiwan hews more closely to a classical logic of restrained rhetoric and a muscular posture. To date, a refusal by successive American presidents (despite some pressure from within their parties) to move away from strategic ambiguity on the defense of Taiwan, and a continuing willingness to put sizeable American military assets at risk in the Taiwan Strait, has helped to keep the situation below the boiling point. Those arguing for increasingly bellicose rhetoric, just as the military balance is starting to tilt away from us, might want to pay careful attention to how effective that precise combination of tactics has been in Ukraine. They might wish to concentrate more on beefing up deterrence and resilience. The defense of Taiwan will not come from starker rhetoric or greater resolve alone.

III

Is the defense of Taiwan in America's interest, or vital to the alliance system in Asia?

America's closest alliances date from the Second World War. They are the countries we fought with to defeat the Nazi regime and Imperial Japan — and in one of history's unusual twists, Japan and Germany, too. Some newer alliances have far less depth, and fewer ties of history, or commerce, or population, or experience. Taiwan is a rare country that is not an ally now but once was, and with whom the United States has the depth of ties that parallel our old wartime alliances — of which, of course, the Republic of China was one. We have long acted in its defense. In 1954, in the face of escalating tensions in the Strait, when an invasion of Taiwan seemed possible, the Eisenhower administration got from Congress the Formosa Resolution, giving it prior authority to wage war with the PRC. In the wake of this crisis, the United States and Taiwan signed the Mutual Defense Treaty Between the United States and the Republic of China, under which both sides agreed to provide aid and military support to the other if it came under attack — as in the NATO charter, an "Article 5" provision. Four years later, in another episode of high tension, President Eisenhower deployed the Seventh Fleet to the Strait.

That alliance held until 1980, one year after the conclusion of normalization with China in 1979. But despite Kissinger's and Nixon's shift towards relations with the People's Republic of China and the adoption of the "One China" policy (according to which the United States recognized Beijing as the sovereign government of China and acknowledges — but does not thereby support — its claim to sovereignty in Taiwan), Congress once again acted fulsomely to support Taiwan, through the passage of the Taiwan Trade Act — which went far beyond trade, including to cover the sale of military equipment to Taipei. Ronald Reagan also pulled back some of Nixon's and Carter's concessions to China over Taiwan, providing Taipei with "six assurances" that the further evolution of America-China relations would not hurt Taiwanese interests, or limit American military sales and trade with Taipei. The Taiwan Relations Act anchors the relationship, and under its provision the United States has maintained unofficial ties with the people of Taiwan; maintained the American Institute in Taiwan, which performs consular and other functions normally associated with an embassy; and engaged in ever deeper trade, most recently in high technology. It was supplemented in 2018 by a new but non-binding Congressional act, the Taiwan Travel Act; which passed a highly divided Congress by — 414 to 0.

Vitally, over the course of the ensuing decades, the United States has used substantial arms sales to Taiwan to help ensure that it can maintain a defense against China — since 2010, roughly $23 billion worth. Those sales have been wide ranging and have included frigates, advanced aircraft (most recently the F-16), surface to air missile systems, anti-tank missiles, transport aircraft, mobile radar, shipborne guided missiles, Patriot missiles, torpedoes, minesweepers, surveillance aircraft, and diesel submarines, along with an array of information and radar technologies. To date, though, America has not sold to Taiwan either of its two most advanced technologies: nuclear submarines and the Aegis radar system. The United States has also persistently (if not entirely consistently) sought to increase space for Taiwanese participation in international bodies such as the WHO, where China persistently and consistently blocks official Taiwanese membership.

The relationship is now governed by a series of diplomatic formula — the Taiwan Relations, the U.S.-China Communiques (which still provide a diplomatic baseline for US-China diplomatic relations), and America's Six Assurances to Taiwan. (All of which sound like they are ripped from the history of nineteenth-century British diplomacy in Asia.) These arcane but highly sensitive formulas have so far allowed for the United States to build and to maintain extensive ties with

Taiwan without strictly speaking breaking the One China policy — and to continue to provide for its defense.

American policy toward Taiwan has long been shaped by a doctrine of so-called "strategic ambiguity" — whereby the United States has not declared explicitly its intention to defend Taiwan in case of a Chinese attack, but merely retained its right to do so if it chooses. This formulation has come under pressure of late, both from scholars who have argued that it does too little to deter China from attack, and arguably from President Biden, who seemed to abandon the formula in a press conference where he stated that the United States would defend Taiwan in case of Chinese aggression — though his team quickly rolled that back and argued that Biden was merely expressing his presidential intention, not a change in American policy.

It is important to recognize that throughout this period Taiwan has continuously deepened its democracy — holding repeated elections, freely and fairly; observing the peaceful transfer of power; sustaining a free press and a free opposition; and routinely scoring highly on the various rankings of democratic standards. President Biden effectively acknowledged this when he invited Taiwan to participate in his Summit for Democracy in November 2021. Does Taiwan's status as a democracy effect the extent of American obligation or interests to defend it? Narrowly, no. But here, of course, we collide with one of the great debates in American foreign policy. In America's grand strategy, its forward presence in Europe and Asia, tied to close allies in both theatres, has been the essential pillar of maintaining American primacy and an order that can deter great power war. In the American-led order from World War II onwards, alliances and democracy are Venn-diagramed concepts: there are several democracies that are not allies, and there are allies that are not democracies, but there is a heavy overlap, and our most robust allies are indeed democracies.

Elsewhere I have argued against democracy promotion as a way to shape or to understand American foreign policy, in particular during an era when our own democracy is challenged. But the *defense* of democracy is a very different business. The defense of democracy within the United States is vital, and the defense of democracy abroad is also essential if the United States wants to retain an order wherein its interests and its political system are secured. If the United States is not willing to extend its power to defend established democracies, then the underlying purpose of much of American forward power and of the alliance system is called into doubt.

Of course, the United States cannot credibly defend democracy everywhere over time, notwithstanding some of the grandiose claims of recent presidents. Would that we lived in a world, as we so briefly did, where American power was so untrammeled as to be able to act to defend any democracy it wished; would that we lived in a world, which we rarely have, where such power was matched by a keen awareness of history, and a solid grounding in the political and cultural realities of other regions, sufficient to allow us to devise wise policy towards that goal. Usually blind to history, and often ignorant of other cultures, American policymakers have repeatedly crafted poor policy to advance democracy (with notable and admirable exceptions), and in so doing they have cast a deep pall over the notion of the use of American hard power in service of democracy. But failures of democracy promotion, especially in the excesses and missteps of America's long "war on terror," do not abnegate the value of defending established democracies. We do, after all, have universal values, and we should not wish to be played for fools by the authoritarians of the world, many of whom are simply exploiting our confusion and our weakness.

There is no danger — anti-interventionists all across America should sleep well — that we are about to become "the cops of the world." Given the reality of the limits on American power, there must of course be choices as to where to defend democracy. It seems obvious, at least to me, that that choice should give preference to democracies with whom we have deep ties, with whom we trade substantially, and with whom we have shared or overlapping strategic interests, especially if they are allies. All of which but the last are features that characterize the situation with Taiwan.

Taiwan is our eighth largest trading partner — only a fraction smaller than the United Kingdom (in American trade), and larger than France, Italy, the Netherlands, and India. Our trade ties with Taiwan are especially important in the area of technology, and specifically in Taiwan's massive role in the manufacture of semiconductors — fully fifty percent of the world's supply of which comes from Taiwanese suppliers. Even more important, Taiwanese manufacturers supply about ninety percent of the bespoke, advanced semiconductors that power the highest end of the technological sector, including most of our advanced military communications and sensor equipment. Would we go to war to defend our economic interests? We certainly have in the past. On its own, though, it is not an adequate reason; leaving aside for the moment any ethical considerations, the fact is that a crisis over Taiwan would also likely rupture our far larger trading relationship

Taiwan: Chronicle of a Crisis Postponed

with China (now our third largest trading partner, recently down from first.) But the trade ties do add weight and depth to the long-standing political relations, its past as an ally, its present fact as a key defense and security partner.

And then there is this: Taiwan is the literal — and littoral — front line in constraining Chinese hard power projection. If China were able to subjugate Taiwan, either politically or militarily, to the point where China's navy could establish bases on its eastern shore, it would tilt the equation in the Pacific. China has launched a bid for extensive global naval power; a long-term but active ambition. It is an understandable ambition: China's economy is vastly dependent on the flow of commercial, industrial, and energy goods in and out of its "Near Seas," and sustained American naval dominance of those waters is understandably an uncomfortable reality for Beijing. A desire to advance its own naval capacity to protect its commercial interests at sea is natural, and on its own terms it is potentially uncomplicated for the United States. Indeed, for a brief period in the early 2000s, it seemed like China's return to the seas for the first time in five hundred years could add to the net global capacity to protect globalization. But, to misuse a metaphor, that ship has long since sailed. In the Xi Jinping era, China has more fully revealed (and arguably more fully developed) its global ambitions, its desire for a blue water navy, and its intent to use this and other features of its growing power to confront and constrain American hegemony, and eventually displace it. As Rush Doshi in his book on China's "long game" documents, this is an ambition both stated and revealed. Yet it is also an ambition constrained by multiple layers of geography and alliances. And those constraints start in the first island chain, of which Taiwan is an essential anchor.

Does China's bid for global naval capacity matter?

Throughout the modern period, global naval power has been the handmaiden of hegemony. Portugal, the Ottomans, the Dutch, Spain, France: all once competed for global naval dominance. The British, securing it in the late 1600s, used it to create its empire and thereby to reshape the modern world, laying the foundation for modern globalization. (They did this with great brutality, with vast slaveholdings, and by becoming history's largest drug cartel.) In the post-colonial world, the United States has been the world's dominant naval power, and found a formula to support an international (now global) trade and financial regime without relying on a colonial infrastructure. Dominance of the high seas has allowed us to foster and to protect the liberal trading system on which so much American and global growth is now predicated (fully eighty-five percent of world trade by value moves by sea); and to protect the flow of oil (and increasingly) gas out of the Strait of Hormuz, on which so much American and global growth is still predicated (and will be for another decade or two); and to wield American power in defense of our interests in literally every corner of the globe; and to help us defeat the Soviet Union. Together with American financial, energy and technological power, our power on the seas has been an essential feature of American dominance. We give it up at great, great cost. Erosion of the first island chain would not collapse American naval dominance or guarantee China's — they still have a long distance to travel to mount a genuinely global navy; but it would certainly be an important shift in the wrong direction.

There is in the United States these days a burgeoning movement, both left and right, that would eschew American dominance or primacy, or at least argue that it is not worth the costs and the risks of maintaining it. This is not the place for a full critical engagement with that argument, but suffice it here to note two essential things. First, that what follows American primacy is not necessarily a period of peaceful multilateralism, as some of the advocates of this argument advance; far more likely is militarized crises in Europe and Asia as the two powers most wrong-footed by the American-led order, Russia and China, push back, and push back hard. As America relinquishes its salience around the world, the world grows more Hobbesian and more cruel and dangerous. And second, for all the ills recently associated with the forward projection of American power, it is easy to forget the roles that American power has played in deterring and defeating illiberal forces, in protecting the global commons, and in generating global public goods. All while the United States profits extensively from the role of the dollar as the world's dominant currency — a different plank of power than our military dominance, but far from unconnected to it. It is hard to imagine any sphere of public life where increased Chinese influence in globalization and global order would not come at a meaningful cost to American interests, and those of close allies. We would cede this territory at great cost and great risk.

The fact that Taiwan is the front line of constraining Chinese global ambition is an argument that cuts both ways: it also makes it much, much more costly to defend. To take a contrasting example: if Tanzania's maturing democracy were threatened by Uganda, the systemic or ordering risks of not responding would be minor; Uganda poses no threat to any other region or to global systems. We could defend Tanzania at very low risk and very low costs. The case with Taiwan is exactly the opposite: the costs to the international order of failing to come to Taiwan's defense are potentially substantial, precisely because it is China that is threatening, but by the same token the costs associated with Taiwan's defense are very large indeed. This will be America's dilemma. It is hard to construct a meaningful and viable concept of the American-led alliance system, the American-led order, or American values that does not incorporate a vital response to Taiwan; but any serious response in Taiwan must reflect the reality that it takes only one or two modest turns of the escalatory dial for us to be engaged in full blown war with China— and perhaps a wider conflagration.

China's reasons to prevent the independence of Taiwan, and/or to incorporate it fully into Chinese sovereignty, are the precise obverse of America's interests. There are reasons of history and reasons of commerce, and there are reasons of legacy. Certainly Xi Jinping has repeatedly stressed the importance of accomplishing this goal, although he has been careful to leave open the option of political outcomes and has set no firm timetable for it. There are issues of ideology, and arguably of the threat posed by the vibrancy of Taiwanese democracy among a nation of Han Chinese — though the virulence of that threat is easily exaggerated, given how tightly the Communist Party is able to control the media narrative and news consumption among its population. But above all there are reasons of strategy.

The most sanguine observers argue that Xi can be satisfied simply by preventing Taiwanese independence. It is possible that that is true, and it certainly seems wise to maintain an American policy aimed at dissuading Taiwan from seeking independence; after all, a Taiwanese bid for independence would most certainly trigger a crisis. But it is hard to rest comfortably on that position. For a start, the underlying logic about China's calculation of its own interests, of the possibility of Chinese forbearance, does not adequately explain its recent behavior in a parallel case: Hong Kong. The *status quo ante* in Hong Kong allowed China to maintain its deep commercial and financial interests in Hong Kong's success, and to prevent any kind of serious move towards more democratic governance, and to control information about what was happening on the island (when the "umbrella protests" took hold, information about it was sparsely available to the population in mainland China). And yet, despite what seemed to most outside observers to be an eminently sustainable situation, Beijing chose to pass a deeply intrusive bill in 2019 designed to improve its ability to arrest Hong Kong citizens and move them to Macau or China. This triggered protests in Hong Kong, and rather than weather the protests as it had successfully done in the past, Beijing passed an even harsher "National Security Law" and moved to implement it through a combination of intense surveillance, intimidation, coercion, arrests, and an unexplainable coincidence of traffic accidents, balcony falls, and other deaths among leading activists. And this, despite the fact that in doing so, it paid two important prices: a measurable flight of citizens from Hong Kong to other major Asian cities, including from the vital financial industry, and an erosion of the "one country, two systems" posture which to date has been an important part of its political strategy for Taiwan. It chose the radical action anyway.

Moreover, the sanguine view of Chinese self-restraint does not adequately contend with the strategic naval role that Taiwan plays in helping to enclose the Chinese PLAN from its wider "far seas" ambitions. China has few options here. Theoretically, it could escape the constrictions of the first island chain if it could convince the Philippines to provide it with basing rights on the Philippine Sea. But despite repeated efforts to woo the authoritarian President Duterte towards

Beijing, China has made little or no progress, owing to stubborn resistance from the Philippine armed forces, who are still deeply enmeshed in the long-standing alliance and defense partnership with the United States. (And yes, there is an irony in China's options being limited by virtue of a questionably democratic posture of the Philippine military.) Taiwan is China's only credible option for improving its strategic position in the Pacific.

Given this, and given uncertainty about Xi's intentions, and given the very real possibility that the PLA's assessment of American capacity and American intent could lead it to overestimate its confidence in victory, it seems wise to assume that, under a range of readily imaginable circumstances, China's temptation to absorb Taiwan will outweigh its calculation of potential costs and risks. So Taiwan and the West have no real choice but to work seriously at deterring war, and at preparing for its possible eventuality.

What would a Chinese effort to take Taiwan look like, and who would win?

In the myriad writings on this, inside and outside the American government, a wide range of strategies are depicted. They start with those sometimes described as gray, namely the use of political and informational tactics, economic inducements, and perhaps private and quiet coercion, to change the political equation in Taiwan without the application of the direct use of military force. This, of course, is China's least costly and least risky tactic. The use of informational warfare, smear campaigns, disinformation campaigns, and possibly more nefarious Russian-style tactics can be combined (more accurately, *are* being combined) with China's naval buildup to create a perception in Taiwan of inevitability: an image of a PLAN with dominance of the bordering seas, doubt about American resolve and response, dissension among those who would pursue independence or deepen the alliance, and ultimately a Taipei capitulation to deeper Chinese political and even military participation in the island's affairs. But Taiwan has been successful so far in rebuffing such tactics, and anyway such tactics do not always succeed — far from it. Russia tried these tactics in Ukraine, for example, and they failed to produce a political outcome favorable to Moscow — at which point Moscow escalated to military options. Beijing might do the same if it sees that political strategies are failing (and if it is confident that it will win.)

By many accounts, what comes next is a Chinese naval blockade of Taiwan, designed to inflict substantial economic costs on the island, sufficient for them to sue for "peace" — that is, to capitulate. This would be relatively straightforward for China to implement. Even though Taiwan has American-made and French-made frigates in its fleet and a wide range of missiles and minesweeping capacities, there is almost no chance that the Republic of China Navy could stand up to the PLA Navy if China determined to enforce a blockade. That is, unless the United States weighed in, and mounted a counter-blockade offensive or deployed parts of the Seventh Fleet (perhaps together with Japan and Australia, perhaps others) to provide a corridor through which ships approaching the Taiwan Strait could sail under our protection. At that stage, China would have to decide whether it was willing to attack American ships, potentially provoking a wider war. Michael O'Hanlon recently undertook a careful table-top estimate of this scenario, and concluded this: the key factor in determining whether China or the United States emerges victorious in this scenario (leaving aside for a moment the deeper question of what it means to "win" in this context) would be the rate at which Chinese submarines could successfully target American and allied naval shipping, versus the commercial shipping that our navies would be trying to protect. His second and essential point is that experience and reasonable estimates of Chinese command and targeting capabilities provide a wide range of outcomes, in some of which the United States "wins," in others of which China "wins" — thus both sides should be in doubt of easy victory here. I am slightly more pessimistic: the narrowness of the sea lane as you approach the Strait, and the swift rise of the seabed to too-shallow levels except in the narrow sea lane, suggest to me that it would be easier than sometimes assumed for China to make well-informed projections about the position of commercial ships and distinguish them from naval ships, meaning that its successful targeting of American ships would likely be at the high end of O'Hanlon's estimate. But even so, this scenario still leaves an option to escalate in American hands.

I am also less certain that a blockade is the low-risk option for China. Modern shipping is a complex business, and there is no such thing as a ship sailing goods only to Taiwanese ports. Ships going in and out of Taiwanese ports will be laden with goods destined for China itself as well, and potentially for several other countries. Those goods form parts of globally integrated supply chains from potentially dozens of countries; indeed, Taiwan is at the very heart of global supply chains. There are essential Taiwanese components in Chinese goods, as there are in German, American, Indian, and French goods, and so on. By squeezing the Taiwanese economy, China would also be hurting several other players, perhaps triggering a

Taiwan: Chronicle of a Crisis Postponed

global economic slowdown. The imposition of a blockade in the Taiwan Strait would likely cause Lloyds of London and other maritime insurers to declare not just the Straits but the adjacent seas a "war risk" zone, creating endless complications for shipping firms in those waters. The disruption to sea-borne trade in the Western Pacific — and thus to the entire global economy — could be substantial. In short, in trying to squeeze Taiwan's jugular, China risks severing one or two of its own arteries. It might still decide that the costs are worth it, but the costs would be real.

What's more, an easier blockade to mount successfully is the one that the United States could do in response: an oil blockade at the Strait of Malacca (through which China imports roughly eighty percent of its liquid fuels, which in turn constitute about fifty percent of its overall energy supply.) At this distance from Chinese mainland ports, the US Navy still has a clear, decisive advantage over the PLA. There are some complexities to an oil blockade here (like the substantial additional costs Japan would have to pay to re-route its oil imports), but they are more manageable than a wider commercial blockade in the Taiwan Strait.

Which leaves more direct military operations. Oversimplifying, there could be two types. One would be a Chinese missile and air campaign to pummel Taiwanese defenses, and thereby to degrade their overall defenses, and to demonstrate Chinese power, and to expose American indecision (if we fail to show up in defense) or incapacity (if our defensive efforts do not substantially diminish the effect of the Chinese campaign). Taiwanese defenses against this kind of attack are not trivial: a combination of hardened bunkers on its eastern coast, anti-missile defense technology, and anti-air defenses would confront China with a number of obstacles.

But not too many, alas: over a protracted campaign China would certainly overwhelm Taiwanese defense (including its cyber defenses, which at present are no match for China's offensive capacity.) Again, unless the United States chose to respond. At which point the scenarios get very wide-ranging and very dangerous.

Most complicated and dangerous for China, of course, is the second military course of action: an actual invasion of the island. History shows, however, that maritime assaults have proved among the hardest and most costly of military options. And in this case Taiwan has substantial mining, missile, and airpower options to make this hard for China — though China in turn has more of all of those instruments and could likely ultimately overwhelm Taiwan's defenses in the Strait itself. But Taiwan also has both 160,000 troops and 1,600,000 reservists who would, in this scenario, presumably be well motivated to fight (though they are not particularly well trained.) That could make it extremely hard for China to get ashore without very high costs, and once ashore to subdue the population. At the very least China would have to prepare for the contingency of a long and costly counter-insurgency campaign. And again, all of this assumes that the United States does not join the fight.

Yet every scenario in which the United States does join the fight comes with a crucial challenge. To increase our confidence of prevailing (in the narrow sense), we must do two very costly things: put large portions of the American fleet at risk, inside the range of Chinese missiles; and make substantial military moves against China's missile batteries and its command and control apparatus, which likely means air or missile attacks on positions inside mainland China. We might well prevail, in the narrow sense of causing greater

Chinese losses than we incur, and in causing China to abandon its military operation against Taiwan. But not before we were in every meaningful sense of the word at war with the PLA, and not before we were risking Chinese nuclear escalation. And if we are not willing to take those risks, we might well lose.

And what if we lose? Would an American loss in any one of a series of Taiwan scenarios constitute a "Suez moment," as Hal Brands and others have argued? Would the American-led order inevitably and inexorably decline? The short answer is: possibly, partially.

In attempting to analyze this properly, we must first ignore the arguments made by many in Washington that the marred American withdrawal from Afghanistan profoundly eroded Western credibility. The evidence for this assertion is exceptionally slim. Anyone following the debate in Beijing, for example, heard the exact opposite: that the American withdrawal, a costly one at that, signaled the arrival of a much greater degree of seriousness in Washington about containing, even potentially confronting, China's mounting power. It seemed as if our much-touted "pivot" to Asia, our promised shift of focus to a rising China, might finally be taking place. The fact that only weeks later, two of our closest allies, the United Kingdom and Australia, chose to substantially deepen their military partnership with us by means of a large nuclear submarine and technology deal shows the limited effect of the Afghan withdrawal. For Beijing our retreat from Afghanistan surely denoted a shift in the priorities of American power, though the extent of our willingness to exercise our power remains an open and vexing question.

Beyond that, credibility — a much beloved concept in American statecraft — is actually quite complicated. While much of the academic literature on international relations is abstract and obscure, one place where it has made a valuable contribution to policy is in puncturing easy claims about credibility, especially the notion that failure to stand up in one domain necessarily erodes credibility in another domain. Think of it this way: would the Poles or the Ukrainians be happy that the United States chose to pour massive quantities of its hard power into the defense of Taiwan? In principle, maybe; but in practice they would be deeply nervous that that effort substantially diminished American capability or willingness to help them defend their eastern borders. Or the reverse: if the United States chose to respond to Russian aggression in Ukraine by mounting a large-scale hard power war in that theater, would Japan and Taiwan feel reassured? Or would they worry that the United States had thereby meaningfully diminished its real material capacity to deter China? In the real world of limited power and mounting challenges, allies are more likely to weigh American actions through the prism of jealous insecurity and worry less about the consistency of our policy.

And yet what seems likely is that whereas a non-defense of Taiwan might not collapse or deeply erode the credibility of our alliance commitments in other theatres, it certainly would have such a damaging effect in Asia. Perhaps if the United States made crystal clear that a non-defense of Taiwan was driven by the fact that Taiwan is not a formal treaty ally, it might ease the sting for other allies in the region. But not by much: given how "alliance-adjacent" Taiwan has been, given how long standing a defense partner it has been, given the economic, democratic, and strategic stakes in Taiwan, it is far more likely that allies such as Korea and Japan, and close defense partners such as Singapore (and increasingly Vietnam), would see the decision in profoundly negative terms, and become far more worried about their own security. An already somewhat unsolid alliance with Korea could be shaken, perhaps irreparably. The alliance with Japan would likely continue, given how profoundly dependent Japan has long been on the American security guarantee, but the odds that Japan would move to develop its own nuclear deterrent would increase substantially and swiftly. Singapore, already divided between elites who see its interests lying in the American security relationship and those who see its commercial interests lying in China, might well feel forced to choose, and to choose China. China's naval, strategic and political position in the Western Pacific would be substantially buttressed, and ours would be weakened. The stability of Asia would be thrown into sharp doubt. Every country in the region — and some beyond — would hedge against American uncertainty and adopt a more accommodating stance to China. China's capacity to project power, military and political, into the wider global system would meaningfully increase, and ours would meaningfully diminish.

We have deep interests in Taiwan's continued autonomy. Even the most cursory glance at the strategic and commercial map of Asia suffices to dismiss the "we have no interests here" argument, even if democracy does not count (*which it does*.) But we cannot be certain of Taiwan's victory, with our help, in limited engagements; and the prospects for our "victory" grow only when we escalate to the point of a wide-ranging war against the PLA, not just across the reaches of the Western

Pacific but also involving attacks on China's mainland. And this is to say nothing of the risk of nuclear escalation — which, as scholars such as Caitlin Talmadge have pointed out, is quite real. All of which combines to make a resoundingly clear point — that the only good version of a war in Taiwan is one that is never fought.

For Xi Jinping and the Chinese leadership, it remains the case that a political and informational strategy to subdue Taiwan is likely preferable to a military option. But only so long as it works. And the success of any such strategy is surely in significant doubt. To move to a military option, however, Xi has to be convinced that the costs can be borne and that the war can be won. Indeed, he would need to be almost certain of victory. To continue to maintain an effective deterrence against war, then, it follows that the United States and its partners must increase the potential costs, and increase the uncertainty.

Much of what needs doing is known — but it needs the doing. Taiwan some time ago adopted an asymmetric defense strategy vis-à-vis China's greater power — that is, a focus on low-cost, resilient defensive capacities designed to deny China a swift, low-cost entry into Taiwanese territory (as opposed, say, to the procurement of ever more expensive frigates that are acutely vulnerable to Chinese missiles). This strategy has only grown in importance. But as the analysts of a bipartisan task force led by Bonnie Glaser, Richard Bush, and Michael Green (among the deans of Taiwan studies in the capital) point out, it has not been implemented in full. Far from it. Indeed, in the vigorous debates between Taiwan hawks and Taiwan doves, one clear point of consensus was the urgency for Taiwan to shift away from a defense focus that involved the purchase and maintenance of large, high-end military assets (which China could likely rapidly defeat in war) and move towards the real implementation of its asymmetric strategy. There is somewhat less of a consensus among China-defense scholars about what the United States needs to do to buttress our deterrent posture against China as a whole — whether by bulking up defenses in fixed positions, shifting to a more distributed defensive posture, investing more in technological counter-moves — but there is wide consensus that implementation of a new posture badly lags behind the recognition of the mounting China challenge. If our objectives are to protect Taiwan and to avoid war, then right now we are asleep at the wheel. Everyone also agrees that the United States should put substantial priority on getting Japan to move beyond the modest steps it has so far taken to possibly, kind of, quasi, semi prepare for coming to Taiwan's defense in the case of an attack.

For Taiwan itself, quite apart from asymmetric defense, there is more work to be done on the issue of political and economic resilience. Taiwan has begun to invest in a range of forms of resilience, but few observers' question that they need to do more. On political and informational resilience: internationally, perhaps the most impressive example of a countries' national resilience strategy is in Finland, which, faced with a range of forms of cyber, political, informational, and threatening pressures from Russia, has revitalized a strategy that engages its military, parliament, media, civil society, the business sector, and the government to share information about Russian tactics, prepare for attacks, and generally decrease the effectiveness of Russia's efforts. Perhaps similar strategies could help buttress Taiwan against Chinese gray tactics. It should also look seriously at the option of building out a port on its eastern shore, perhaps in the estuary that is much easier to defend or resupply than any of its ports in the Taiwan Strait. On economic resilience, there are a number of preparatory steps such as Taiwan can take to increase its options. That involves steps such as stockpiling reserves of war munitions, medical equipment and supplies, some essential food stocks, and essential fuels (including air fuel.)

What is often missing from discussion of Taiwan's defense options is a wider global strategy. The defense of Taiwan is principally its own responsibility, and secondarily that of the United States. But there are stakes here, too, for all of those allies and partners whose interests are impinged upon by instability in Asia, those who would not like to see China in a position increasingly to exert its power in world affairs; those who have stakes in the free flow of energy and commerce on the high seas; those with a deep interest in resisting a world in which authoritarian powers move by coercion to establish spheres of influence in which they could be entangled. Many of these countries will face similar dilemmas to ours — many of them (ironically including Japan) have vast trade and financial relationships with China that they will be reluctant to risk. But the United States must work to convince them that the risks are much greater if war breaks out than through deliberate deterrence. If you wish peace, prepare for war: the old Latin adage certainly applies in this new era of Chinese power.

For the allies that are less likely to put military assets in play, there are still a number of steps that they can prepare themselves to take in the case of a Taiwan emergency. Just a partial list includes: votes in defense of the Republic of China in key international institutions; curtailment of visas for Chinese students and scientists, especially in key technology domains; targeted technology sanctions; targeted economic sanctions; targeted individual sanctions; energy sanctions; disinvestment from key sectors; blocking Chinese firms from acquiring nationally registered firms (or shares of firms) in the energy, technology and agricultural sectors; recognition of Taiwan; joint investment in supply chain diversification; joint investment in strategic minerals production. And crucially, this includes allies in Europe and other regions, not just in the Pacific. Making Taiwan a global — and not just a regional — problem will play to American strengths and exploit China's continuing weaknesses. If we think about deterrence only in the seas on China's eastern borders, we cede a massive geographical advantage to Beijing. At present China has far flung economic, energy and diplomatic interests, but its capacity to reinforce those by hard power projection lags far behind. This is China's global dilemma, and we should do nothing to help them find a way out of it.

We are not ready for a Taiwan emergency. Despite repeated alarms, 2021 did not see such an emergency, and there are reasons for calm about the short term. But over the medium term, the possibility of a Chinese military action in the Taiwan Strait or on the island cannot be ruled out. The United States and its Asian allies have major interests in preventing that outcome. We also have a major interest in avoiding war with China.

All this being said, it seems unwise to me that the United States should move off of its declaratory policy of strategic ambiguity. Richard Hass and others have made the case for this shift, arguing that the current policy does not adequately deter China. If we were confident of victory in low-threshold crises and confident also of our ability to maintain "escalation dominance," or to control the level of violence in the event of hostilities, perhaps this would be wise policy. But we are not. Speaking more loudly does not increase the size of our stick.

We would be much wiser to increase the size — or at least the potency, the unpredictability, and the survivability — of our stick. And wiser, too, to communicate privately to China about the steps that we and other allies would be prepared to undertake in the case of a military move against Taiwan. At the same time, we can and should stipulate our continued conviction that, short of a military crisis, we oppose Taiwan's independence, all the while retaining a freedom of tactical maneuver. We need to get this right: to keep our heads and stay calm, build our strength and rouse our allies, recognize our strategic responsibilities and be prepared to act with moral courage. Otherwise we are headed for costly abandonment or consequential failure.

DURS GRÜNBEIN

Expressionist Film

We arrived at our goal in the dark,
via the Avus. The green eye
of the Radio Tower winking, as we
saw the city sprawled below us.

The broad streets radiated inwards
reaching towards a center,
monsters' fingers, from the days
of silent film, closing round a throat.

The journey passed by ditches,
new building sites, gaps between houses,
where excavated earth lay in heaps
glinting like slaughtered beasts on the hook.

Under S-Bahn bridges they sat on their
mattress thrones, wrapped in blankets,
figures of the night from all the countries
of Europe, the princes of alcohol.

The jagged shadows emerging from
courtyards met in front of posters
for a retrospective of UFA-films
called From Caligari to Hitler.

In Cold Arms of Water

I picked roses on the Wannsee
and don't know who to give them to.
Jakob van Hoddis

We left the city on muddy paths
along the riverbank. Bare trees
dogged us unseen like shadows
in the icy water, the grey cross hatching.
We brushed past blackthorn, breaking
off alder branches with our shoulders.
We tramped through unmined terrain.
With us the dead, the fog of breath.
Dangers almost all banished. That was new.

It was those days that fall between the years.
The fear was nameless now. But the forest
stood in quarantine, an unpassable zone.
Through tree trunks we glimpsed its sparkle:
the Wannsee, lake of madness, lake of silver.
This is where the poet fell through the ice, this
is where he was beyond all earthly help.
A mask was caught in the bramble thorns.
And night was enclosed in cold arms of water.

East-West-Axis

The cold glint of gold in the winter sun.
The monuments no longer blaze like back
in the day, the barrels of anti-aircraft guns, clumsy tanks.
The old capital of terror turns over in its sleep,
shifts from one side to the other: East-West.

A great listening ear hovers in the air
above the Tiergarten trees, a funnel
filled with the echoes of victory and love parades.
And no one on the axis, the vanishing point
where war and post-war disappeared, eerie,
the spine of the city, broken over again.

How small one feels here, and especially
after so many decades living in this place,
where the dead read the living the riot act.
Where perspective is all, and memories become
anniversaries. Where houses in the distance
hum and high above the oily waters
the overhead railway rushes on by.

Lumière

This black train, puffing out
clouds of white smoke, still
races towards the viewers.
They say some
jumped up in fright,
thinking the catastrophe was about to occur.

The light on the wall of the salon, light
from an incarnate summer's day – so different
from the Paris light at the same moment,
outside on the squares, the boulevards –
flooding over them as they sat in the dark.

Perhaps it was panic, maybe also concern
for the child on the hand of the elderly lady
(Madame Lumière, as we know now),
toddling so close to the edge of the platform.

Concern perhaps, also shock,
but not yet horror
at all the implacable trains
that have criss-crossed the century,
the endless rows of sealed trucks.

The tracks heading straight towards them,
past them and out of the frame.
And like the smoke from the chimney,
the shadows of those waiting impatiently,
like the film itself, ghostly,
the fatal locomotive of time.

Flea Market

Enough of these silver spoons and tropical helmets,
widows' brooches and porcelain;
enough of these old bird cages, bent out of shape
and the photo portraits of dead children.
Set up in rows on wobbly tables,
under canvas in wind or bad weather, what
do they say, what do they hide, these
remnants of the nameless crimes
about which the uniforms and daggers of honour
say almost nothing.
How can one's thoughts not go astray
faced with the piles of glasses,
and old leather suitcases?
Sorry stuff. The miserable junk
recalls the former owners, all long dead.

We are the discarded things, they cry.
Time has vanquished us, the wonder:
modernity has never taken place.

Translated by Karen Leeder

DAVID GREENBERG

The War on Objectivity in American Journalism

In May 2021, a newly hired journalist at the Associated Press, a twenty-two-year-old Stanford graduate named Emily Wilder, began posting provocative musings on Twitter about fighting between Israel and Hamas. Wilder had not been assigned to write about the Middle East. She may have thought she was tweeting as a private citizen. But the Associated Press had just reminded its employees that they are prohibited "from openly expressing their opinions on political matters and other public issues," as the wire service reported about her case, "for fear that could damage the news organization's reputation for objectivity and jeopardize its many reporters around the world." Two weeks on the job, Wilder had run afoul of one of her employer's sacrosanct rules.

But Wilder's mistake was bigger than that. Not only was she failing to uphold journalistic objectivity by sounding off about a sensitive issue while still a cub reporter, she also derided the AP's very commitment to objectivity. "'Objectivity' feels fickle when the basic terms we use to report news implicitly take a claim," she tweeted, making an argument at once convoluted and sophomoric. "Using 'israel' but never 'palestine,' or 'war' but not 'siege and occupation' are political choices — yet media make those exact choices all the time without being flagged as biased." Setting aside Wilder's confusions about the Middle East — the AP does, for example, use the terms "occupation" and "siege" — her words showed no appreciation that editors at the Associated Press, as at most top-tier news outlets, think hard about and often revisit the content of their stylebooks: when to say "war" and when to say "occupation," when to use "Palestine" and when to avoid it. It is precisely because of this diligence that the wire service is rarely "flagged as biased."

Most of us would agree that the AP's blue-chip reputation for telling it like it is — which endures, for the most part, even in our age of near-total politicization — is a good thing. The world needs high-quality professional reporting on issues far and wide, presented in a way that diverse readers can trust as accurate and not colored by politics. For over one hundred seventy years, the AP has shared its stories with hundreds and even thousands of subscribing newspapers, radio and TV stations, and web portals. Small-town dailies use it as their prime source of foreign and national news. Its analyses of election outcomes are so well respected that almost everyone else relies on them.

It was not surprising, then, that the AP fired Wilder. "Emily Wilder was let go because she had a series of social media posts that showed a clear bias toward one side and against another in one of the most divisive and difficult stories we cover," Brian Carovillano, the AP's managing editor, explained. That didn't stop a mudslide of hypocritical outrage. On the right, fair-weather free-speech fans wallowed in her dismissal. On the left, pundits who had pitilessly shrugged off scores of unfair firings piously intoned that no one should be punished for expressing opinions. And they had a point: Wilder's superiors could have simply reprimanded her and suspended her from Twitter until she recommitted to her organization's rules.

Beyond the politics of cancellation, however, there was a larger inconsistency at work.

That inconsistency concerned journalistic objectivity. Wilder's firing came as most liberals were lamenting — properly — the collapse of trust in mainstream journalism. Over several years, millions of Americans had forsaken their faith in the traditional "objective" news providers, which they came to conclude were ideologically skewed. As institutions ceded their nonpartisan reputations, willingly or unwillingly, the void was filled by mostly inferior news sources: partisan mouthpieces, fulminating talking heads, trashy internet sites, amateur punditry, dashed-off Facebook comments, unverified viral retweets, late-night comedians, state-of-the-art misinformation, out-and-out fake news, and other varieties of click bait.

The consequences are well-known and grim. We saw that when a huge portion of the citizenry, prodded by Donald Trump and his apparatchiks, determined the coronavirus pandemic to be a giant hoax. That delusion led many to spurn medical advice to get vaccinated, deepening the crisis.

Indeed, throughout the pandemic, the breakdown of trust in journalism helped to politicize the crisis, so that what should have been utterly apolitical questions — technical and scientific questions, such as whether to close schools or mandate masks — ended up turning on ideological leanings and parochial loyalties, not on a dispassionate assessment of the facts.

We saw the same stupendous distortion with the presidential election in 2020. Again Trump and company urged Americans to disbelieve traditional news sources in order to sow doubt about his loss to Joe Biden. The Capitol riot followed. One bulwark against Trump's disinformation was the sober-minded work of the Associated Press, which four days after Election Day concluded its professional review of the Pennsylvania vote to declare Biden the winner. The factuality of Biden's victory and the AP's role in establishing that truth played a crucial role in those uneasy transition months. They reaffirmed that, despite our partisan echo chambers, dependable sources of information are still in place, still doing their job, still a mainstay of our democracy. We were not yet hopelessly trapped in an irresolvable clash of narratives, because responsible empirical analyses of the narratives could still be made.

These two headline stories, Trump's fraud claims and the coronavirus, highlighted democracy's need for politically uninflected journalism that is committed to as complete and accurate an account of the facts as possible. In both cases, what we call objective reporting served as a stabilizing force in a destabilized time. That should have led objectivity's detractors to tip their hats to the Associated Press and other news agencies that try to uphold it. But in the Emily Wilder case and in our debates since, we are hearing only whooping and hollering over objectivity's imminent demise.

Actually the war on objectivity began many years ago. It is one of the distinguishing features of the cultural and intellectual history of our time.

Objectivity in journalism, an ideal that took root early in the early twentieth century, can be understood by considering the regime that preceded it. In the nineteenth century, newspapers were proudly partisan, not only in their editorials but also in their news columns—and sometimes in their names: the *St. Louis Democrat*, the *Plattsburgh Republican*. They openly rooted for candidates and causes and made no pretense of speaking to anyone else. That style of news never disappeared. Into the twentieth century, papers such as the McCormick family's *Chicago Tribune* blatantly slanted their coverage to promote a political program. What's more, there always were (and still are) an endless variety of magazine writers, editorialists, polemicists, radio hosts, and others who aim not to report but to interpret, explain, argue, advocate, preach, or ridicule. The rise of the ideal of objectivity never eliminated or threatened the prevalence of opinion in journalism. But in the new century it became standard for newspapers — which were the chief source of news — to avow that they would, as *The New York Times* famously said in 1896, "give the news impartially, without fear or favor, regardless of party, sect, or interests involved." *This* was the intellectual and journalistic innovation. The *Times'* approach quickly shaped print journalism and, later, radio and television.

Journalistic objectivity was rooted in several assumptions. For a start, it was based on the view that reporting — news-gathering — was the press' central task. It was thus informed by the hardscrabble reporter's "just the facts" empiricism. This in turn was premised on the philosophical idea that empiricism was possible, despite the biases that inevitably attend each of our positions, and that it was valuable. Yet objectivity must not be supported in its naïve version: there is no such thing as pure investigation, research, and fact-finding. The influence of subjectivity, its unavoidable presence, had to be acknowledged and confronted. As Michael Schudson argued in *Discovering the News* — still, four decades later, the best history of the subject — newsmen of the 1920s (there were not yet many women) were not oblivious to the limitations of their own perspectives. To the contrary, they were quite aware of them. That is why journalistic objectivity, and the corollary notion of identifying, neutralizing, and even eliminating biases, emerged. Objectivity is the unceasing attempt to correct subjectivity and thereby come closer to what people of many standpoints can agree is the truth.

It was easy enough to be accurate, as Walter Lippmann wrote in *Public Opinion*, when reporting on the stock exchange or a baseball score. Numbers defeat prejudices, at least for honest people. But the size and the complexity of modern society, the unquantifiability of the large human stories that had to be covered, made most subjects hard for even a skilled, knowledgeable correspondent to know with certainty. The attempt to do so was further impeded by the rise of corporate public relations and government spin doctors, who made it risky to accept officials' claims at face value. Above all, Lippmann reminded us, human beings have only a partial view of the world — a perspective that creates biases that can distort, even benignly, their transmission of the facts. Lippmann and others of his era thus conceived of journalistic objectivity not as some uncanny ability that reporters possess to divine God's Honest Truth, but as an epistemological safeguard — a disciplined bulwark against the ever-present pitfalls of subjectivity and bias. "As our minds become more deeply aware of their own subjectivism," Lippmann wrote, "we find a zest in objective method that is not otherwise there." As Thomas Nagel, perhaps our most influential contemporary defender of philosophical objectivity, elaborates in *The View from Nowhere*: "Objectivity is a method of understanding... To acquire a more objective understanding of some aspect of life or the world we step back from our initial view of it and form a new conception which has that view and its relation to the world as its object. In other words, we place ourselves in the world that is to be understood."

Reporters in the 1920s didn't need to read Lippmann (or philosophy) to know that perfect objectivity is not attainable. It is an ideal supported by a set of procedures and norms, meant to remedy as much as possible the biases that afflict everyone. Upholding objectivity means not that journalists will never succumb to bias. It means that they will identify bias and think critically about it — that they will follow policies and practices to minimize and to correct for it, in the realistic but rigorous spirit of what Amartya Sen has called "positional objectivity." The impossibility of pure objectivity is not an excuse for collapsing into subjectivity. Objectivity is an asymptotic pursuit, but when taken seriously it can certainly suffice for a credible and "checkable" account of events. And it can always get better.

For a century, then, policies and practices designed to promote objectivity have underpinned reported journalism. In the reporting stage, they call for independently verifying sources'

claims and talking to a mix of sources so as not to fall captive to one person's perspective. In the writing stage, they prescribe an antiseptic tone: no ideology, snark, self-righteousness, anger, euphoria, invective, or exaggeration. They call for furnishing evidence to substantiate doubtful assertions. They stipulate the attribution of claims to let readers judge their validity. They require the inclusion of multiple, competing explanations about complex or controversial issues. Similar practices exist for editing (having multiple editors review a story); photojournalism (no staging or doctoring images); even anchoring the news (the Olympian Cronkite delivery). Large news agencies concerned with protecting their reputation for objectivity also impose rules to reassure readers that their employees approach stories with an open mind. While correspondents may offer considered judgments about the events they cover, they must not have conflicts of interest — a scruple that is a small moral revolution in itself. And they may not crusade on behalf of a cause or spout off carelessly. Doing otherwise would compromise their credibility, as Emily Wilder learned the hard way.

To support these practices, individuals internalized professional norms and values. For most newsmen and newswomen, a job well done came to mean breaking stories, revealing important information, exposing high-level wrongdoing, delivering a thorough and reliable account of events. Newsroom reporters do not always consciously think of themselves as objective, but their practices adhere to the objective method. As Jack Shafer, an uncommonly thoughtful observer of the media, puts it, they "follow a hunch with reporting that could undermine the hunch, address possible criticisms, remain open to criticism and refutation, correct meaningful errors of fact, abandon dry wells instead of pretending they're gushers." The tenets of aspirationally objective journalists are not those of influence-seeking but of truth-seeking: skepticism, independent-mind-edness, scrupulousness. The professional reporter doesn't care if the official whom he caught in a lie is a Democrat or a Republican, or whether the subject of her thorough exposé is a corporate CEO or a union boss. Bob Woodward and Carl Bernstein insisted during Watergate that they weren't going after the president, just after the story. For those who view everything as politicized, or measured for its political effects, such impartiality may be hard to fathom.

It is important to keep in mind, too, that since perfect objectivity is unattainable, journalists inevitably have fallen short. Sometimes they have been insufficiently vigilant and let editorializing creep into their copy. Puff pieces, hatchet jobs, scandal-mongering, sensationalism, and loaded comments are occupational hazards. At other times, overly literal-minded or plodding journalists have committed the opposite error: letting the duty to air multiple viewpoints keep them from giving a true picture of events. This second fallacy was concisely summarized by the intellectual historian Thomas Haskell in an essay called "Objectivity Is Not Neutrality." Today it often goes by the inelegant name "both sides-ism," and today's media critics seem to think that they discovered it. In fact, the critique has induced bouts of self-scrutiny for decades. "It is current-day fancy to consider a journalist objective if he hands out slaps and compliments with evenhanded impartiality on both sides of the question," Archibald MacLeish wrote in 1941. "Such an idea is, of course, infantile. Objectivity consists in keeping your eye on the object [and] describing the object as it is — without regard to the feelings of anyone." In the 1950s, conscientious journalists saw how Senator Joe McCarthy manipulated them into publicizing charges that some prominent person was a Communist. "Our rigid formulae of so-called objectivity," complained Eric Sevareid of CBS, "... have given the lie the same prominence and impact that truth is given; they have elevated the influence of fools to that of wise men; the ignorant to the level of the learned; the evil to the level of the good."

Reminders like MacLeish's and Sevareid's were salutary. They forced journalists to stay alert to the dangers of a rote, unthinking application of their rules. They strengthened the cause of objectivity. MacLeish saw that the adherence to the "rigid formulae" of even-handedness represented a corruption, not a consummation, of the ideal. Objectivity did not require allowing liars to take advantage of the press. A lie, if widely proclaimed and believed, should be neither ignored nor suppressed; it should be reported in context, along with the truth. The public needs to know about falsehoods being spread, whether by demagogues, propagandists, knaves, or fools. Nothing prevents the news reporter from dispassionately adducing the evidence that would make clear when claims are simple or complicated, broadly accepted or hotly contested, false or true. To believe otherwise is to misunderstand how journalism works.

Whereas a critique of mindlessly balanced coverage developed early in the twentieth century, only in the 1960s did there arise a call to jettison objectivity outright. In that turbulent era, liberalism was suffering a pincer attack. Both the New Left and the New Right assailed "establishment" liberalism not just over public policy choices but also on foundational grounds — for assuming its own values as normal or natural, rather than created and maintained to keep power. Part and parcel of this attack was a dual offensive against mainstream journalism. The left argued that that news sources were captive to their corporate owners and advertisers, that reporters were too deferential to governmental sources, that the pose of neutrality reinforced the status quo — that objectivity was a disguise for power. Marxists, post-modernists, and neo-pragmatists alike, from Noam Chomsky to Michel Foucault to Richard Rorty, promulgated variations on this crude theme; Chomsky, after attacking objectivity in 1968 in *American Power and the New Mandarins*, argued more sweepingly in the 1980s that the media writ large were engaged in the sinister project of "manufacturing consent" (its title a misreading of Lippmann) on behalf of the powerful. On the right, meanwhile, Southern racists such as George Wallace and Jesse Helms rallied conservatives by demonizing the news media as having abandoned their charge to be balanced; the correspondents jetting in to cover Montgomery, Little Rock, and Birmingham, they argued, were hostile to the segregationist South. ("The trouble with this country," declared Birmingham's public safety commissioner Eugene "Bull" Connor, "is communism, socialism, and journalism.") Others on the right argued sociologically. They held that the progressive college-educated arrivals in the newsrooms and the broadcast studios — "a small and unelected elite," in Spiro Agnew's phrase — were smuggling into ostensibly nonpartisan accounts beliefs that were in fact liberal: pro-civil rights, pro-counterculture, anti-Vietnam War, anti-Nixon. Both right and left saw objectivity as a cover for the liberal party line.

These critiques provoked enough soul-searching in the news business to keep the *Columbia Journalism Review* and a small army of journalism reviews, press critics, and ombudsmen in clover for decades. But objective journalism not only survived, it thrived. It did so by undertaking a thoughtful, incremental renegotiation of what the concept properly allowed: incorporating more context into news reports, creating space for interpretive and personal writing, revising cramped assumptions about what constituted excessive editorializing. The Fourth Estate bent so as not to break. *The Washington Post*'s Style section welcomed forays into New Journalism, letting literary-minded writers indulge a cheeky subjectivity and a hip flair. Newsrooms founded investigative teams that ignored daily deadlines in pursuit of depth. Veteran reporters were given license to venture into "news analysis," sharing their informed sense of what developments meant. *The New York Times* created its Op-Ed page to showcase a gamut of voices at variance with the staid unsigned editorials. And objectivity remained a bedrock principle.

This renegotiation led to a modus vivendi that Michael Schudson calls "Objectivity 2.0." Critics still found fault with the media — for the superficiality of television news, the post-Watergate lust for scandal, the perennial blight of pack journalism, and a lot more. Conservatives still pounded the press as skewed toward the left, and the left still charged that it was skewed to the right. Many journalists, having absorbed the attacks on "objectivity," now eschewed the word, talking instead about fairness and balance (terms that were not necessarily improvements). When, in 1996, the Society of Professional Journalists revised its ethics code, it replaced a line calling for "objectivity in reporting the news" with a reminder to "distinguish between advocacy and news reporting." But if the term fell from favor, the creation of escape valves for journalists' desire to interpret, contextualize, and opine left intact the underlying insistence on the dispassionate empirical reporting of "hard news" carried out without fear or favor.

Yet it was not long before Objectivity 2.0 came under fire as well. One reason was a changed mediasphere that greatly magnified the space for opinion compared to hard news. As Ronald N. Jacobs and Eleanor Townsley remark in their book *The Space for Opinion,* the "dramatic expansion in news commentary and opinion ... accelerated particularly rapidly after the 1970s." There were many reasons for this, but perhaps none was more important than the lure of punditry. In the midcentury years, journalists would spend their early careers reporting the news and then, at mid-career, perhaps graduate to a column, depart for a magazine, or make it onto television. But for journalists of the 1980s and 1990s — coming of age with television having eclipsed print — punditry beckoned early. (The term "pundit," first applied in the 1920s to sage columnists such as Lippmann, now meant garrulous television commentators.) Pundits were celebrities, stars. Why toil away at a local paper in Oklahoma or work the metro desk when you could head straight to Washington and the limelight? Opinion journalism also cost less than reporting. Objective reporting had regained its prestige, or at least its footing, but it was being pushed aside by opinion.

With the rehabilitation of subjectivity under the mantle of opinion came a vogue for the once-taboo first person. The old culture frowned on the use of *I* in the news columns. By the late twentieth century, however, *I* was everywhere: confessional talk shows such as *Oprah*, the memoir boom, blogging, internet writing in general. Even academics clotted their articles with clunkers like "I mean to suggest..." and "I want to propose..." and "I think it is a mistake to assume..." (One academic claimed that "the suppression of the authorial *I* in academic writing, is, ultimately, a rhetorical ploy" meant to foster "the appearance of objectivity.") In 2015 a critic in *Slate* bemoaned "The First-Person Industrial Complex," a torrent of experiential hot takes in online journalism that editors liked because they got traffic and writers liked because they could "build relationships with readers via self-exposure." It was the age of the "personal essay." Far from a mark of unreliable subjectivity, for many the first person was now an emblem of authenticity. Journalists — not only commentators but also news-gatherers — were themselves becoming public figures and then "brands." No brand distinguishes itself from the pack, or achieves "self-exposure," with a voiceless neutrality. (That is what fact-checkers are for, we think, even though fact-checkers perform a function we used to call reporting.) "Voice" has become a high-end journalistic virtue.

Then the internet pitched in to the new subjectivity. It did more than merely exalt the first person. Blogs, webzines, and *Drudge Report*-style portals elevated armchair analysts to the level of veteran beat reporters or experts. Every reader became a potential media critic, poking holes in authoritative statements, posting criticisms online, catapulting them through cyberspace. In a universe without objectivity as the lodestar, opinions came to be valued not for their veracity or their intellectual rigor, but for their authenticity, their sincerity, their provenance, or their wit (or what passes for it). Though some of it consisted in an admirable application of critical thinking to the issues of the day, there developed a larger climate of suspicion and mockery that ate away at the idea of journalistic authority itself. Digital commerce also played a role: web publications learned to boost traffic — that is, to produce the data that satisfied advertisers — by throwing up two or three times as much content as before, much of it with only cursory reviewing, since web journalism was usually edited much less rigorously than print journalism.

The War on Objectivity in American Journalism

(Writing a piece for, say, the *Atlantic* magazine involves many more rounds of scrutiny and fact-checking than writing for the *Atlantic* online.) Since the online stuff was so fleeting, the relaxation of rigor seemed less objectionable. The booming number of websites, all equally accessible to any reader with an internet connection, opened pathways to circumvent the gatekeepers who once would have nixed all those churned-out commentaries that now made passing sensations on *Salon*, the *Daily Kos, Powerline, The Huffington Post, Gizmodo*, or wherever.

In no time at all subjectivity evolved into partisanship. The move online hastened the reign of proudly partisan media. This tendency started on the right, which believed that "non-partisan" media were instruments of liberal partisanship. Although Americans had always consumed their share of ideologically oriented fare, conservatives under Nixon set out to institutionalize right-wing journalism as a full-blown alternative to the mainstream press, which they portrayed as an appendage to the liberal elite. Nixon's attacks on the media mobilized the political energies of conservatives who resented the progressive attitudes they detected in the news; just as important, they eroded the news outlets' credibility. Over time, as growing numbers of Americans concluded that the press was biased, their disaffection fed a market for partisan substitutes. In the 1980s, Rush Limbaugh and a legion of radio hosts forged a wildly popular subculture of right-wing news and puerile entertainment. Within another decade, Roger Ailes, Nixon's old TV coach, had unveiled Fox News, the fruit of two decades' labor to set up a full-fledged rival to the networks. It soon became the leading cable news channel.

While the right was battling liberalism in politics, the left was making incursions in academia — an important station in its long march through the institutions. To some, victories there meant little. "They got the White House," the late and estimable Todd Gitlin observed "and we got the English departments." But culture shapes politics, and the triumph of the left-wing campaign against objectivity in the universities — it flew under the flags of postmodernism, perspectivism, anti-foundationalism, pragmatism, and identity — indirectly shaped the climate of opinion that came after, including in journalism. In time the students brought their corrosive attitudes toward objectivity out of the campus and into the profession, marching now through different institutions. What all the strains of anti-objectivist dogma had in common was a militant skepticism toward Enlightenment liberalism, including the idea that knowledge could be distinct from power. One line of illiberal thinking, drawing eclectically from Nietzsche, the pragmatists, Gramsci, and the Frankfurt School, insisted that what passed for rationality and knowledge were constructs deployed for a cunning form of social control. The ground for this "sociology of knowledge" had been prepared by the Marxist notions of ideology and class. The war on objectivity, in this respect, is not a new war.

The emerging subjectivism of the 1980s and 1990s raised troubling and meretricious questions, but it usually stopped short of outright epistemological nihilism. As the intellectual historian Daniel Rodgers has noted, "For most of those who tried to think through the politics and epistemology of a world beyond certainties, truths were not dead. Truths needed to be argued out. ... Truth-seeking demanded doubt, demanded the ability to entertain more than one hypothesis, demanded patience." In the new century, however, patience in research and reasoning would be in short supply.

All of these trends converged in a perfect storm during the presidency of George W. Bush. Like their Nixon- and Reagan-era forerunners, Bush-era conservatives viewed the bastions of the knowledge class — the universities, the think tanks, the foundations, the cultural industries — exactly as they viewed the media: as ideological organs that hid their liberalism behind a mask of expertise and authority. But now, three decades after Nixon began the project, the right had its own counter-establishment of institutions to push back.

Trotting out their own experts from their own think-tanks and their own foundations, the Bushies and their allies baited reporters into the old false-balance trap. Too many news stories about climate change, for example, gave roughly equal weight to the preponderance of scientists who saw peril in the warming planet and the fringe minority who did not. On birth control, abortion, second-hand cigarette smoke, and other issues, too, the Bush team spun its ill-supported science as one side of a legitimate debate. You have your experts, we have ours. Wags dubbed them postmodern Republicans.

The biggest controversy centered on the case for war against Saddam Hussein's Iraq, including the shaky claims that Saddam was rebuilding his nuclear program. Since the White House kept its intelligence secret, skeptics were hard pressed to introduce dispositive facts into the discussion. Still, reporters managed to discover evidence that cast doubt on the case for war, and a long and robust public debate followed. Ultimately, the public backed the Iraq adventure not because Bush presented a watertight case or because the press relayed it credulously, but because a lot of Americans nursed a desire to exorcise the shame and humiliation of 9/11, however tenuous its connection to Saddam. Still, the perception that the press corps failed to ward off a disastrous war revived complaints that journalists were pursuing a cramped notion of evenhandedness at the expense of truth.

A bit surprisingly, however, Bush's critics — whether liberals in the opposition or workaday reporters — mostly doubled down on objectivity. Liberals took to boasting of their membership in "the reality-based community" after a Bush official used that enchanting term to mock people who "believe that solutions emerge from your judicious study of discernible reality." Stephen Colbert coined "truthiness" to satirize the idea, embodied by Bush, that it mattered not that an idea was true but that it felt true. News organs renewed their objectivity vows, too. An internal *New York Times* self-assessment entitled "Preserving Our Readers' Trust" urged employees to "strengthen and better define the boundary between news and opinion." It called for reining in reporters' appearances on the shoutfests, setting up a system to avoid "conveying an impression of one-sidedness," and pursuing diversity of viewpoint as well as of race and gender. These were ways to fortify objectivity, not to abandon it.

That was one response, anyway. Others wanted to be done with the whole thing. Liberals wrote books that simply branded their proponents "liars" rather than arguing against conservative ideas. Although Bush did lie (all politicians do), and although conservatives may lie more than liberals do (at least about the science behind certain policies), this rhetoric took the critics into treacherous terrain. A lie is a falsehood uttered with the intent to deceive. Were all those claims about projected tax cuts or the wisdom of military action abroad really outright lies, or might they have stemmed from alternative assumptions, values, priorities, and analyses? Would they all violate a courtroom oath, or might they be better classed with those partial, sometimes tendentious, but technically truthful claims that we call spin, of which nobody in politics is innocent?

The "liar" charge revealed not tougher scrutiny on the part of left toward false political claims, but greater laziness toward refuting those claims. (The right also lazily slung the term at Democrats, as South Carolina Congressman Joe Wilson did at President Obama from the House floor.) Paul Krugman, rightly irritated at the credulity shown to Bush's economic plans, cracked that if the president called the world flat, headlines would read, "Opinions Differ on Shape of the Earth." But if Krugman was correct to chide headline-writers not to dignify flat-earthers, he was wrong to liken economic policy disputes — rooted in real ideological and analytical differences — to a clash between the enlightened and the benighted. Declaring one side of a policy debate illegitimate from the get-go represents is another form of retreat from actual intellectual argument.

Some on the left amplified this tendency by redoubling their efforts to create their own partisan apparatus, in mimicry of the right. For decades, of course, leftists had always had their magazines, such as *The Nation* and *Mother Jones,* and their coterie of syndicated columnists. But the left's impresarios never found their "liberal Limbaugh." ("It was never exactly a disgrace to American liberalism," Leon Wieseltier wrote in 2004, "that it lacked its Limbaugh.") When, in 2003, the activists Anita and Sheldon Drobny launched a left-wing radio network, Hendrik Hertzberg of *The New Yorker* was politely skeptical. "The main obstacle," he wrote, "is neither financial nor ideological but temperamental." The typical liberal political junkie, he noted, didn't revel in "expressions of raw contempt for conservatives" as a substitute for reporting. Hertzberg was partly correct. Most liberals (back then, at least) did prefer something like National Public Radio (back then, at least) — where a high-toned collegiate-class progressive attitude infused the sensibility and the story selection, but journalistic values, not ideology, largely governed the content. Yet the Drobnys were also partly correct. Their network, "Air America," did not last long, but it bequeathed to the airwaves Rachel Maddow and Al Franken, among others, and soon MSNBC started down the road toward becoming a left-wing Fox, if never as vicious or heedless of facts.

In 2001, the legal scholar Cass R. Sunstein warned, in a little book called *Republic.com*, that while the internet was expanding the tableau of available political viewpoints, it was also narrowing our horizons, steering us into pods of the like-minded. The ability to "customize" or "personalize" news feeds would blockade inconvenient information and promote groupthink. The book was prescient. If we are not quite in Sunstein's dystopia, there is no denying that the diminished audience for general-interest, common-carrier news outlets — those that try to speak to us all — has fractured our polity. Reason and deliberation — genuine deliberation, not what passes for it in our media — are now rare in public discourse, and consensus and compromise distressingly elusive in matters of state.

131

Recently the calculus on objectivity has been scrambled again. The right still complains about a liberal bias in the media, but the hubristic boasts of "creating our own reality" have reverted back to a traditionalist (and seemingly disingenuous) espousal of the time-honored principles of unpoliticized reporting. "Whatever happened to professional journalism and the promise or at least suggestion that the press ought to pursue the *objective truth* in the gathering and reporting of news?" asks the right-wing radio host Mark R. Levin, in his book *Unfreedom of the Press*. Perspectivist, heal thyself!

Meanwhile some on the left are now arguing for a journalism of "moral certainty" or "moral clarity." Those newly fashionable phrases should make us pause, not only because they were first popularized by Bush during the war on terrorism, but also because determining the correct moral posture on a political or policy issue is almost always difficult and certainly beyond the capacity of a daily journalist working at digital speed. Yet the Manichaean language is unmistakably there today. Lewis Raven Wallace, author of the anti-objectivity tract *The View from Somewhere* (the title is a jab at Nagel), declares that our dire times necessitate "a moral stance" from reporters. Wesley Lowery of *60 Minutes*, another prominent critic of objectivity, likewise decrees on Twitter: "American view-from-nowhere, 'objectivity'-obsessed, both-sides journalism is a failed experiment. We need to fundamentally reset the norms of our field. The old way must go. We need to rebuild our industry as one that operates from a place of moral clarity." None of the new critics elaborates an understanding of the relationship between moral clarity and intellectual clarity, or how such clarity can be achieved without first adopting a scrupulous regard for truth.

What changed? How did the happy, scrappy membership in the "reality-based community" of the Bush years give way to the righteousness of the Trump years? How did countering right-wing propaganda with searched-for empirical truth give way to countering right-wing propaganda with quips and exclamation points? We do not have to be technological determinists to refer back to the role of the internet. The newfound glut of accessible news, instead of producing a better-informed public, led everyone — given the polarized climate — to seek out sources that confirmed what they already believed. "Confirmation bias" is one of the epitaphs for our time. Instead of grappling with unwelcome facts and arguments, Americans now find it simpler to declare those arguments out of bounds. Hence the new fondness for deplatforming, cancellations, and censorship. Ideas once considered misguided, incorrect, or just objectionable have been recast as evil and intolerable. Being wrong became the same thing as being bad.

Two major political events of the last decade helped to spark the newest war on objectivity. The first was the racial ferment that seized the country toward the end of Barack Obama's presidency, especially after a police officer in Ferguson, Missouri killed Michael Brown in August 2014. With the ensuing protests and the harsh police reprisals that followed, a surge of long-needed reform agitation took hold on the left. But so, in some quarters, did a wide-ranging race-centered worldview. Certain newly prevalent ideas condemned as irredeemably racist first police departments and then the criminal justice system and then many other institutions and cultures. Eventually a whole panoply of individuals, concepts, practices, and entities that might seem race-neutral or even progressive were implicated as racist or "white supremacist." Some critiques indicted journalistic objectivity, too. What was objectivity, if not a cover for white power?

The race-centered attack on objectivity charges that the historic arbiters of journalistic fairness were often blind to their own racist assumptions. That argument is not wrong. But neither is it new. As the post-1960s debates had shown, white-led news organizations had indeed at times failed to consider how black reporters or readers might view certain stories, to their detriment. As Matthew Pressman shows in his superb history *On Press*, the churn of the 1960s and 1970s led editors to incorporate black and other minority perspectives. But they did so slowly and incompletely. By the mid-2010s, with racial conflict spilling over, the patience of many black journalists was spent, and a new generation, much less forgiving toward those in power, was entering the profession or becoming politically activated.

As in the 1960s, a sense of urgency, even desperation, encouraged the issuing of demands, many of which we are now debating. Some of these are sensible, wise, even overdue. Lowery has argued that knowing how frequently law-enforcement authorities have twisted the facts of police shootings means that editors should "consider not publishing any significant account of a police shooting until the staff has tracked down the perspective — the 'side' — of the person the police had shot." This proposal seems reasonable and practicable, although we should note that it is a call for stronger, not weaker, fidelity to the principle of presenting "both sides" of a story. It is an unwitting recognition of a point that is tragically missing from our bitter disputations: that objectivity is one of the conditions for justice.

What does not hold up in the new attack on objectivity is the far-reaching and suddenly popular claim that objectivity is itself inherently racist and therefore fatally compromised as an ideal. "The views and inclinations of whiteness are accepted as the objective neutral," Lowery has written. When it comes to how to do journalism, however, "whiteness" has no intrinsic "views or inclinations" or indeed any autonomous power. Yes, journalistic objectivity took shape when the mainstream press corps consisted mainly of white men, and the manner in which they pursued the ideal reflected prejudices that black journalists may well have been less likely to share. But if that tells us something about the ideal's implementation, it says nothing about the merit of the ideal itself. The flawed implementation of a justified ideal may not suffice to discredit the ideal. Walter Lippmann's skin color does not invalidate the concept of objectivity any more than Isaac Newton's skin color invalidates the concept of gravity. And as a historical matter, white journalists have shared no consensus at all about race and racism. The editors of *Newsweek* in the 1960s, which covered the civil rights movement aggressively, were far readier to include black perspectives than were the editors of Southern dailies.

Lewis Raven Wallace, too, decries objectivity as racist, faulting it for the press' historical neglect of the views of not just African Americans but also gays, lesbians, and trans people, and many other minorities. Many of the examples in Wallace's book, from nineteenth-century accounts of lynchings to Reagan-era journalism about AIDS, will make readers cringe. But they don't expose flaws in the objectivity ideal any more than Lowery's arguments do. What they show is that newspapers and news networks, like other social institutions, express the prevailing outlook of the culture, including their biases against minority groups. In the past, not only straight-news reporters but also opinion journalists — journalists of a moralizing bent, journalists who scorned objectivity — tended to neglect minority groups and causes. The problem was not peculiar to big-time newsrooms or networks. Coverage of lynching and of gay rights improved not because objectivity was junked (it wasn't), but because society evolved. Journalists came to revise their assumptions and attitudes not about objectivity but about lynching and gay rights. But Wallace — who justifiably deems stamping out bigotry and racial injustice

135

an urgent matter — shows no interest in even elementary historicism. The fierceness of his conviction leads him to assert that the gravity of our injustices today should compel journalists to put aside traditional reporting and take up the cause of "fighting back against racism and authoritarianism."

Wallace's pairing of "racism" with "authoritarianism" here is revealing. It suggests that the racial ferment of the 2010s was only one impetus for the new moralism, the usurpation (to borrow Rorty's words) of objectivity by solidarity, that he prescribes. The other impetus, of course, was Trump.

Early in Trump's presidential campaign, it was clear that he enjoyed a super-strength Teflon that Ronald Reagan would have envied. Vulgar, hateful, and obnoxious in ways that would have sunk most politicians, Trump regularly crossed over into ugly racist or sexist or xenophobic statements. He lied constantly, and with a surpassing brazenness and indifference to the consequences. Journalists microscopically examined his sordid business behaviors, the sexual harassment and corruption charges against him, his fondness for dictators, his inflammatory tweets. But among Republicans his standing only rose.

Trump's stunning upset in 2016 and his unflagging support from a sizable minority of the electorate maddened his detractors, including those in the press corps. Many concluded that he could not be stopped without changing the rules. "If you're a working journalist and you believe that Donald J. Trump is a demagogue playing to the nation's worst racist and nationalistic tendencies, that he cozies up to anti-American dictators and that he would be dangerous with control of the United States nuclear codes, how the heck are you supposed to cover him?" asked Jim Rutenberg, a reporter-turned-columnist at the *Times*. "Because if you believe all of those things, you have to throw out the textbook American journalism has been using for the better part of the past half-century, if not longer, and approach it in a way you've never approached anything in your career." The blogger and journalism professor Jay Rosen said much the same. In order to defeat Trump, he wrote, journalists "have to do things they have never done. They may even have to shock us... Hardest of all, they will have to explain to the public that Trump is a special case, and the normal rules do not apply."

Not everyone agreed. After Trump's inauguration, Reuters editor-in-chief Steve Adler sent a memo to his staff bucking the tide and insisting that traditional reporting methods were still the order of the day. Those methods, which worked for Reuters in covering the Iranian mullahs and the Chinese dictatorship, didn't need to be tossed out because of Trump's authoritarian impulses. Marty Baron, the editor of the *Washington Post,* took a similar stance, declaring, "We're not at war, we're at work." But over the next four years, straight-news journalists seemed to follow Rutenberg's and Rosen's advice as often as Adler's and Baron's. Political imperatives frequently overrode journalistic ones. Sometimes the politicization of reporting was intentional; other times it happened unwittingly, as journalists breathed the air around them. Whether it was conscious or not, subjectivity, opinion, and moralism suffused the coverage of a president as never before.

In the newspapers, headlines and articles used pejorative and loaded language where they once would have striven for a clinical tone. Descriptive language dripped with scorn for the president and his agenda. CNN, which had upheld a nonpartisan space on cable TV as MSNBC swung left, now stuffed its evening line-up with anti-Trump programming. As White House correspondent, a role that called for an adversarial but impartial posture, Jim Acosta flew the resistance flag. Elsewhere on the cable channels, reporters who might once have donned a temperate persona for a PBS discussion or a Sunday-morning roundtable outdid one another in attesting to their antipathy to Trump. In November, 2017 a Pew Research Center study compared coverage of Trump's first months to those of previous presidents. It found that media — including straight news sources — dwelled on Trump's character more than on his policies, and with a "far more negative" valence than in the past. Harvard's Shorenstein Center found the same, concluding its report: "Trump has received unsparing coverage for most weeks of his presidency, without a single major topic where Trump's coverage, on balance, was more positive than negative, setting a new standard for unfavorable press coverage of a president." A pair of RAND studies in 2018 and 2019, which linguistically analyzed print, broadcast, and internet news, showed that the new subjectivity was not limited to coverage of Trump. "Our research provides quantitative evidence for what we all can see in the media landscape," said Jennifer Kavanaugh, the lead author. "Journalism in the U.S. has become more subjective and consists less of the detailed event- or context-based reporting that used to characterize news coverage." Reports now included fewer detached, factual accounts of events. Writers regularly blurred lines between fact and opinion. News contained more subjective — and more dogmatic — judgments.

Worst of all was Twitter. For journalists, hanging out on Twitter can feel like going to a private party or a bull session. You let slip your professionalism and fire off the sort of mean-spirited, impetuous, pointed, or opinionated *bon mots* that you might otherwise have shared over beers after work. But Twitter is a public forum, and a *New York Times* or AP reporter commenting there is heard by distant readers of all stripes. Your tweets shape how your reporting is received. If your job calls for you to banish editorializing from your stories, then you must do that on Twitter, too. Yet many normally responsible correspondents at the *Post* and the *Times* spent the Trump years tapping out sassy, hostile, nit-picking, pompous, or ill-considered takes — all with scarcely a half-sentence of context to orient readers — eroding their credibility with each barb. As a result, when reporters did produce damaging facts to report about Trump, which was often, they could not so credibly claim, in the tradition of Woodward and Bernstein, that they were going after the story, not the president.

Some journalists justified the soapbox editorializing by saying that desperate times call for desperate measures. Wallace wants journalists to ask whether their reporting will help advance "fascism or democracy," "capitalism or collectivity." Rosen, whose previous hobbyhorse was promoting the idea of "the citizen journalist," also insists, in effect, that reporters must choose between adhering to objectivity and saving democracy. In an interview with the historian Nicole Hemmer, he called Trump's denial of his defeat in 2020 "a breakthrough moment where journalists said, yeah, I mean, we could really lose this democracy if Trump succeeds in his campaign to throw out the results, ... a moment there where I think they looked into the abyss and they said we have to cross this." Rosen applauded "direct statements" on CNN that "there's nothing to these claims, and this is a lie."

Rosen made a number of errors. First, what debunked Trump's spurious claims of victory was not the say-so of CNN personalities. What mattered was hard-headed reporting — objective reporting — on the vote counts in key swing states. That reporting investigated and refuted the claims of fraud; and detailed Trump's many legal challenges and why they failed; and aired testimony from local Republicans officials who judged any election irregularities too few to matter; and produced evidence that Trump pressured state officials to break the rules. Traditional empirical reporting — not moral clarity — exposed Trump's lies.

Rosen also erred, like many, in imagining that it is self-evident what being pro-democracy entails. The reality is less obliging and edifying. How to serve or to strengthen American democracy must be searched for, reported out, and argued about. For many of us it is perfectly obvious that Republicans today are trying to constrain democracy by imposing state-level limits on voting. But that judgment, even if universally accepted, will not dictate how to write about those laws. Should the statehouse reporter at the *Atlanta Journal Constitution* or the *Austin American Statesman* bellow that a new Jim Crow era is at hand? Or can that be left to the columnists and the cable blowhards, while reporters coolly present the debates about these laws — alongside a dispassionate analysis of who will be purged from the rolls, deterred from the polls, and given control over vote counting? What about the analyses of the *Times'* Nate Cohn, whose review of the academic research found that Georgia's new voting law is "unlikely to significantly affect turnout or Democratic chances"? Should newspapers ignore that conclusion because it might sap the urgency from the Democrats' efforts? Does it make Cohn's journalism insufficiently "pro-democracy"? To assume that there is only one pro-democracy position — or only one anti-racist position — which is knowable in advance of events is a form of subjectivity whose logic is to deprive audiences of information and ideas and to impede the search for truth.

Lovers of democracy and enemies of racism have nothing to fear from a journalism that uses conventional methods. The biggest mistake of Rosen and others like him is to fail to see that objectivity was never Donald Trump's friend. On the contrary: rarely if ever has a president's behavior been so self-incriminating. Trump's conduct in office was so manifestly ugly, dishonest, and irresponsible that the most bland and clinical description of it forms a damning indictment. Trump's support endured — insofar as it did — not because the namby-pamby media failed to slap his dim-witted followers out of their willful ignorance, but because those followers shared Trump's worldview, liked his policies, thrilled to his will to power, or hated the Democrats more. These followers could read the compendia of Trump's lies that newspapers published and the minute coverage of his impeachments; they could witness his groveling before Vladimir Putin; they could watch the Capitol riot with their own eyes. If anything, the rampant editorializing in the media worsened the perception of liberal bias and drove them further into their dark bubbles. A second Pew study found that trust in CNN, *The New York Times, the Washington Post*, and other major news outlets plummeted between 2014 and 2019 — led by Republicans — as these media were letting subjectivity and opinion flood into once-neutral spaces. If the journalism of moral clarity was supposed to persuade everyone that Trump was a fascist, it didn't work.

Although it has now become a mark of one's progressive bona fides to disparage objectivity, many of its critics will actually concede, when pressed, that it is worth preserving, at least in large part. Jay Rosen keeps on his website a backgrounder where he admits that if objectivity means "trying to see things in that fuller perspective Thomas Nagel talked about ... pulling the camera back, revealing our previous position as only one of many" — which it does — then "I second the motion. We need more of that, not less." Wallace writes that pursuing truth "still requires the rigorous practice of report-ing," including "the careful observation of events," "verifica-tion through a variety of means," and "analysis of data." (These parts of objectivity, presumably, are not expressions of white supremacy.) Even Lowery, while saying on Twitter that "the old way must go," modifies this position substantially in a *Times* op-ed, holding that journalists should "devote ourselves to accuracy," solicit perspectives they disagree with, and ask hard questions of everyone. Funny: that sounds an awful lot like the old way.

If Rosen, Wallace, and Lowery all concede the importance of so many components of objectivity, if they don't really want to kill off the "failed experiment" of twentieth-centu-ry-style reporting, what are they asking for? Rosen, according to his university biography, had only "a very brief career in journalism at the *Buffalo Courier-Express*" before entering academia, but in the cases of Wallace and Lowery, the origins of their anti-objectivity activism may be telling. Wallace took up his crusade in 2017 while a reporter for the public-radio show *Marketplace*. After he wrote a brief against traditional journal-istic values titled, "Objectivity Is Dead, and I'm Okay with It" on *Medium*, a supervisor expressed concerns about it. He decided to keep it up anyway. The next week his boss told Wallace that in her view he "didn't want to do the kind of journalism we do at *Marketplace*" — a seemingly accurate statement — and fired him. Lowery got into the game under similar circumstances. As a *Washington Post* reporter, he chafed at the constraints that his straight-news job placed on his public behavior. Editors had grown frustrated by his social media posts and comments on TV which they considered political, unprofessional, and contrary to *Post* policies: attacking *New York Times* reporters, calling Maureen Dowd a "decadent aristocrat," getting in Twitter fights with a Republican official. Ultimately Marty Baron reprimanded Lowery, leading to his departure. Both Wallace and Lowery, in other words, did what Emily Wilder did: they violated rules safeguarding their institutions' professional credibility. Perhaps what they are seeking, then, is not really an end to objectivity. Perhaps what they are seeking is the right to tweet.

There is nothing wrong with reporters tweeting. Lowery was part of a Pulitzer prize-winning *Boston Globe* team that covered the Boston marathon bombing in 2013. The portfolio that the *Globe* submitted included some of Lowery's tweets. One read, "7:25 a.m. Now in Cambridge, outside of apartment believed to be shared by suspects. State police have street blocked off." Another said: "3:08 a.m. Parade of more than 25 cruisers just peeled out. Headed away from original scene/ current perimeter." This is one kind of tweeting that reporters should do, sharing on-the-spot, factual information that they are in a unique position to deliver. It's not exactly the same as calling a rival paper's columnist "a decadent aristocrat."

Which behaviors should be allowed or denied to straight-news reporters is open to discussion. Donating to candidates? Working for campaigns? Attending a pro-choice or pro-life rally? Writing polemical pieces for outside publications or on social media platforms? Giving ideological speeches on campuses? Voting? (There have been journalists and editors

143

who have felt professionally compromised by casting a vote in an election.) Wherever an institution draws the line, making rules to ensure that the tone and the approach of reporters' public statements match that of their journalism hardly infringes unfairly on their freedom. Nor does the enforcement of such rules fatally impugn the idea of objectivity. Any journalist who wants to be argumentative or partisan, snide or nasty, vocally opinionated or morally judgmental, can do so. It just entails moving clearly to a different role. No one has criticized Lowery or Wallace for the act of voicing strong views from their new positions. What's problematic is holding a straight-news job while at the same time acting like an opinion journalist.

Engaging in advocacy through your journalism is a perfectly respectable course of action, one chosen every day by libertarians at *Reason*, liberals at *The Atlantic*, conservatives at *National Review*, left-wingers at *The Nation*, wokesters at *Vox*, and anti-wokesters on Substack. Opinion journalism in America has never been so plentiful. Jay Rosen, in his conciliatory mood, says he simply wants to be "ecumenical" and "pluralistic," letting "some in the press continue on with the mask of impartiality" while "others experiment with transparency," or wearing one's ideology on one's sleeve. But this makes no sense. There is no need to "experiment." We have always had journalists who are open about their politics, and the current configuration of American journalism could hardly be more ecumenical or pluralistic. The question that we are debating is not whether to permit *more* opinion journalism. The question before us is whether *any* journalism that aspires to objectivity should be maintained.

Forsaking the studious detachment of the newsroom for the moral clarity of Twitter may be permissible or even desirable for an activist-freelancer such as Wallace, an academic blogger such as Rosen, or a crusading TV journalist such as Lowery. Yet it is a terribly wrongheaded idea for straight reporters, whose job requires searching for truth, not virtue. Unless journalists remain genuinely open to viewpoints different from those of their own circles, they will not do their jobs well. In 2012, Fox News watchers and pundits alike had become so entombed in their own assumptions about the world that they could not believe Mitt Romney lost the election to Obama; the anchor Megyn Kelly had to traipse into the studio's back rooms to interview the network's own number-crunchers on air. Over the last twenty years we have seen countless other examples of the right's isolation from factual reporting — its "epistemic closure," as another ungainly neologism from a few years back called it. But the same problem is now surfacing in the mainstream media. The violence that occurred amid the largely peaceful protests in 2020, the misbehavior of some FBI agents during the Trump-Russia investigation, the anger among Virginia parents over racial pedagogy, Kyle Rittenhouse's case for having killed two men in self-defense in Kenosha, the "lab leak" theory of the coronavirus' origins — the failure to take seriously all of these things occurred when journalists neglected to scout out and listen to sources and viewpoints at odds with their own. They happened because journalists chose moral certainty over objectivity.

145

Objectivity will always have its points of weakness. Every story will admit of different ways to be written and presented, and no one can ever correct for all of his or her biases. Sometimes journalists will veer into unwarranted opinion or attitudinizing. Other times they will slavishly hew to rigid formulae that make matters sound more uncertain than they really are. But just as Churchill described democracy as the worst form of government except for all the others, objectivity looks badly flawed only until you consider the alternatives. Objectivity will always be a stronger basis for finding the truth than subjectivity, because it rests on external evidence, on verifiable and falsifiable claims, on impartial methods. The alternative is nothing less than a wild dystopia of unchecked feelings and unchallenged falsehoods in which shared ground has given way to shared contempt. The abandonment of objectivity would be a catastrophe for democracy.

146

INGRID ROWLAND

Thucydides 2022

Whenever sabers begin to rattle somewhere in the world, I am irresistibly drawn back to Thucydides, the Athenian general who wrote a history of the Peloponnesian War, the deadly clash between Athens and Sparta that raged from 431 to 404 BCE and engulfed most of the Greek-speaking world in its chaos. He wrote, perhaps, precisely for people like us: in the first of the three introductions that he eventually added to his masterwork, he declared that he intended it as a "possession for all time," and so it has been for over two millennia.

No one has ever turned to Thucydides' history for any sensation that could be called comfort. He presents a clear-eyed chronicle of war both as a constant of human life and as the ultimate form of human folly. But his clarity, won at a terrible personal price (he suffered both plague and exile because of it), has its own harsh beauty, and makes his work as piercing now, and as precious, as it has ever been to previous centuries. Our weaponry and the theaters of our conflicts may have changed, but the same basic forces still drive human beings to destroy one another, and everything else around them, for evanescent promises. The war between Athens and Sparta, at least as Thucydides presents it, may have been the inevitable result of too much power concentrated in two rival polities, but battling over their differences benefited neither state in the end; indeed, it came close to destroying them both. The conflict hinged on too many variables for anyone, however insightful, to predict, and thus Thucydides' history of the Peloponnesian War becomes a vast spectacle of misjudgment and its consequences. The fact that Thucydides himself provides that *History* with three separate introductions at three separative points in the narrative shows how radically he was compelled, by time and circumstance, to broaden his own point of view as the conflict dragged on for a generation. What he first may have seen as a straightforward duel turned out to be a bitter lesson in geopolitics.

The first introduction appears where we would expect it, at the beginning, when he presents the object of his scrutiny as the war between Athens and Sparta. "Thucydides, an Athenian, recorded the war between the Peloponnesians and the Athenians, beginning at the moment that it broke out, and believing that it would be a great war, and more worthy of relation than any that had preceded it. The preparations of both the combatants were in every department at the peak of perfection, and he could see the rest of the Greeks taking sides in the quarrel." But when he reaches the moment when Athens and Sparta strike a peace treaty in 421, after ten years of battle, Thucydides recasts his enterprise. The war may be officially over, but the peace is illusory:

> Though for six years and ten months they abstained from invasion of each other's territory, yet abroad an unstable armistice did not prevent either party doing the other serious injury, until they were finally obliged to break the treaty... The history of this period has also been written by the same Thucydides, an Athenian... Only a mistaken judgment can object to including the interval of treaty in the war. I lived through the whole of it, being of an age to comprehend events, and giving my attention to them in order to know the exact truth about them. It was also my fate to be an exile from my country for twenty years ..., and being present with both parties, and more especially with the Peloponnesians by reason of my exile, I had leisure to observe affairs more closely.

In 423, as one of the ten generals elected each year in Athens, Thucydides had been put in charge of an Athenian fleet stationed in the north Aegean, a territory he knew intimately. When a Spartan army began to draw near Amphipolis, the chief Athenian outpost in the region, Thucydides mobilized his navy, but he arrived too late: a quick-moving Spartan general named Brasidas had reached Amphipolis ahead of him, though Thucydides did manage to save the settlement's port from the hands of his dashing adversary.

We know virtually nothing about Thucydides' exile "after my command at Amphipolis"; the word he uses to describe his situation, *phygé*, can mean both voluntary flight and official banishment. Athens passed a general amnesty for exiles in 403, which fits exactly with Thucydides' mention of a *phygé* lasting twenty years, but the Italian scholar Luciano Canfora has argued recently that the historian returned home much earlier, in time to participate in the oligarchic coup d'état that shook the city in 411. Without implicating Thucydides in a rather vicious political plot (which included discreetly assassinating a host of "inconvenient people"), we can take Canfora's point that our knowledge about the twenty-year exile is based on little more than those two statements in Book Five of the *History*. We can guess that Thucydides might have been punished by the Athenian assembly as a scapegoat for their frustration, drummed up to fever pitch by the demagogue who, as general in his own right, would seize back Amphipolis the following year (and perish in the victory): Cleon, the harsh-voiced ruthless power broker who acts as a negative foil in the *History* to the charismatic Pericles. The *History* is full of instances when an overstimulated crowd passes insensate laws for the basest of reasons.

But we also know that in any body politic, the length of a judicial sentence may well differ from the length of time served, especially when the sentence involves a person with friends in high places. And Thucydides was not only wealthy and well-connected; he also maintained a privileged grip on three of the commodities most central to the Athenian economy during the years of conflict with Sparta. He had been stationed on remote duty near Amphipolis because the area was his second home: his father's unusual name, Olorus, suggests that they probably had family ties in that region, which was Thrace, a borderland between Greek and non-Greek states, including the rising local power, Macedon. Thucydides managed the lease to the gold and silver mines of Pangaion, the mountain looming beyond Amphipolis, shipping bullion to Athens by the same routes as the Thracian timber that helped to build the Athenian navy, that is, through Amphipolis and its port, which, it is worth remembering, Thucydides and his fleet had managed to preserve from the Spartan assault in 423 — not exactly a minor detail. The conquest of Amphipolis is one of the many surprising reverses that make Thucydides' *History* so real: Brasidas, contrary to the slow-moving Spartan stereotype, had mounted a *Blitzkrieg*, and then used his uncommon eloquence, another strikingly non-Spartan trait, to convince the Amphipolitans that this new takeover was really a liberation. Perhaps Thucydides, in his Athenian complacency, had been blind to the possibility of a quick-witted Spartan, and perhaps there was nothing he could have done to prevent the capture of Amphipolis in any case, because ships, especially in groups, move over water at a different pace than troops over land.

Back at home, the loss of Amphipolis would have raised the Athenians' ire because it served as so crucial an emporium for essential resources. When the war broke out, Athens, with a population that scholars estimate at a hundred thousand, lived on imported grain, imported timber, and the tribute it exacted from a series of other Greek city-states, exchanged for olive oil and protection, ostensibly from Persia, by the Athenian navy. Its surrounding region, Attica, had grown rich on the local silver mines of Laurion, but their ore had already begun to peter out. If Thucydides the elected official was condemned to exile, in one of the capricious moves for which the *History* implicitly and explicitly damns his city's democratic regime on many occasions, did he also lose his properties within Athens along with his right to live there, or did the metal magnate and his ungrateful city-state come to some kind of convenient working arrangement that kept the commodities moving as smoothly as ever? It sounds as if, to some extent, Thucydides managed to play both sides of his situation. "Being present with both parties" sounds as if he became, if anything, more of a cosmopolitan than he must have been already, a cosmopolitan with open eyes and open ears, to be sure, but also, perhaps, with an open purse.

As the war moved into a new phase, Thucidydes' view of it was destined to change yet again. At the beginning of Book Six, as he introduces the *History's* most harrowing episode, the botched Athenian attempt to invade Sicily, Thucydides reintroduces his work by providing a history of the island that mirrors the history of Greece with which he began his whole analysis of the war. In effect, he confesses that his guiding scheme for the previous five books, the conflict between two great powers, turns out to have been completely inadequate to the real situation all along. Whether he had seen it before or not, the great powers in the Greek world that he inhabited had always been not two but three: Athens, Sparta, and Syracuse. The latter, he writes, is the city most like Athens in the entire Greek world.

But Syracuse is also different. It wages war in a different way from both Athens and Sparta, by relying on the cavalry that thrived on the broad plains around the city. Sparta was renowned for its heavy-armed infantry (and the brutally stratified society that sustained it) and Athens for its fleet (and hence the broadly based democracy that gave a voice to rowers as well as soldiers and horsemen), but Syracuse commanded Sicily through its mounted troops, an elite force that neither Athens nor Sparta had taken into serious consideration until they were both overwhelmed by it, and which, at the moment when we and Thucydides encounter the Syracusan state, provides no easy correlation with its governmental system. Before and after the democratic moment of the Athenian assault, Syracuse was ruled by tyrants, that is, monarchs, and that form of government, the most rarefied of all elites, just as cavalry was the most rarefied of all military formations, would have fit suggestively into a simple three-way scheme. Life, however, is more complicated than that.

The power of the Syracusan cavalry should not have been news to anyone; Syracusan chariots were legendary performers at the Olympic Games, celebrated by the great poet Pindar, but Athens and Sparta (and Thucydides) were so concentrated on their duel that they lost a broader vision of the world — until they were plunged headfirst into a larger reality.

Thus the Athenian plans to invade should have hinged, like all wartime plans, as Thucydides insists everywhere in his *History*, on *paraskeué*, preparedness (a subject about which the manager of the mines of Pangaion must have known a good deal). But for moving hearts and minds in the Athenian assembly, *paraskeué* turns out to be no match for a pipe dream. The pipe dream is Sicily. It is supplied to the Athenian assembly by Alcibiades, one of the year's ten generals in 415, silver-tongued, dissolute, utterly selfish, and apparently irresistible (though I have never managed to see the charm in his self-absorption, either in Thucydides or in Plato). "Be convinced," he

153

declares (after going on at wearisome length about himself), "that we shall augment our power at home by this adventure abroad. . . At the same time, we shall either become masters, as we very easily may, of the whole of Greece, or in any case ruin the Syracusans" The more prosaic discussion of *paraskeué* is left to his fellow general Nicias, who tries to deter the Assembly from their fool's errand by exaggerating the amount of provisions they will need, confident that they will balk at such an immense investment. Instead, Thucydides reports, "everyone fell in love with the enterprise" and voted for every extravagance that Nicias proposed (which in the event, like so many projected estimates of total expenditures for large projects, would fall well short of the mark).

Scholars have often wondered why Thucydides seems to know so much about what Nicias is thinking throughout the dramatic ups and downs that make the tragic tale of the Sicilian Expedition so gripping. Friendship would provide an excellent explanation. The two of them were respected figures in Athens (Nicias, a great benefactor, was probably the most influential man in the city when he was sent off to Sicily with Alcibiades), but neither belonged to the oldest aristocracy of Athens, the Eupatridae or the "well-fathered," the ancient landowners who traced their lineage back to the Bronze Age and to the city's protective gods and heroes. Thucydides had that foreign, Thracian, ancestry, and Nicias was the first person in his family to attain conspicuous wealth. Both of them rose to their exalted status, of course, by managing mining operations. If the Laurion mines had made Nicias the richest man in Athens, then Thucydides could not have lagged far behind. Their social circle also included Cephalus, a Syracusan shield maker — that is, arms merchant — who had settled permanently in the Athenian port of Piraeus, where his sons kept company with the privileged youth of Athenian society: Niceratus, the son of Nicias, and Plato's two brothers, Glaucon and Adeimantus.

The fortunes of all three men, like every ancient fortune, rested on the shoulders of slave labor. Both Laurion and Pangaion, like all ancient mines, were worked by gangs of men, most of them probably captured as prisoners of war, and Thucydides shows clearly that war and slavery have ever gone hand in hand, like war and plague. One year into the Sicilian venture, a cash-strapped Nicias raises money for his struggling forces by falling on the helpless fishing village of Hykkara, populated by indigenous Sicilian refugees from the Greek colonization of the island, and selling them all at the slave market of the city that has become his reluctant ally, Katane. It is one tiny tragedy within the sweep of a far greater tragedy, the life of a village bartered for 120 bushels of silver, but it stings. Protracted war had long since turned the Athenians, whom Pericles once praised as "the school of Hellas," into brutes.

Nicias, before he set forth with the Sicilian Expedition, had been the *proxenos*, or goodwill ambassador of Syracuse in Athens. In Sicily, he continued to maintain constant contact with a pro-Athenian faction within Syracuse, hoping that a swift coup d'état would eliminate the need for a protracted battle; this may be one of the reasons he hesitated so long before attacking, thereby setting off the chain of calamities that finally overtook the Athenian force. Relying on the promise of treachery was only one of his many errors of judgment, but nearly everyone on both sides of the Sicilian Expedition would make cataclysmic mistakes before the ordeal was over, two years after it began. One wonders whether Nicias, like Alcibiades, imagined Syracuse as yet another tributary state in the Athenian empire, or whether he

155

had a more visionary idea of striking an alliance between the two leading democracies of the Greek world, with attendant benefits to trade. That alliance would have upended the traditional rivalry between Ionian and Dorian Greeks; if he had any thoughts along such lines, they were truly perceptive. But instead, in the real world, the old ties provided the chief excuse for dragging the city-states of Hellas one by one into the war between Ionian Athens and Dorian Sparta, to the ultimate benefit of none.

In the end, the war brought Athens and Sparta mutually assured insignificance and left Syracuse firmly positioned in its place as a major Mediterranean power, but no longer as a democracy. The monarchs returned to Syracuse, just as a dynasty of Macedonian kings came to fill the power vacuum on mainland Greece. Both Philip of Macedon and his son Alexander knew better than to rouse that Sicilian giant as they expanded their kingdom into an empire; they led their armies eastward, setting their sights on Persia. It was Plato, with his arsenal of persuasion by peaceful means, who hoped to conquer Syracuse for philosophy (until circumstance got the best of him, too). Thucydides himself came to acknowledge a broader vision of the Greek world as something more than simply Greek. By the time he reaches Book Eight of his *History,* which suddenly breaks off in mid-sentence, he is acutely aware that political events in Athens, Sparta and Syracuse are constantly conditioned by what goes on in Carthage, Persia, and Etruria.

What does Thucydides provide, then, aside from a chronicle of stupid, unrelenting, avoidable human misery? Like the tragic poets who evidently shaped his sensibilities,

156

he plays out, with an unerring sense of contrast, a series of misjudgments, the occasional insight, and their consequences when put into action. Aristotle would later declare that watching a tragic performance gives us comfort by filling us with pity and fear, and somehow cleansing us through our exposure to those extremes of feeling. He called the process *katharsis*, cleansing, or purification, and perhaps catharsis is what Thucydides offers: a continual clearing of his own vision and ours, a regular exchange of illusion for sobriety.

This time, you hope when the sabers start to rattle, maybe it will not happen in the Thucydidean manner: this time the Athenian fleet will say "no" rather than set out for Sicily with promises of conquest that will end in the blood-soaked mud of the River Assinaros, as the horsemen of Syracuse mow down the last remnants of Athens' finest; this time the people will hear the demagogue's screech for the bad omen it always is; this time we will remember that all wars breed atrocity as a natural development, but civil war most of all. This time we will stop and think before we lay waste to an Earth we barely understand in all its complexity, least of all our inextricable connection to it. This time we will put aside Thucydides at last, and begin to rewrite the history of what it means to be human.

157

DAVID A. BELL

Marat/Zemmour

To understand Éric Zemmour, the ultra-right candidate who has garnered so much attention in the French presidential election this spring, it helps to go back all the way to April, 1793. On the thirteenth of that month, France's ruling National Convention voted the arrest of the deputy and journalist Jean-Paul Marat. The violent rhetoric that he spewed out on a regular basis in his newspaper, *L'ami du peuple*, had long shocked even radical revolutionaries. On one occasion he demanded that two-hundred thousand heads roll, so as "to save a million." Earlier in April, he had called for a popular insurrection to purge the Convention of supposed counterrevolutionaries. Now his enemies hoped that his downfall had finally arrived. But on July 24 the Revolutionary Tribunal acquitted Marat, and his jubilant supporters carried him in triumph on their shoulders through the halls of the Paris Palace of Justice. France's revolutionary First Republic did not have a presidency, but Marat was now indisputably one of the two or three most influential men in the country.

Marat, a figure of the revolutionary ultra-left, might not seem to have much in common with the reactionary Zemmour, a journalist who first gained public notoriety with his ferocious attacks on feminists, immigrants, Islam, and the European Union, and his embrace of the noxious "great replacement" theory. But France is a country in which, as the French saying goes, the extremes meet. Decades before attempting to enact a radical socialist program as President in 1981, François Mitterrand belonged to the far-right Cagoule. The leader of France's mid-twentieth century fascist party, Jacques Doriot, started his career as a communist. In fact, a high proportion of the older men and women who are voting for Zemmour this spring once voted for the French Communist Party. Zemmour himself voted for Mitterrand in 1981, and once counted a far-left rival for the presidency, Jean-Luc Mélenchon, as a friend and regular dinner companion.

Beyond their shared extremism, Marat and Zemmour have other similarities. In both cases, there is an outsider quality: Marat was Swiss, Zemmour the son of Algerian Jews. In both cases, the men conjure up specters of vast, evil, alien forces threatening France: counterrevolutionaries and foreign enemies for Marat, Muslim immigrants for Zemmour. Like Marat, Zemmour has repeatedly, and deliberately, provoked formal prosecution. Courts have twice convicted him of hate speech, although he has been acquitted of denying France's

159

crimes against humanity in the Second World War. He recently went on trial yet again for "public insult" and "incitement to hatred or violence." Unlike Marat, he does not risk the guillotine if convicted.

The most important similarity, however, lies in the two men's backgrounds as journalists and would-be men of letters. To be sure, Éric Zemmour fits into an all-too-prevalent global pattern: that of the populist provocateur who openly appeals to racial and xenophobic ressentiment. He hopes to benefit from the same forces that earlier swept to power such figures as Jair Bolsonaro, Viktor Orbán, Narendra Modi, and, of course, Donald Trump. But he still belongs to a distinctly French variety of the species. In France, more than anywhere else on the globe, even populists who rail against elites can still pose as intellectuals.

Although Zemmour spent most of his career as a daily journalist, he is also a prolific essayist and author. Among his works is a five-hundred-page tome called *French Destiny,* which tries to summarize a thousand years of the country's history, attacking professional historians for "deconstructing" the country's past glories and praising past leaders (including even Robespierre!) who did not hesitate to use fiercely repressive measures against supposed internal enemies. He cemented his appeal to the traditionalist far-right through a detailed, splenetic, and mendacious critique of Robert Paxton, a formidable American historian of Vichy France. If Donald Trump's Twitter feed generally seemed like the ravings of a demented racist uncle, Zemmour's often reads like a series of pseudo-literary aphorisms ("my political family is France eternal"). He calls Balzac's *Lost Illusions* his favorite novel and compares himself to its ill-fated hero, Lucien de Rubempré, another outsider who made it into the elite circles of French journalism. He even professes a respect for the Italian Marxist Antonio Gramsci, from whom he claims to have derived the idea that seizing political power depends upon first establishing cultural hegemony.

Most French intellectuals of the center and left scoff at Zemmour's pretensions, mock his history-writing as alternately false and banal (which it is), and dismiss his literary references as superficial and trite (also true). Yet he belongs to a long tradition of intellectuals and pseudo-intellectuals in French politics, of which he himself is perfectly aware. To quote a recent series of his tweets: "Our greatest writers and journalists have thrown themselves with fervor into political life... Journalism, literature, and politics: a magical trio, a French trio, for the best and for the worst... The best is style, grand ideas, grand ideals. The worst is bad faith, invective, sectarianism." It's a fine summary, except that Zemmour himself exemplifies only the very worst aspects of the tradition.

The grand tradition of the *engagé* intellectual did not proceed by tweets, of course; and it might seem antiquated and unsuited to the new media universe of Twitter, Instagram posts, viral video clips, and twenty-four-hour news networks. But in fact something of the opposite is true. This new universe favors men and women who can write prolifically and fast, with a knack for delivering memorable quips and insults at a moment's notice. Twitter was made for *bon mots*. Zemmour certainly fits this pattern, and it helps to explain his recent success.

His intellectual background also explains one of the strangest things about his recent political success, namely how the son of Algerian Jews has been able to assume the leadership of a political current long associated with some of the deepest and most virulent forms of European anti-Semitism.

161

Put simply, Zemmour, thanks to his literary background, has developed a note-perfect imitation of blood-and-soil French Christian nationalism that no actual Gaul-descended Christian could get away with today — and that has more than a few anti-Semitic motifs. Remarks of the sort that put previous ultra-right leaders like Jean-Marie Le Pen, founder of the National Front, firmly beyond the pale of mainstream French politics have not yet had the same effect for Zemmour, who may yet appeal to enough supposedly more moderate conservatives to come within reach of the presidency.

Jean-Paul Marat today is mostly remembered as an unhinged demagogue who helped drive forward the revolutionary Reign of Terror. It is not an inaccurate characterization, but it is incomplete. Marat, born in 1743, had a serious classical education, which he deployed to considerable effect in early philosophical essays and then in a radical tract called *The Chains of Slavery*. He wrote this work in English, in the course of a decade-long stay in Britain during which he also qualified as a medical doctor. After moving to France in 1776, he secured a position as a court physician, established a laboratory, and began carrying out scientific experiments. Although never accepted by the Academy of Sciences, he received serious attention from the press and from fellow scientists (including Benjamin Franklin), notably for an attempt to refute Newton's work on optics. His own translation of Newton remained the standard French version long after his death.

Marat's revolutionary journalism, while crude, violent, and full of outlandish conspiracy theories, was also undeniably brilliant. He created an astonishing rapport with his readers, making them feel as if only he and they were privy to hidden truths about the forces shaping revolutionary politics. He had a remarkable talent for spurring fear and outrage — France, in his telling, was always half an inch from the edge of the abyss. He cast himself as a heroically persecuted victim, perennially in danger from a dark constellation of enemies. After his assassination in July 1793, frenzied supporters carried his heart through the streets of Paris chanting "heart of Jesus, heart of Marat." The municipality briefly renamed Montmartre as Mont Marat. The great painter Jacques-Louis David cast his death scene as a revolutionary Pietà.

The list of intellectuals who have had serious political careers in France since Marat is long and illustrious. The great Romantic writer Chateaubriand, after composing polemical tracts against Napoleon, became a key figure in conservative politics and served as Foreign Minister in the early 1820s. France's greatest political thinker, Alexis de Tocqueville, spent twelve years in the French parliament and also had a stint as Foreign Minister. Two of the most prolific and popular French history-writers of the nineteenth century, François Guizot and Adolphe Thiers, became the nineteenth century's most consequential French prime ministers. The great poet and author Alphonse de Lamartine briefly led the government during the Revolution of 1848. The Socialist leader Jean Jaurès, assassinated on the eve of World War I, wrote a classic history of the French Revolution. The past century, it is true, has seen fewer figures make the leap from writing to political office. While the most famous French intellectuals have rarely hesitated to seize the political megaphone (think Jean-Paul Sartre or Bernard-Henri Lévy), they mostly have not stood for election. Still, Socialist Prime Minister Léon Blum first had a career as a prolific literary journalist; the reactionary writer Léon Daudet spent several years in parliament; and the novelist André Malraux served as Charles de Gaulle's enormously influential Culture Minister. De Gaulle himself — no intellectual, but a well-read and gifted writer — composed one of the greatest of French memoirs.

Until 2011, it seemed very unlikely that Zemmour could ever be included in this company. He was born in 1958, the son of Berber Jews who had moved to France six years earlier, when Algeria was still an integral part of France and its Jews (unlike its Muslims) had full French citizenship. His father was a paramedic. He grew up first in the Parisian suburb of Drancy, notorious for the detention camp through which Jews passed on the way to Auschwitz, and then in a lower-middle-class neighborhood of Paris itself. He attended Jewish schools and had a conventional Jewish upbringing. Quick-witted and ambitious, he received his university education at the prestigious Institut d'Études Politiques ("Sciences-Po") but failed to gain admission to the even more prestigious École Nationale d'Administration, which trained the country's administrative and political elite, including four of its last six presidents. Instead, at the start of the 1980s, after a brief stint at an advertising agency, he turned to journalism, writing political analysis and profiles for several daily newspapers. In 1996 he joined the staff of *Le Figaro*, the venerable newspaper of the French right and center-right. (Raymond Aron wrote a column there for thirty years.)

Over the years his career flourished. Zemmour the journalist had a reputation for fluid, elegant, witty writing, produced at high speed and in large quantity. According to his biographer Étienne Girard, in 2002 he whipped off an influential profile of the far-right leader Jean-Marie Le Pen in less than an hour. He started publishing books as well, beginning with a biography of then-Prime Minister Édouard Balladur in 1995. Personally charming, he was soon on close personal terms with many of the country's leading politicians, using them to procure information and being used by them in turn, in classic insider fashion. Paris has its own equivalent of the chummy Georgetown cocktail circuit —with considerably better hors d'oeuvres — and Zemmour was very much a member in good standing. But he was desperately ambitious, and wanted a higher public profile.

In these years Zemmour still fit comfortably into the French political mainstream. Although associated with the right, his early vote for Mitterrand long behind him, he did not yet have particularly radical views. To the extent that he belonged to what the French call a political "current," it was that of Philippe Séguin, who in 1997 became head of the party founded by Charles de Gaulle (its descendant is now known as Les Républic-ains). Unlike most centrist and center-left politicians, Séguin had fought in 1992 against the ratification of the Maastricht Treaty creating the European Union and opposed further French integration into it, but he favored a strong social safety net and on most issues had thoroughly conventional views.

Zemmour's move to the far right seems to have been more a matter of ambition and calculated strategy than an expression of deep conviction. (In this he resembles Trump.) In 2006, in his first piece of outrageous Marat-style provocation, he published a slim volume entitled *Le premier sexe*, an attempt to refute Simone de Beauvoir's feminist masterpiece *Le deuxième sexe*. In it, he condemned the feminization (or "de-virilization") of French society and called for a return to traditional patriarchal values. Although studded with historical references, the book was crudely written, with Zemmour writing in one instance that in modern France "the ideal man is in fact a woman. He has surrendered. The weight between his legs has become too heavy for him." In a post-publication interview he argued that men "should be civilized sexual predators. There is an expectation of violence, so they need virility and violence." Zemmour has faced several accusations of groping and kissing women against their will.-

Mainstream commentators largely dismissed *Le premier sexe*, but it succeeded in raising Zemmour's profile, and encouraged him to take even more provocatively radical stances. Soon afterward he started to appear on a combative *Crossfire*-style television show, in which he regularly accused leading political and cultural figures of wanting to destroy the country. And then in 2014 his radicalization took a further leap forward with a much longer book entitled *Le suicide français*. Modeled loosely on Victor Hugo's *Choses Vues*, a posthumous collection of the great writer's recollections and reflections on the history of his times, it consists of a long series of vignettes arranged in chronological order and covering the period from the 1960s to the 2010s. It has both literary and academic pretentions, citing a bevy of famous French authors, and social scientists including Christopher Lasch on the "culture of narcissism" and Samuel Huntington on "the clash of civilizations." Much of it reads like a series of mediocre aphorisms. "Debates are like women: the best are the ones that you haven't had." "The French long thought that Europe would be France writ large. They are beginning to realize, bitterly, that it will be Germany writ large." "We are continuously told that May 1968 was a failed revolution, but in fact it triumphed." The book's thesis was simple: starting with the student uprising of 1968, France's feckless elites had destroyed a once-great country. "We have eliminated our borders, renounced our sovereignty; our political elites have forbidden Europe even to refer to

its Christian roots... France is killing itself, France is dead."
Le suicide français sold over half a million copies and made
Zemmour a celebrity.

One chapter in particular turned out to be key for
Zemmour's future career, and at first glance its inclusion
seemed quite strange. In the midst of his crude attacks on
feminists, homosexuals, judges, professors, and parliamen-
tarians, Zemmour also devoted several pages to a detailed
critique of Columbia University historian Robert Paxton, on
two of his extremely erudite books on Vichy France. Why did
Zemmour bother with this apparent digression, and why was
it so important? To answer these questions, a little history is
in order. It is a past that still matters enormously, and disturb-
ingly, in France.

When the Germans overran France in June 1940, the parlia-
ment voted full powers to Marshal Philippe Pétain, an aged hero
of World War I. His new regime, based in the spa town of Vichy,
governed the free zone that the Nazis allowed to exist in south-
ern France, and its legislation also applied in the northern and
coastal areas occupied by the German army. Although at first
professing nothing but a desire to protect the French, Pétain
and his allies soon began what they called a "national revolu-
tion" to remake the country in a conservative mold and to fit it
into Hitler's apparently triumphant new European order. For
a time, Pétain enjoyed massive popular support from a trauma-
tized population that saw him as its savior.

Some members of the Vichy government were genuine
fascists, but many more belonged to the traditional "legiti-
mist" French right wing. This was a political current which

defined itself largely against the legacy of the French Revolution and its supposed destruction of a cohesive, organic, and pious society, bound together by the monarchy and the Catholic Church. The legitimists excoriated the left, and the successive regimes that had preserved and extended the Revolution's principal reforms. They particularly loathed the Third Republic, established in the 1870s, which had secularized public education and deprived the Catholic Church of any official standing. Increasingly, they also fixated on Jews as both the cause and the symbol of everything they hated about the Republic, and about modernity in general. Best-selling books and newspapers depicted Jews as rootless, unpatriotic, money-grubbing, parasitic, conspiratorial, and sexually deviant. Within months of taking office, the Vichy government on its own initiative passed laws expelling French Jews from the professions and stripping them of legal protections. By 1942 it was willingly collaborating with the Nazis in rounding up Jews, confining them in transit camps, and deporting them into the machinery of the Holocaust. More than seventy-five thousand eventually perished.

The Liberation left both Vichy and the legitimist right thoroughly discredited, but for decades the country failed to engage in a true reckoning with its wartime record. It was far easier to believe the convenient myth, peddled by Charles de Gaulle in the interest of national unity, that nearly all the French had resisted both the Nazis and Vichy, and that with the punishment of the most flagrant collaborators (Pétain himself received a life sentence, others were shot) the book could be closed on the episode. The deportation of the Jews was laid firmly at the feet of the Germans. Only in the 1970s did a new generation of historians, less marked by wartime experience, start to insist on both the depth of popular support for Vichy, and also on the active, independent role that Pétain's state had played in deporting Jews to their deaths.

And central to this development was Robert Paxton, who also had the advantage of writing as a foreigner, from a seemingly more neutral viewpoint. His books *Vichy France,* from 1972, and *Vichy France and the Jews,* from 1981 and co-written with Michael Marrus, spurred agonized debates, and also a wave of new research that largely confirmed their findings. Traditional French conservatives who had largely lain low since the war, giving tepid support to de Gaulle's political parties, now found themselves in the dock, both metaphorically and in some cases literally (as with the trials of two Vichy officials, René Bousquet and Maurice Papon, who had slid frictionlessly into prominent post-war careers). In a landmark speech in 1995, President Jacques Chirac formally acknowledged the country's guilt for wartime crimes. "These dark hours," he declared, "forever sully our history."

It was this reckoning that Zemmour sought to undo in his critique of Paxton. In his chapter in *Le suicide français,* he repeated claims first made by Vichy officials themselves immediately after the war. The collaborationist regime, he insisted, mostly deported foreign Jews, not Jews with French citizenship. In fact, Vichy strove to protect those French Jews. Pétain, he added, reprising an old line of the far right, had engaged in an effective partnership with de Gaulle, serving as the country's "shield" while the leader of the Free French abroad acted as its "sword." These arguments are entirely spurious, ignoring Vichy's eager collaboration with the Nazis and its quick implementation of Nuremberg-style laws against all Jews, French-born and foreign alike. It is true that some Vichy officials initially attempted to save French Jewish citizens from deportation, but many others, such as the vile

169

"Commissioner for Jewish Affairs" Louis Darquier, aimed to deport them all, and worked to strip French citizenship from thousands. In any case, what ultimately enabled the majority of French Jewish citizens to survive the war was not Vichy but the allied armies and their defeat of Germany. Had Hitler's new order lasted only a year or two more, the rest of French Jewry would have ended up in the camps, with the enthusiastic cooperation of French officials. The difference between France and other European states under Nazi control was a difference, above all, of timing.

Zemmour's chapter marked the first time that a well-known mainstream cultural figure, who also professed an admiration for Charles de Gaulle, had publicly defended Vichy in this manner. Jean-Marie Le Pen, founder of the reactionary and xenophobic National Front, had often done the same, but Le Pen remained beyond the political pale. He had a well-deserved reputation as an anti-Semite, having once called the gas chambers a mere "detail" in the history of World War II. President Chirac went so far as to formally forbid any members of his neo-Gaullist party from allying in local elections with members of Le Pen's National Front. Zemmour, however, managed to avoid such anathema, at least to a certain extent. One reason was his long-standing cozy relations with so much of the French political class. Another, of course, was his Jewish identity, which sheltered him from accusations of anti-Semitism and fascism.

Over the years, Zemmour has made very canny use of this Jewish identity. He claims to be proud of it and still attends synagogue, but at the same time he defends an extreme version of French republican secularism with reference to it. In keeping with a tradition that goes back to the Revolution, he insists that religion should be strictly confined to a private sphere of life. He condemns the very idea that the Jewish community should have an active political voice, and sharply disassociates himself from any connection with the state of Israel. (He has very little interest in any country other than France.) He has spoken critically of "militant Zionism" and "the Jewish lobby," says "Tel Aviv" rather than Jerusalem when referring to the Jewish state by its capital, and has speculated that the Jews possessed too much influence in France before World War II. After a terrorist attack against a Jewish school in Toulouse in 2012, Zemmour condemned the decision of Jewish families to have their murdered children buried in Israel. He even compared it to the demand by the family of the killer, Mohammed Merah, to have him buried in Algeria, in both cases saying that the dead "do not belong to France." A gentile would have received far more opprobrium for such a statement. Among French Jews themselves, community leaders have condemned Zemmour almost without exception, but according to press reports he has considerable support among the ultra-orthodox, and among the largely Sephardic Jews who live in heavily Muslim neighborhoods.

Zemmour also exploits his vision of French Jewry to measure French Muslims against the same strict secularist standards, and of course he finds them wanting. He has claimed that Islam, because it allegedly makes no distinction between public and private, "is not compatible with France." He has repeatedly called for the closure of any mosque associated with radical Islam, and while a controversial law already forbids girls from wearing veils in public schools, Zemmour wants to ban veils from public streets and buildings as well. He has hesitated, however, to endorse a ban on ritual animal slaughter, well aware that it would apply to kosher butchers as well. His secularism, you might say, stops at the delicatessen door.

The defense of Vichy, for Zemmour, became the crucial opening for trying to effect a full-fledged rehabilitation of the old legitimist right wing, and to establish an electorally powerful "union of the right" between it and mainstream conservatives. In the years since publishing *Le suicide français* he has increasingly taken to praising and citing the leading nationalist and reactionary intellectuals of the Third Republic, including Hippolyte Taine, Maurice Barrès, Charles Maurras, and Jacques Bainville. In his columns and his speeches, he rarely fails to say that France must return to its Christian "roots," reprising a favorite theme of Barrès, whose most famous novel was an attack on the secular left entitled *Les déracinés*, or *The Uprooted*. It apparently does not trouble him that Barrès and Maurras were vicious anti-Semites who fought against attempts to exonerate the Jewish Captain Alfred Dreyfus, unjustly convicted on charges of spying for Germany, even after copious evidence of the man's innocence arose. Zemmour has gone so far as to speculate that Dreyfus might have been guilty, again using his Jewish identity to shield him from charges of anti-Semitism.

172 Zemmour does not, it is true, advocate a full return to the ideology of the pre-war legitimist right. Maurras and Bainville led a movement called the Action Française, which excoriated the Republic and demanded that France restore its Old Regime monarchy. Zemmour accepts the Republic and plays the republican anthem, the Marseillaise, at his campaign rallies. His extreme secularism — at least as far as Jews and Muslims are concerned — comes straight out of the secular republican playbook. He professes an admiration for Napoleon, whom the Action Française despised as an heir and torchbearer of the French Revolution, and has even had kind things to say,

as noted, about Robespierre. Yet Zemmour does not hesitate to speak rapturously about France's Christian identity. He has called for abolishing birthright citizenship. And he has taken to concluding his campaign rallies with the cry: "Long live the Republic, but, above all, long live France!" His supporters are not slow to hear the nuance.

In his copious recent writings (including a recent book called *La France n'a pas dit son dernier mot*, or *France Has Not Said its Last Word*) and in his campaign, Zemmour joins this xenophobic, bigoted, blood-and-soil nationalism to a vision of where the country stands that is even more apocalyptic than the one he peddled in *Le suicide français*. He has now fully and openly embraced the "great replacement" theory — originally developed a decade ago by the French writer and activist Renaud Camus, who calls it "genocide by substitution" and supports Zemmour — in which he accuses French elites of deliberately stimulating immigration so as to replace the native French population with barbarous Muslim newcomers. In the Zemmourian worldview, the elites have also wantonly laid waste to the glories of French cinema, French art, the French universities, the French public school system, French architecture (he particularly loathes the abstract "Buren columns" erected in the gardens of the Paris Palais Royal), and much else. Radical Muslims have turned the suburbs around major cities into no-go zones for the police where sharia law rules supreme. A surrender to the European Union has destroyed French sovereignty and corrupted French law. Multi-national corporations threaten the small businesses that represent the soul of French capitalism.

173

Only a return to Christian roots (of which Zemmour himself of course has none), to "France for the French," and to strong, even authoritarian leadership will save the country from complete ruin. The message has considerable resonance for French people still traumatized by the terror attacks of the past decade, mostly committed by home-grown radical Muslims, and who recoil from the violent anti-Semitism of radicalized Muslims in the depressed suburbs around major French cities. You would never know from Zemmour that France has one of the most secular Muslim communities in the world, and that despite the massive problems in the suburbs, post-war immigrants have overall integrated very successfully into French life.

In the years since *Le suicide français* appeared, Zemmour's public profile rose like an untethered balloon. In 2019, the cable television mogul Vincent Bolloré recruited him to join the daily prime-time broadcast of his channel CNews, France's equivalent of Fox News. Viewership tripled. Although Zemmour stepped down from the channel in September to prepare his presidential campaign, it gave him yet another forum in which to promote his proposed "union of the right."

Zemmour is an inexperienced campaigner, and his speaking style is stiff and punctuated, unsettlingly, by small giggles. Yet even if he does not fulfill his dream of power, he has already done a great deal — far too much, in fact — to transform and debase the French political landscape. During the campaign, the nominee of Les Républicains, Valerie Pécresse, steadily drifted towards the right in her own positions, in an attempt to coopt his electorate. Marine Le Pen, the daughter and heir of Jean-Marie, found herself in a particularly uncomfortable dilemma. After taking over the National Front (now called the National Rally) from her father, she spent years trying to "de-demonize" it, in an attempt to bring it sufficiently into the mainstream to win elections. Among other things, she worked hard to appeal to Jewish voters. In 2017 she came in second after Macron in the first round, only to lose badly in the runoff round after a disastrous debate in which she came off as ignorant and slow. Zemmour, in addition to being anything but ignorant or slow, has now demonstrated authoritatively that the nationalist, reactionary base does not want de-demonization. It wants more demonization, more rhetoric of total war against Muslims and the French elite, more blood and more soil. Whether or not it chooses Zemmour as its standard-bearer, his lesson will resound for many years to come. And Zemmour himself is unlikely to fade from the scene.

In this respect, of course, Zemmour has performed much the same role as his better-known counterparts elsewhere in the world. He is a populist nationalist in a period in which the species has flourished almost everywhere. Splenetic attacks on feckless liberal elites, on international organizations, on immigrants who have the wrong skin color and worship the wrong God, and on critics who dare point out blots on a country's historical record, are today common currency almost everywhere, from Modi's India to Putin's Russia to Xi's China to Bolsonaro's Brazil to the United States.

What distinguishes Zemmour from Trump and other populist counterparts elsewhere is his pseudo-intellectual background and pretensions, which owe so much to the strong and unusual French tradition of intellectuals in politics, going all the way back to Marat. In the United States, journalists and professors who have seriously attempted the leap to political office generally fit into a liberal elite, whereas Ivy-league educated conservatives dumb down their vocabulary, don tractor caps and flannel shirts and try to talk like good ol' boys (and girls), as J.D. Vance has scurrilously done.

But if Zemmour in one sense seems redolent of the French past, he may also represent something of a model for the global future. Across the globe, the COVID-19 pandemic has only accelerated a move of democratic political life into virtual reality. More and more of it takes place on social media, in endlessly circulating video clips and in viral aphoristic tweets and posts. The communication skills that successful candidates need are changing. The ability to give grand and inspiring speeches matters less and less. Our new media environment requires more and more an ability to come up with memorable, juicy, viral epithets and phrases, all done on the fly — and here journalists and some varieties of intellectual have an obvious advantage. They are also, it must be said, often experts in knowing how to lie fluently, and with conviction.

Donald Trump might seem the polar opposite of Éric Zemmour in his contempt for learning, his crude and limited vocabulary, his frequent verbal stumbles. But he, too, fits the bill in some surprising ways. Remember that he got his real political start as a media star. The coastal elites who were already laughing at Trump the hyperactive real estate mogul in the 1980s tend to forget that most Americans only encountered the man through his reality television show, and then through his Twitter feed. It is also worth remembering just how closely Trump's rambling speeches, with their endless self-congratulations, deliberate provocations, boundless mendacity, and dark warnings about foreign plots, resemble the monologues of conservative talk radio shock jocks, the late unlamented Rush Limbaugh first and foremost. Trump's political success derived in the first instance from his ability to cultivate a close, almost intimate relationship with his supporters through these endless, repetitive, easily digestible performances. The crude mockery of his enemies made the rants and the tweets entertaining, while solidifying Trump's own reputation as the embodiment of common sense, the one who sees through the fantasies and deceptions of the "libs." The daily conjuring of the alien threat stimulated fear and outrage, along with admiration for the only man seemingly capable of defending the country against it. (Remember "I alone can fix it?") His off-the-cuff remarks are anything but eloquent, but they are often memorable. They make great entertainment. And while Trump has no sense whatsoever of the American conservative intellectual tradition, he still instinctively channels it with his "America First" rhetoric, just as Zemmour, in a very different and more sophisticated register, channels Taine, Barrès, Maurras, and Bainville.

So it is not just in France where the likes of Éric Zemmour may flourish in the years to come. If Tucker Carlson ever decides to make a run for president, he will not be larding his speeches with quotations from poets and novelists, let alone name-checking Antonio Gramsci. But he will be drawing on the same skills, the same demagogic articulateness, the same anti-intellectual intellectualism, that has brought Éric Zemmour to such lamentable promise in France today, much as it did for the frightful Jean-Paul Marat over two centuries ago.

177

NATHANIEL MACKEY

Song of the Andoumboulou: 266

—book of the there we'd have been—

We remained entranced by words positing
    a world beyond their reach, that words don't
go there said with words. They were speaking
                              for
    the we that was no we they knew. It wasn't
music went where words were unable, it was
    aroma consubstantial with crease and declivity,
                                  the
    beloved's cleavage's remit... There was a we
      so whole it couldn't be added to, the lover
and the beloved's extrapolative extent. An arche-
    type, some had said, auguring more, a certain
                             polis
bound up in it, sort-of more than certain, the we
    or the would-be we we'd be. Doubletalk ob-
    tained its lease. It felt good to be where words
                           did
    not go and we were glad, no matter they didn't
sound like what they were... All was not lost we
    were secretly believing, a host insistence we held
                          or

that held us. Another nakedness had overtaken
us, deeper than before and affording no glamor, the
   is of as-it-is exactly as it was, as with nothing not
                                      said
   nothing left. A too-late eternity chimed at every stop
      on the train we were on, the boat we rode, the bus
we were on... Who was to know a banana Nub was the
                                 Nub
      we'd be in we were asking. The body's propensities
      the mind's obsession, the remanding of which was
meat for the lit season spring would be, a garland for the
                                          lit-
up wind, bodies dressed in cloves and rosemary. "These,"
   we declared, "begin to be auspicious, as though am-
   bage never happened our way, a sign of the return of
                                    signs."
   We had all gone off to hibernate, inside or astride   179
the exploding moment or aside from it, we the unexcited
   excitable ones. All was not lost we were secretly be-
lieving... "Density, be our boon," we stood intoning,
                                       some-
   thing said in another tongue it seemed. One spoke
      with a balloon in one's jaw and with bubbles coming
out of one's head, all the gathered-up glory's urgency
                                     and

ferment no longer one's own, had it ever been. An
unacted-on whim, an adamantine desire, our place was
no place but polis manqué. A spectral world it was
we were in, cracks in our heads the bubbles came out of.
Some-
thing like fate moved among them. "Everything I have
is yours" had been said, toxins at large and afoot. A
violin grew out of one's neck, one's body's propensities
baf-
fling, be-
set

•

No words did Andreannette's churchical girth justice,
her Lespugue-like buxomness gathered into one em-
brace. We were the tribe whose madonna she was, she
of
the auto-apocalypse we moment to moment were
shot back by. A continuing book of the there we'd have
been we were in, a book that, hung up and caught out,
was
a book that wasn't one... Whatever it was and wher-
ever it was, it came back to there being a body to be or
not be in, a beyond words knew no way of reaching, a
where that they already were. Did it make it different if
there

was a different name for it we were wondering, rhythmic
      remit shown to be what soul was, fetishized back and but-
tocks, the width of the world in our grasp addressing her,
                                                        the
      so-called sodality we
were

———————————

We dreamt everyone had gone away, no one could
be reached. We sensed eternity existing without us,
   more where than when, the where words would not

                                             go.

   Something like fate or like foreboding moved
among us, Andreannette's thick madonna, thin with
   late-life proffer, thick for the occasion again...
                                        We'd
been busy looking for signs, each the one that had
   no name according to lore, Philippé's "Well, well,
   well, well, well" spun us around, the going away of

                                             love
   being liberty the lie Nub told itself... They were each
the one lore said had no name, the signs we saw, lore
   itself a kind of naming we could see, a there there were

                                             no

   words in, might
it be

                •

What it was was there we were among the muses,
 a ladling of sand on the shore up and down Lone
Coast. It would not explain itself. All manner of

                                                    crev-
ice and curvature abounded, foothill, grass light,
late afternoon sun, a tenuous bond between body
 and shoreline, scrub and eucalypti farther in. We

                                               bit
 our bottom lips. We pounded the heels of our
hands together, the is of what it was under epic sur-
 mise... "There's a there the word 'there' makes

                                          us
 think there is," Andreannette proclaimed, Andre-
 annette our priest, our possessor, "a there no word
not 'there' can reach." A longing for where it was

                                      over-
 came us. We were wanting a there the word that   183
was whose rumor was whose location. We were
 wanting to be the word itself... What to say was our
question again, what to say, momentary apocalypse.

                                   Epic
 surmise bought us time, our cheeks grew hot...
Earthly extent, gratuitous beauty, fell away disconso-
 late. Sweet churchical girth, a celestrial spread, we

                                   saw

it as. What to be done with it, we asked, but, could we,
coexist, all bodily amenities exiting or exited from.
We were on decapitism's cutting edge reminiscing when
life

was more wonder... They were calling everything so-
called, a there that wasn't there of late the propriocep-
tive, rattling fit we called soul... They were not calling
it

that

——————

A referendum on soul what had seemed a matter
of location, locution, the word and the where of
   there, the wear of it over space across time. There-
by and by then seeming to say there was nothing to   185

                             .   say,
   a referendum on that about which no one wanted
to know, the whereness of its there deeply in doubt...
  A valedictory bequest what had begun as query, a

                            won-
dering what out loud or in the meated mind's chamber,
  whose bounty or its bearing the altar we worshipped at,

                           a dis-
  crepant rap, soul's knock upon
body

ROBERT COOPER

Atrocity in the Garden of Eden: Myanmar

Something new and unexpected is happening in Myanmar. No, not the most recent coup d'état. Few countries have had so many coups as Myanmar. The surprise is that, a year later, the military are still not in control. *That* is what has never happened before.

On February 1, 2021, when a new parliament was due to convene, General Min Aung Hlaing, commander-in-chief of Myanmar's army, known as the Tatmadaw, decided to act on his dislike of the result of the elections held in November 2020 and took over the government. Again, no other country has a history of coups to rival Myanmar's, or has endured such long periods of military misrule. But this time it is different. This time the coup has been launched but it has not landed. The military are in government and they occupy the buildings of the state — but they are not in power. The government does not function, not even in the incompetent and brutal fashion in which it usually operates under the military. Resistance continues, and it is everywhere. For a military that has been in power on and off since 1958, this suggests that something has gone wrong. Or more precisely, gone right.

No one explains Myanmar, from both personal experience and academic study, as well as Thant Myint-U, and in his book *The Hidden History of Burma: Race, Capitalism, and the Crisis of Democracy in the 21st Century* he records an apposite question asked by Frank Smithuis, a Dutch doctor who worked in Myanmar since 1994: "Why is there severe malnutrition in this Garden of Eden?" The doctor's image is not accurate: Myanmar is hardly the Garden of Eden. For decades it has been one of the poorest countries in the world. And yet, even on a short visit, you cannot escape the feeling that it *ought* to be the Garden of Eden. The country's assets and its potential are visible even to the casual visitor. It is a big country, roughly the size of Ukraine; it has some of the most fertile soil in Asia; from the foothills of the Himalayas to the warm waters of the Andaman Sea it has every climate you could wish for. The mangoes are legendary, but climb a bit higher and you can create a first-class vineyard. The seas are full of fish; Myanmar's great rivers have been the arteries of civilisation for a thousand years. The forests have a wonderful legacy of hardwoods, not to mention tigers and elephants. The teak inheritance has been pillaged,

Atrocity in the Garden of Eden: Myanmar

but the forests can be restored; and handled well they would be a unique asset. There are beaches, lakes, and wooded hills to please the most discerning tourist. In the hills you can find every mineral, every rare earth, every gemstone (including diamonds, it is said). There is oil and gas, too. Myanmar's potential for looting and drug production has already been plentifully exploited, but in a well-governed country the prospects for development would be unlimited.

Well-governed: there is the catch. Myanmar has never been well governed. That is not the fault of the people. According to Thant Myint-U, his country "ranks consistently as one of the most generous countries on earth." Some ten years ago, in Myanmar on official business, and tired of meetings with government officials in air-conditioned offices, I stopped in a remote village to visit a small project, and to see how ordinary people lived. The head of the village organized a meeting, providing local peanuts and milk. Everyone came. One remark in particular, from the collective conversation, sticks in the memory: "The government doesn't help us, so we help each other." This spirit runs through the whole society: no matter how poor the people, they look after their children, and are proud of them; they keep themselves and their villages as clean as they can. They do not have many opportunities, but there is a respect for learning and a great desire of education. Nor is this just my own view of today's Myanmar: Viscount William Slim, who commanded British forces in Burma in the war against Japan, described his impression of a Burmese village when he first arrived there in 1942: it seemed, he wrote "much cleaner and better kept than similar places in India — as indeed are all Burmese towns and villages." All Myanmar needs is a break from the wars, and a halfway decent government.

Britain began to annex Burma in 1852 and it became one of

the last additions to the British Empire, a province of British India, in 1886, a time when its older possessions, notably Ireland, were beginning to press for home rule. It lost Burma, briefly, to Japan in World War II, and gave it independence in 1948. The movement for independence had begun in the interwar years among the students at Rangoon University, partly inspired by Ireland. That movement included many individuals who would matter later: U Nu, the country's first prime minister; U Thant, the first non-European UN Secretary General; and Aung San, Burma's first elected leader. Aung San was expelled from university for an article attacking its principal, but reinstated after a student strike. He admired Abraham Lincoln, read voraciously, learned some of Edmund Burke's speeches by heart, and at different times embraced every ideology from left or right, provided it pointed to independence.

The British government, meanwhile, was beginning to experiment with pseudo-democratic institutions: a Burmese parliament and a council of ministers. These were all a façade: power remained in the hands of the Governor — including direct rule over the hills of the periphery, the regions of minority peoples such as the Shan, the Karen, and the Kachin, seen by the British as good war-like material for the British army. It is important to understand that Burma, now Myanmar, is an uncommonly diverse country. No less than 135 ethnic groups have been officially recognized, and they have been grouped into eight "major national ethnic races." The largest is the Burmese, or Bama. Burma is where China meets India and where both meet Thailand, Laos and Bangladesh. To an outsider the Wa seem Chinese, and the Chin might be from Nagaland, and the Karen and Shan resemble Thais. (And there are villages in Vietnam where everyone looks and dresses like

189

the Burmese). Belonging to one of these groups is a way of qualifying as a citizen — which has made the absence of the Rohingya from the official list a serious problem.

The first military intervention in British Burma was the Japanese invasion in 1942. The Japanese claimed to come as liberators and brought with them a small "Burmese Independence Army" (BIA), led by Aung San. Despairing of change under the British, and with help from Japanese intelligence, he had made his way to Tokyo, returning secretly to recruit other young men — the "thirty comrades" who arrived with him in Burma as auxiliaries to the Japanese army. As Japan moved into Burma, Aung San and his comrades recruited more Burmese, so that his "independence army" grew to approximately three thousand — still a tiny number when compared with British or Japanese forces. But the sight of Burmese people in uniform, helping to drive the British out, inspired patriotism among some Burmese. For others, such as the Karen, who were stalwarts of the British colonial army, it brought anxiety. The arrival of the BIA thus set off communal violence among Burma's different peoples. The Japanese intervened to stop it. (The Kachin, who had fought in Flanders in World War I, also fought the Japanese, but as part of the campaign to liberate China, and under the auspices of the OSS, which was the predecessor of the CIA.)

In 1943, the Japanese organized an independence ceremony, appointing Dr. Ba Maw as Leader — this was, after all, a fascist regime. Both the independence and the office were hollow, as the office of prime minister under the British had been. The same Ba Maw had held that position too; but now Aung San was his number two and his minister of defense. By 1944, it became increasingly clear that independence under the Japanese was not the real thing; also that they were losing the war. Aung San, in secret, created a new movement: the Anti-Fascist People's Freedom League. When the British got word of this, they signalled that they would be ready to arm and work with his new organization. A few weeks later Aung San and his men joined a Japanese parade in front of Government House, but instead of marching back to barracks they turned in a different direction, to join the war against Japan. Another few weeks, and Aung San arrived, by invitation, in General Slim's headquarters — causing a stir, since he was still in the uniform of a Japanese general. Slim asked Aung San if he was not taking a rather large risk in coming: after all, he had committed innumerable offenses and had only oral promises of safe conduct. "No" he replied, and, when Slim asked him why not, he said: "Because you are a *British* officer." But had he not come now only because the British side was winning? Aung San replied that it would not have done much good to come to Slim if the British had been losing. Slim liked his frankness, and judged him to be a patriot, straightforward and bold. And so he was.

Shortly afterwards, parties of Burmese soldiers began to arrive in Japanese uniforms, announcing that they were reporting for duty with the British. By then Japan was being beaten in Burma. A few months later, after Hiroshima and Nagasaki, they surrendered. The British side had plans for the peace: an orderly transition to independence under British supervision, including a new Burmese Advisory Council, based on a British White Paper. Aung San's Anti-Fascist League would have a special position in this body. But they had also made promises of independence for the Karen, the Kachin, and others. Aung San's message was simpler: only independence mattered. By now he had a private army and a growing public following. The "strength of the League appears to depend on the personality of Aung San," wrote the British colonial Governor, Sir Reginald Dorman-Smith.

In late 1946, Aung San made four demands: elections the following spring; the inclusion of all Burmese territory — including the hills of the periphery, where the Shan, the Karen, the Chin, the Kachin and others lived; a review of economic reconstruction and the role of British companies, and above all, independence by early 1948. As always: clear and concise. Britain was already dealing with the post-war complications of India and Palestine, the occupation of Germany, and its own domestic wreckage and debt; it had every incentive to settle Burma quickly. The government invited Aung San and a delegation to London in the freezing January of 1947. Aung San went with his deputy Tin Tut, an able lawyer, but none of the delegates with him were from the minority peoples. Karen and Shan leaders warned that they would not be bound by an agreement where representation for them was absent.

By comparison with Burma's internal complications, the negotiation with Britain was easy — the Attlee government was committed to independence for India and had no reason to hang on to Burma. The only question left open was that of membership of the Commonwealth. Rivals on the right — U Saw — and on the left — the clever Communist Party leader Thakin Than Tun — joined the conference in London, but they refused to sign the agreement and they also opposed membership in the Commonwealth. In practice, this was never a runner. The name "British Commonwealth" did not sound very different from "British Empire." And it was headed by the Queen. It would be hard to explain to a newly independent country (itself a former monarchy) that Her Royal Highness was not a real sovereign and would have no power. The shape of the Burmese constitution, and the position

192

of non-Burmese peoples, such as the Karen, was hardly discussed. (The ethnic minorities tended to favor the idea of being part of the Commonwealth and were nervous that the end of the Commonwealth might put them "at the mercy of Burmese-dominated Burma.")

Aung San was in his early thirties. His life had been full of drama: as a student he had joined any number of dissident groups, including Dobama Asiayone, or the We Burmese Association, whose members gave themselves the ironic title Thakin, or Lord; he had been expelled from university, along with U Nu, but reinstated after a three-month strike by the other students. After graduating he became Secretary General of the Burmese Communist Party and left it twice. All of these activities were unpaid, so he had lived in poverty. Then he had been a soldier on both sides in the war, and now, as Governor Dorman-Smith said to him, he was "the people's idol." "I did not seek that," Aung San said, "but only to free my country. But now it is so lonely." And then he wept.

The path to independence began with parliamentary elections in April 1947. Before the elections Aung San gathered the leaders of non-Burmese peoples, Shan, Karen, Kachin, and Chin, together in the town of Panglong in the Shan Hills. The Shan agreed to join the new republic on condition that they had the right to secede in ten years. The Karen refused. They had fought on the British side against the Japanese, and against Aung San's small army too; they had promises of independence from Britain. They boycotted the elections, which unwittingly helped Aung San's party to win a huge majority.

The Panglong meeting is still remembered in Myanmar as a bid for national reconciliation. So it was, but just as significant was the composition of Aung San's Executive Council — which he nominated after the elections as the interim government, under British authority, until independence. It included neither the extreme right (U Saw) nor the Communist Party; but Aung San persuaded important Shan, Kachin, and Chin leaders and to join it, as well as a well-regarded Moslem figure from Mandalay.

Independence was scheduled for January 4, 1948 — a date identified by the astrologers as auspicious. Until then the British Governor, now Sir Hubert Rance, presided. On July 19, 1947, the Executive Council met for an informal session under Aung San. As the meeting began, three men in military fatigues burst in, firing sub-machine guns. Aung San died instantly, and so did many members of his cabinet and staff. U Saw, who had organised the slaughter, was later hanged. Aung San left behind him his wife, Daw Khin Kyi, and three children. The youngest, his daughter Aung San Suu Kyi, was two years old.

The death of Aung San was a calamity. It was as though Abraham Lincoln had been assassinated *before* the Civil War. With him died the best men of his generation: he had brought them together to rebuild the country as an independent state and a union. He was young, but he was the creator of Burma as an independent state, and also of its army.

Instead of Aung San, the Prime Minister at independence in January 1948 was U Nu. He was older than Aung San, but they had been expelled together from Rangoon University many years before and had been active in the same movements. U Nu had a different temperament. He was charming, thoughtful, and a devout Buddhist. Perhaps he had some of the naivete of someone who is essentially a good man. What is certain is that he did not have Aung San's hard edge,

194

nor his decisiveness, nor the authority that his experience of military command had brought him.

In retrospect U Nu's time as Prime Minister is commonly regarded as a golden age. In fact it was a time of turmoil, shaken by rebellions of every sort, especially by the Karen. U Tin Tut, an experienced colleague of U Nu (and they were few) was killed by a bomb that was planted in his car, no one knows by whom. At this time too, the civil war in China spilled over the borders into northeast Burma, where some of hill tribes are cousins of the Chinese. U Nu's closest friend and adviser was U Thant; but he, too, was a man of words and of peace. The Burmese army had much to do, and did it well enough; but increasingly the military became a separate entity, led by General Ne Win, responsible only to its own command structure. It was at this time that the military began to run private businesses for profit — the beginning of the military-commercial-political complex that has been a disaster for Myanmar.

U Nu offered U Thant the job of Burmese ambassador to the United Nations in 1957. A few years later, as Secretary General, he became the most famous Burmese in the world. But U Nu himself was left more isolated. In the following summer some of his own party proposed a vote of no confidence in the government; U Nu won the ballot, but rumors circulated of plots by army field commanders for Ne Win and the army to take the government "under its protection." U Nu then announced that, "because of the situation," he had invited General Ne Win to "assume the reins of government" as a "caretaker."

Strictly speaking, this was not the first of the military's coups d'état, but that is how it is remembered. There was no violence, but it was in part a result of the killing of Aung San and his government in waiting. In hindsight it also looks a lot like a dry run. The military governed rather well, if also rather brutally. They cleaned up Rangoon and other cities; they dealt with rebels and with corruption, except their own (the army's commercial interests continued to expand). And they handed power back on time, through elections in February, 1960. U Nu won by a landslide. The people clearly preferred civilian government, but it seemed also that the military could be trusted with power.

Wrong! After the dry run, came the real thing. On March 3, 1962, tanks and armored units moved into downtown Rangoon. Prime Minister U Nu, other ministers, and the chief justice were arrested; so were a number of Shan and Karen leaders. With a few exceptions the coup was bloodless, but now there was no promise of future elections. When, in July, students in Rangoon University demanded the restoration of democracy, troops arrived and fifteen students were killed. The next morning the army blew up the Students Union building where, as students, Aung San, U Nu and U Thant had all spoken.

Ne Win, like Aung San, was from the middle classes. He went to Rangoon University to read natural sciences, hoping to become a doctor. But he failed his examinations and, after two years, dropped out. He tried different kinds of work, but found that small business was dominated by the Indian community. He ended up working for the Post Office. When he was not selling stamps, his free time was spent with politically minded students, and he helped to translate *The Communist Manifesto* into Burmese. With Aung San and others he was a Thakin in the We Burmese association. Then he joined Aung San as one of the thirty, taking "Ne Win" (meaning "bright sun") as his *nom de guerre*, and it stuck. He was Aung San's second in command, and after independence he became the army chief of staff. In private life he was happily married several times, and known as a playboy.

Anyone who thought that in power the army would repeat the technocratic pattern of its previous two years was incorrect. As chairman of the Revolutionary Council, Ne Win declared that "parliamentary democracy was not suitable for Burma," created the Burma Socialist Programme Party, and declared all other political parties illegal. When there were riots at Rangoon University, he shut all universities down. Health care was nationalized, and so was almost everything else, including major private enterprises. Foreign trade and development aid — except some Soviet programs — were banned. This was "the Burmese road to socialism."

Officially, Burmese foreign policy was "non-aligned," or unaffiliated with either the United States or the Soviet Union, the great power rivals in the Cold War; but it would be more accurate to say that it was isolationist. The country turned inwards. In 1964, Ne Win expelled Burma's large Indian community, some three hundred thousand people. Burma also had a substantial Chinese population, with its own school system, and as they became more visible — with flags and badges — during the Cultural Revolution in 1967, they too became a target. But China sent troops into Burma, to join related ethnic communities in the Kokang and Wa hills, close to the border with China's Yunnan province, where traffickers ran opium, and today, methamphetamines. The government did not touch Chinese schools or communities.

In 1966 U Nu was released from prison. He met Ne Win and discussed the possibility of a return to democracy. Ne Win was against it, but he gave U Nu permission to leave the country. He did, and promptly set up an organisation to over-throw Ne Win. It failed. In 1974, U Thant died. His family brought his body back to Burma. Ne Win, who believed that U Thant had been conspiring with U Nu against him, refused any official recognition. His family arranged for his coffin to be displayed in a dignified way in a public space (the old racecourse) with flowers and his portrait; and when a torrent of well-wishers came to pay their respects, the government reluctantly gave permission for a (private) burial. Anti-government students hijacked the coffin and took it to Rangoon University and the site of the Students Union, where monks watched over it with the students, who wanted it buried on the spot. Thousands of soldiers and police arrived: they arrested many of those who had gathered, probably killing some. Eventually U Thant was buried close to the great Schwedagon Pagoda.

The Burmese road to socialism turned out to be a road to nowhere. The country grew isolated and impoverished. Ne Win contributed to the decline with a series of demonetizations. In 1964 he decreed that 50 and 100 Kyat notes would cease to be legal tender. This was a clumsy effort against the black market, but its main effect was to wipe out the savings of the poor. Later, in 1987, having been told that the number nine was astrologically auspicious for him, Ne Win introduced 45 and 90 Kyat notes — both numbers being multiples of, and adding up to, nine. That is not a sound basis for monetary policy. Around this time, I visited Rangoon briefly for the first time. Two memories are especially vivid. The first was the complaint of a woman that to buy a bag of cement she had had to fill in twenty-four forms and obtain permission from almost as many ministries. The second was the story that Ne Win had been told by a soothsayer that in the coming

198

year Burma would turn to the right. As a pre-emptive strike against the prediction coming true through the overthrow of his left-wing government, he announced that traffic would henceforth drive on the right. This made no sense, as cars were largely imported from Britain or Japan and they suddenly had the steering wheel on the wrong side. No matter: it was done and everyone drove on the wrong side. As usual, the Burmese people managed.

In the end numerology and bad luck got the better of Ne Win. In 1988 he announced that he would resign, thoughtfully suggesting that this might be the moment to return to multi-party democracy, but leaving the details to his military successors. They accepted the resignation and forgot the rest. The students, as usual, wanted better; their demonstrations met a violent response and many were killed. Then came the numerology: the number eight is lucky in Burma, so on 8/8/88 the students tried again. A massive demonstration was put down with massive force, but this time others joined in: workers, civil servants, and even policemen and soldiers.

Then the bad luck: Aung San Suu Kyi was in Rangoon. She had left Burma long ago, when U Nu had sent her mother to India as ambassador; and from India she had gone to Oxford University, and then to New York, where she had worked in the Secretariat of U Thant's UN, returning to Britain to marry Michael Aris, a quiet, serious scholar of Tibetan Buddhism. They had lived in Bhutan and were living in Oxford, with their two children, when in 1988 Aung San Suu Kyi returned to Burma to care for her mother, who was dying. That being her purpose, she had no wish to involve herself in politics. But after many approaches, from old friends and from young people, she agreed to address the students. Her first words were: "I never left Burma." They were true: whether she was enjoying herself in New York, or looking after her children in Oxford, a part of her mind had always been in Burma.

In 1988, hundreds of the protesters were imprisoned, usually far from their families to worsen their isolation. A year later Aung San Suu Kyi herself was placed under house arrest. She was now committed to the fight for democracy in Burma and, with one or two breaks, when the political atmosphere improved, she spent most of the next twenty years isolated in her mother's house in Rangoon. During this time her husband died of cancer. She had declined the government's offer to let her visit him when his illness worsened, being sure they would not let her return.

Soon a new general would rule in 1992: Than Shwe had replaced Ne Win, and the State Law and Order Restoration Commission (SLORC) replaced the Burmese road to socialism. In 1990 they held elections. Remarkably, they were well conducted. We know this because the National League for Democracy (NLD) — Aung San Suu Kyi's party created in 1988 — won over eighty percent of the seats. (The army has never understood how unpopular it is). The new military government, renamed the State Peace and Development Commission (SPDC), declared that the implementation of the election results would have to wait for the new constitution that they were starting work on. The United States and the European Union adopted a policy of sanctions and isolation, out of sympathy for Aung San Suu Kyi and the NLD. This approach often punished the people more than the rulers who profited from illegal trade in timber, gemstones, and drugs. But what else can you do? The West also criticized ASEAN when it admitted Burma (now calling itself Myanmar) to its ranks. In retrospect this had a good side: visiting thriving countries such as Indonesia and Thailand gave Myanmar's generals a sense of how far their own country was falling behind their regional peers, whom they had always looked down on. But at home nothing changed, unless for the worse. Inflation and seizures of land made the lives of peasant farmers — most of the population — even poorer.

In 2007 the monks took up the cause of the people in what the West has called "the Saffron Revolution." As their protests were beginning, recent newspaper photographs of Than Shwe's daughter in a wedding dress covered with diamonds added fuel to the dissident fire. The demonstrations began in late August and continued through September. In many places, contrary to Buddhist custom and doctrine, the monks were met with force. On September 24, demonstrations were held in twenty-five cities; in Rangoon a long line of monks walked in front of Aung San Suu Kyi's house. She opened the gates, watched them in silence, and received their blessing. But there was no revolution. Instead the SPDC carried out its plan to move the capital from crowded Yangon (the former Rangoon) — always at risk from mass protests — to an empty Disneyland capital in the middle of nowhere, called Naypyitaw. There the government would not have to worry about unsightly and dangerous demonstrations.

Then, in May 2008, Cyclone Nargis struck. It made landfall on the flatlands of the Irrawaddy Delta, with the wind at more than a hundred miles per hour and a storm surge reaching twenty-five miles inland in a densely populated area. The government refused to acknowledge either the damage or its incapacity to deal with it. Eventually UN Secretary General Ban Ki-Moon persuaded Than Shwe to accept foreign aid and aid workers, with a promise that no military would be involved. The death toll of Nargis is thought to have been more than a hundred thousand people. In other countries it would have been natural to involve the military in relief operations; eventually this happened in Myanmar too, though the Tatmadaw had no plans for civil emergencies and no experience in helping, as opposed to oppressing, the people.

And right after Nargis, another storm hit, not natural but political: the referendum on the new constitution. This had been drawn up by the National Convention, which was almost entirely from the military. The NLD had been invited to join, but it refused when it was offered only a small number of the seats. It had won a big majority in the election of 1997, but the SPDC decided to set this aside until the new constitution was agreed upon. Government figures claimed that, despite the chaos brought by Nargis, turnout for the referendum was at 99%, with 92.4% voting for the new constitution.

That constitution, which would be in force today had the Tatmadaw not set it aside, promises Myanmar a "flourishing of a genuine, disciplined multi-party democratic system." But it has some unusual features. Three are especially important: a quarter of the members of each of the two parliamentary chambers are military officers nominated by the Commander in Chief of the army, and they vote according to his orders; one of the qualifications for the office of the presidency, as specified in Article 59, is that he or she must not have a spouse or a child who is a foreign citizen (this was designed to exclude Aung San Suu Kyi); the president appoints all ministers, but the ministers of defense, home affairs, and border affairs are appointed from a list of "suitable Defence Services personnel" who are "nominated by the Commander-in-Chief of the Defence Services." Constitutional change in Myanmar requires a majority of 75% plus one in a vote in Parliament. In other words, military control is secure.

Yet the constitution does provide for elections. When elections were held under the new constitution in 2010, Aung San Suu Kyi was under house arrest and the NLD did not register as a political party. A few NLD members, seeing no other way forward, broke away from the party and ran in the elections. When votes were counted and it began to look as though they might win, sacks of advance votes were "discovered" to ensure that they did not. A rigged election that followed a rigged constitution seemed to suggest that nothing was going to change.

But when the new government, with U Thein Sein (the general who had chaired the National Convention) as president, took over, a series of surprises followed. A controversial and unpopular mega-dam was put on hold, greatly to the annoyance of China; some political prisoners were released; and then "the Lady's" house arrest was not renewed. She was invited to meet the president in private, and after much thought and consultation she agreed to register the NLD under the new constitution and to contest forty-four seats in upcoming by-elections. (The constitution is based on the separation of powers, so members of parliament must resign their seats if they become ministers. Montesquieu might have wondered whether a constitution where the head of the army appoints members of parliament really embody a separation of powers.) The by-elections, when held, were visibly free and fair: the proof of this was that the NLD won all the seats but one. Aung San Suu Kyi and the NLD were now in the Burmese parliament for the first time. But they were far from being in power.

In 2012, the NLD was a small minority party in parliament, though Aung San Suu Kyi played a prominent role. In the general election four years later, she and her party contested every seat, and won a large majority. Admiration for her and her father was a factor — at rallies many carried his picture as well as hers. So was the unpopularity of the military, who had corruptly enriched themselves and who were fighting a never-ending series of wars against the non-Burmese peoples of the border lands. Aung San Suu Kyi dealt with the problem of Article 59 by having a trusted friend elected president, inventing the title "state counsellor" for herself, and acting as if she were president. Yet there was no way to get around the impossible parliamentary threshold needed for constitutional change: the military vote under orders and acted as a permanent blocking minority.

Nor did it prove easy to make peace in the border regions, though U Thein Sein's government tried hard. Peace is a condition for both development and a secure democracy. Long-term conflicts have their own momentum, especially if some of those involved benefit commercially. The NLD is seen by some as a Bama party. Aung San Suu Kyi herself is a heroine in regions such as Kachin, but minority peoples are not well represented in her party. The heart of the problem, however, was and is the Tatmadaw: Bama in its composition, and from the day of independence under no one's control except its own. Abroad Aung San Suu Kyis was seen as a saint, but her government was unable to perform miracles. On reflection, a long period of solitary confinement is poor preparation for government. (Nelson Mandela's prison on Robben Island was much less comfortable, but he was with his comrades and they planned the future together.)

The area where Aung San Suu Kyi took the boldest approach was the one for which she has been most criticized. To tackle the problem of the Rohingya, an unloved Muslim

204

minority who are mostly not citizens, she persuaded Kofi Annan to chair a commission and promised to follow his recommendations. She knew that these would include a path to citizenship, and that this would be unpopular. Only hours after his report came out, a Rohingya group attacked Burmese forces, provoking massive and wildly disproportionate retaliation against the whole Rohingya community, driving hundreds of thousands across the border to Bangladesh. A mass exodus of refugees followed — an unconscionable episode of ethnic cruelty and ethnic cleansing. Later Aung San Suu Kyi shocked many people by defending the Burmese army's harsh actions against the Rohingya in court at The Hague. Those who had thought she was a saint now decided that she was a war criminal. In fact, the transition that she had made was from heroine to politician. She had an election to win in 2020, and seeming unpatriotic is a bad election strategy. A cold-hearted calculation perhaps, but to help the Rohingya, if that was her intention, she needed power, and she won again by another massive majority.

And so, on February 1, 2021, there occurred yet another coup d'état, this one led by Min Aung Hlaing. There were multiple arrests, including Aung San Suu Kyi herself, who was charged with possession of an illegal walkie-talkie and "incitement" — presumably to overthrow the constitution, which of course is precisely what Min Aung Hlaing had just done. With her, many NLD members were arrested too, elected parliamentarians and veteran detainees (and also her Australian economic adviser Sean Turnell, who is one of the least conspiratorial people I have ever met). Now it is more than a year since the

Atrocity in the Garden of Eden: Myanmar

coup, and the army is still not in control. But neither are those who won the election. They were never going to be allowed full and legitimate control under this constitution; but now they are in prison. We can describe such events properly only when we know their outcome. Is this the start of a doomed if heroic struggle against overwhelming odds? Or are these the first steps on a path that will unite everyone against the military?

Immediately after the coup people took to the streets all across Myanmar — not only the students of Yangon University, but people of all ages. Everyone has been involved, poor as well as middle class, women as well men, their elders are joining them, and the kids are not giving up. On the streets the leadership comes from Generation Z, who have grown up digital and connected. (For better or for worse, life in Myanmar is dominated by Facebook). And they are able to organize themselves. One woman wore a wedding dress to the protests and held a placard that read, "I am supposed to be getting married; but it's more important for me to be on the street demonstrating for democracy." Others are banging pots and pans, a traditional way to express scorn and to ward off evil spirits. The protests started spontaneously after the coup. Everything stopped: trains did not run; government offices emptied; doctors left their hospitals for the day. The Commander in Chief, now the leader of the junta, Min Aung Hlaing, has admitted that he did not foresee such resistance. But he still ordered his troops to shoot and kill demonstrators. Arrest warrants were issued for those who did not turn up for work, and for health care workers ministering to the wounded, and for people in the fields of television, journalism, literature, music, and theater arts.

One of the first to lose her life was a twenty-year-old named Mya Thwate Thwate Khaing, in Naypyitaw. In Yangon,

206

seeing young people being shot, fifty-nine-year-old Daw Tin Nwee Yee put on her school-teacher's uniform and joined her colleagues and her pupils. She was shot on the street by a rubber bullet and died of an immediate heart attack. In Mandalay, Kyal Sin, singer, dancer, and taekwondo champion, was shot dead. As the mass marches were driven from the streets of the big cities, the small towns took up the struggle. Myanmar people abroad are providing money for food and for guns. Eleven months after the coup, a silent strike was organized to show that the people have not forgotten, have not given in: fifty-five million people vanished for the day.

Away from the streets there are dissident organizations: an underground government, the National Unity Government (NUG), brings together those who have been elected and are not yet in prison. Under its auspices, supporters in local areas have established People's Defence Forces (PDFs) to protect the people against the Tatmadaw. The NUG would like to win the support of the Ethnic Armed Organizations (EAOs) who for years have fought the Tatmadaw. That the NUG now speaks of establishing a federal democracy — putting the word "federal" first — is itself a sign of change. It has also put aside Aung San Suu Kyi's longstanding policy of non-violent resistance.

In some areas there has been a positive response from the minority peoples who have been fighting the Tadmadaw for years. Some are helping to train PDFs; some are fighting alongside them. Others are offering refuge to those fleeing the Tadmadaw. Here are two small examples of what might be described as the battle for the hills. The battle began in 1948, when the state was founded. The objective has always been to change the state's shape, and the enemy has usually been the army. In Chin State on the Indian border, an area that until recently was relatively peaceful, the local Chinland Defense

Force has clashed with Tatmadaw units, who have abducted citizens, including children, to use as human shields. The Chin National Front now has an agreement with the National Unity Government; it works with the parallel NUG administration to deal with COVID-19, and it offers training for the new People's Defense Forces.

Several hundred miles away over bad roads and across wide rivers, on the border with Thailand, is the township of Lay Kay Kaw in Kayin state. Here the forces of the Karen National Union (KNU) are giving shelter to members of the civil disobedience movement, who are organizing demonstrations and urban resistance. The picture is grim. In December the military attacked the town of Lay Kay Kaw, using, they said, "limited force," claiming that the town was sheltering "terrorists." The KNU spokesperson denied there were terrorists in the town: "We accepted the guests on the basis of human rights. Those people wouldn't have to seek refuge in Lay Kay Kaw if the military didn't keep killing and torturing people." Twenty-one people were arrested, including members of the National Unity Government, and public servants taking part in the Civil Disobedience Movement. When junta troops returned to Lay Kay Kaw the next day, they found themselves under siege. What triggered the conflict, according to the KNU, was the behaviour of the Tatmadaw. who did not just make arrests but also stole and destroyed property belonging to residents. "We couldn't stand by and do nothing. They have acted with impunity for their actions for too long."

People were fleeing by the thousands. By December 20, 2021 the clashes in Lay Kay Kaw had become so serious that the KNU made an appeal to the United Nations to declare a no-fly zone over the area. Three days later the regime launched airstrikes and heavy artillery attacks that forced thousands more to flee their homes. The junta said the attack was in accordance with its rules of engagement. The KNU spokesperson memorably retorted, "What rules of engagement did they follow? The entire world knows that they've been indiscriminately shelling entire villages... The military keeps sending reinforcements. The battles are bound to continue... the locals can't come back." A woman (who did not want to give her name) from the nearby Thai-Myanmar border town of Myawaddy had this to say about the regime's professed attempts to repatriate displaced villagers: "It's pure fantasy. No one believes a word of it. People here know the real situation, and so do those who fled the fighting. Everyone knows the military even fired shells into Thailand. They're only telling lies about this to maintain stability inside the army." Another KNU spokesperson summed it up: "The more the military treat the people as enemies, the more enemies they will have."

The eventual settlement in Myanmar will have to be far-reaching: not just elections, but a constitution that recognizes ethnic diversity in a federal framework, and offers a better electoral system than the colonial legacy of first-past-the-post, the most primitive of all electoral systems. This is still a long way off. But there are grounds for hope. The battle for the streets and the battle for the hills are becoming the same battle in some places. This is a development of enormous significance. Those who seek democracy and those who seek autonomy have joined forces. The wish for autonomy is old, of course; it goes back before independence. What is new is the realization that the two fights can be made one — that democratic majorities and protection of minorities can be a single cause.

What has made this national solidarity possible is the other new factor in the struggle against military dictatorship in Myanmar: the experience of democracy, from 2010 to 2020. This was a mediocre democracy in every way, with the military taking a quarter of the seats in parliament, and a primitive electoral system inherited from Britain — but even that experience of flawed and limited democracy has had such a powerful effect that people are risking their lives for it.

The catalogue of arrests, torture, trials, and killings grows long. By the abysmal standards of Myanmar justice, Aung San Suu Kyi has gotten off lightly so far: in December she was convicted of violating COVID-19 restrictions during the election campaign and of calling for public opposition to the coup, and was sentenced to six years in prison; this was reduced to two years in a show of magnanimity by the military; and more recently she was given a four-year sentence for owning a walkie talkie, also reduced to two years. Many other charges against her remain, and if she is found guilty she could spend the rest of her life in prison. The Assistance Association for Political Prisoners, an organization based in Thailand, founded and staffed by Burmese former political prisoners, does its best to keep a record: their latest update since the most recent coup, as of late January, records 1,503 killed, 8,778 arrested, and 1,672 on the run. The numbers go up every day.

That inexperienced city kids and disparate ethnic organizations might win against the ruthless, disciplined, well-armed Tatmadaw may seem impossible, but they are many in number, and their courage and endurance is extraordinary. A year after the coup, the military is still not in control of the country. Yet the authoritarians in power in Yangon, like the authoritarians in power in other capitals around the world, may believe that there is a new historical trend in their favor: the indifference of the West, and particularly the United States, to the global attrition of democracy. Democratization no longer figures among our foreign policy priorities; indeed, it is increasingly described as imperialism.

We who live in democratic countries have increasingly lost sight of the worth of democracy, both for ourselves and as a way of making the world more peaceful and more decent. The tyrants in Myanmar will persist in their vicious policies until they encounter not only serious resistance at home but also serious resistance abroad. But who among the powers will put up the impediments to their cruelty?

STEVEN M. NADLER

Bans, Then and Now

Can anything surprise us anymore? A madman with no political experience who boasts of sexually assaulting women is elected president of the United States, and the only thing that keeps him from doing irreparable harm to the American republic is his own stupidity and incompetence. A rabid mob of citizens, incited by his lies and the misinformation promulgated by right-wing pundits, attacks and ransacks the United States Capitol while Congress is in session. In America, books are being banned from libraries and schools. Meanwhile, the planet is on what seems to be an irreversible path to environmental disaster, while a global pandemic continues to rage and disrupt our social, economic, and political welfare. Conspiracy theories are everywhere. And none of this is keeping billionaires from devoting their immense wealth to a competition that involves sending themselves (on round-trips, alas) into space. We deserve to be the least surprisable, the most jaded and disabused, people who ever lived.

And yet, out of a usually quiet corner of the beautiful, peaceful, and tolerant city of Amsterdam, late in the year of 2021, came this gem of a letter, addressed by a prominent Dutch rabbi to an Israeli-American professor of philosophy:

Amsterdam, 28 November 2021 / 24 Kislev 5782

To the attention of Professor Yitzhak Melamed,

The chachamim [rabbis] and parnassim [lay directors] of Kahal Kados Talmud Torah [Talmud Torah Congregation] excommunicated Spinoza and his writings with the severest possible ban, a ban that remains in force for all time and cannot be rescinded.

You have devoted your life to the study of Spinoza's banned works and the development of his ideas.

Your request to visit our complex and create a film about this Epicouros [heretic] in our Esnoga [synagogue] and Yeshiva (Ets Haïm) is incompatible with our centuries-old halachic, historic, and ethical tradition and an unacceptable assault on our identity and heritage.

I therefore deny your request and declare you persona non grata in the Portuguese Synagogue complex.

213

The letter is signed by Rabbi Joseph Serfaty of the city's Portugees-Israëlitiesche Gemeente (Portuguese-Jewish Community), who closes by wishing Professor Melamed "a meaningful Chanuka."

As the Dutch might say, *Wat in Godsnaam?!*

In the spring of 1656, Bento de Spinoza was not yet the infamous philosopher, the bold and radical thinker who would scandalize Europe by identifying God with Nature, denying the possibility of miracles, and proclaiming the Bible to be a "corrupt" and "mutilated" collection of human writings whose only value is that its stories are morally edifying. At this point Spinoza was, in fact, an importer of dried fruit — just another merchant from a prominent family in Amsterdam's Sephardic community, the same community that Rabbi Serfaty now serves. Just a few years earlier, at the age of twenty-one, when his father Michael de Spinoza died, Spinoza had to cut short his formal schooling and take over the family business. As far as we can tell from the extant documentation, everything was fine. Spinoza was still donating (or at least pledging) his semi-annual dues and charity payments to the Talmud Torah congregation, although the amounts were gradually diminishing. An indication of a loss of faith? More likely just a consequence of the serious debts that he had inherited from his father. To all appearances, Bento was still an upstanding (if financially struggling) member of the community.

Thus, what happened next comes — to us, at least — as a bit of a shock. On July 27, 1656, or the 6th of Av, 5416 on the Jewish calendar, the following ferocious proclamation was read out from in front of the ark of the Torah in the congregation's synagogue on the Houtgracht, the "Wood Canal," filled in during the nineteenth century and now the Waterlooplein, site of the city hall, the opera house, and a flea market.

The *Senhores* of the *ma'amad* make known to you that having for some time reports of the bad opinions and acts of Baruch de Spinoza, they have endeavored by various means and promises to turn him from his bad ways. But being unable to effect any remedy, on the contrary, each day receiving more information about the abominable heresies which he practiced and taught and about the monstrous deeds which he performed, and having many trustworthy witnesses who have reported and testified on all of this in the presence of the said Espinoza, who has been found guilty; after all of this has been examined in the presence of the rabbis, they [the members of the *ma'amad*] have decided, with their [the rabbis'] consent, that the said Espinoza should be banned and separated from the Nation of Israel, as they now put him under *herem* with the following *herem*:

With the judgment of the angels and with that of the saints, we put under *herem*, ostracize, and curse and damn Baruch de Espinoza, with the consent of Blessed God and with the consent of this entire holy congregation, before these holy scrolls, with the 613 precepts which are written in them; with the *herem* that Joshua put upon Jericho, with the curse with which Elisha cursed the youth, and with all the curses that are written in the law. Cursed be he by day and cursed be he by night; cursed be he when he lies down and cursed be he when he rises up. Cursed be he when he goes out and cursed be he when he comes in. *Adonai* will not forgive him. The fury and zeal of *Adonai* will burn against this man and bring upon him all the curses that are written in this book of the law. And may *Adonai* erase his name from under the heavens. And may *Adonai* separate him for evil from all of the tribes of Israel, with all the curses of the covenant that are written in this book of the law. And you that cleave unto *Adonai* your God, all of you alive today: We warn that no one should communicate with him orally or in writing, nor provide him any favor, nor be with him under the same roof, nor be within four cubits of him, nor read any paper composed or written by him.

The young Spinoza was now formally — and irrevocably — ostracized from the Portuguese-Jewish community of Amsterdam by the *parnassim* (directors) sitting that year on the *ma'amad* (board of directors) of the Talmud Torah congregation. The writ of ostracism, the ban called a *herem*, may originally have been composed in Hebrew. It is extant only in a Portuguese version entered into the community's record book, the *Livro dos Acordos da Naçao e Ascamot*, the sole copy of which is now in the Portuguese-Jewish Archives of the Municipal Archives of the City of Amsterdam. Spinoza was only twenty-three years old when he was issued the *herem*; as far as we know he had not yet made public anything he may have written.

Herem as a coercive or punitive measure exercised by a Jewish community upon recalcitrant and rebellious members goes back at least to the period of the Mishnah, in the first and second centuries CE. Originally, in its biblical use, the term *herem* designated separating something or someone from all other things and forbidding ordinary use or contact; in some cases, it could mean destroying that thing or person. The reason for separation might be that the item or individual is sacred or holy, or it might be that it is polluted or an abomination to God. The Torah, for example, declares that anyone who sacrifices to any god other than the Israelite God is *herem* (Exodus 22:19). He is to be killed, and the idols that he worshiped are to be burned. Deuteronomy (7:1–2) declares that the nations occupying the land that God has promised to the Israelites are *herem* and thus must be destroyed. On the other hand, something that has been devoted to the Lord (*herem le-Adonai*) is "most holy" (Leviticus 27:29) and therefore cannot be sold or redeemed. There are also in the Hebrew Bible occasions when a separation or destruction is used to threaten or punish someone who disobeys a command. The people of Israel are ordered to destroy (*taharimu*) the population of Yavesh-gil'ad because they failed to heed the call to battle against the tribe of Benjamin (Judges 21:5–11). In the post-exile period, Ezra declared that anyone who did not obey the proclamation to gather in Jerusalem within three days would "lose [*yoh'ram*] all of his property and . . . be separated from the congregation of the exiles" (Ezra 10:7–8).

By the late medieval and early modern era, *herem* had become a regular congregational instrument of punitive ostracism. A person who has violated Jewish law or commandment, or even just a local community's regulations, could be punished by being put under *herem*. The harshness and duration of the punishment usually depended upon the seriousness of the offense, and the terms varied from place to place. What could earn one a *herem* in Amsterdam might lead to only a slap on the wrist in Venice or Hamburg. In pretty much all cases of *herem*, though, the sanctioned individual is to be isolated from the rest of the community and treated with contempt. To be put under a *herem* was of great consequence for an observant Jew, affecting his or her life and the life of the family in both the religious and secular domains. The person under a *herem* was cut off, to one degree or another, from participating in the rituals of the community and thus from performing many of the ceremonies and tasks that make everyday Jewish life meaningful.

A man under *herem* would likely be forbidden from serving as one of the ten males required for a *minyan* (prayer quorum), or from being called to the Torah in synagogue, or from serving in a leadership post of the congregation, or from performing any number of *mitzvot*, deeds that fulfill halakhic (legal) obligations. In extreme cases, the punishment extended to the offender's relatives: as long as he was under a *herem,* his sons were not to be circumcised, his children were off-limits for marriage, and no member of his family could be given a proper Jewish burial. This is all very harsh. Owing to the ban's restrictions on any kind of conversation or dealing, a person under *herem* was also forbidden from engaging in ordinary social and business contacts. Clearly, a *herem* carried tremendous emotional and even economic impact. As the historian Yosef Kaplan has put it, "the excommunicated individual felt himself losing his place in both this world and the next."

The power to ban an individual was typically vested in a community's rabbinical court, the Beth Din. Among the Sephardim in seventeenth-century Amsterdam, however, such prerogative belonged to the community's lay leaders. They were certainly permitted and even encouraged to seek the advice of the rabbis before issuing a ban against someone, particularly if the alleged offense involved a matter of Jewish law. But such consultation was not required. The

Amsterdam *ma'amad's* exclusive right to ban members of the community went virtually unchallenged in the seventeenth century (although it was a source of some tension between the *parnassim* and the rabbinate, and apparently it remains so, as we shall see).

Disregarding Maimonides' admonition to be sparing in the use of this most severe form of punishment, Amsterdam's Sephardim employed the *herem* quite broadly. A *herem* was primarily attached to the violation of certain rules regarding religious and devotional matters, such as attendance at synagogue, the observance of the dietary laws of *kashrut*, and the observance of holidays. A Portuguese Jew in Amsterdam was forbidden, for example, from buying meat from an Ashkenazic (German or Eastern European Jewish) butcher. Then there were ethical regulations: one could be banned for gambling or for lewd behavior in the streets. Social precepts protected by the ban included a rule against marrying in secret, without parental consent and not in the presence of a rabbi. There were also regulations deriving from the political and financial structure of the community. One could be banned for failing to pay one's taxes, or for showing disrespect to a member of the *ma'amad*. Jewish women were forbidden, under threat of *herem*, to cut the hair of gentile women, and members of the community were warned not to engage gentiles in theological discussions. Sexual relations between Jews and gentiles were also prohibited (but, it seems, at least in the case of Jewish men and gentile women, rarely punished). It goes without saying that the public expression (orally or in writing) of certain heretical or blasphemous opinions — such as denying the divine origin of the Torah or slighting any precept of God's law or demeaning the reputation of the Jewish people — would also warrant a *herem*.

In all, between 1622 and 1683, as Kaplan has discovered, thirty-nine men and one woman were banned by Spinoza's congregation, for periods ranging from one day to eleven years. Rarely — as in the case of Spinoza — was the ban never removed. All of this indicates that a *herem* was not intended by the Jewish community of Amsterdam to be, by definition, a permanent end to all religious and personal relations. It might, on occasion, turn out to have that result, as it did for Spinoza. But it seems usually to have been within the power of the individual being punished to determine how long it would be before he or she fulfilled the conditions set for reconciliation with the congregation — usually a matter of apologizing and paying a fine.

The *herem,* then, was used in Amsterdam to enforce the religious, social, and ethical conduct thought appropriate to a Jewish community, to discourage deviancy not just in matters of liturgical practice but also in everyday behavior and the expression of ideas. This was particularly important for a community founded by the descendants of "conversos" — forced converts to Christianity — who, for generations in Spain and Portugal, had been cut off from Jewish texts and practices and who had only recently been re-introduced to Jewish orthodoxy and were still being educated in its norms. The leaders of the Talmud Torah congregation, formed from the merger of three congregations established at the beginning of the seventeenth century, had to work hard to maintain religious cohesion among a community of Jews whose faith and practices were still rather unstable and often tainted by unorthodox beliefs and practices, some of which stemmed from their lives within Iberian Catholicism. (The Purim festival, for example, was apparently called the Feast of St. Esther.) Moreover, such a community might have felt insecure about its Judaism, and thus in compensation would

220

have been inclined to resort frequently to the most rigorous means to keep things "kosher."

In its vehemence and its fury, the text of Spinoza's *herem* exceeds all the others proclaimed on the Houtgracht. There is no other *herem* document of the period issued by the Amsterdam Sephardic community that contains the wrath and the maledictions directed at Spinoza when he was expelled from the congregation. More typical was the *herem* against Isaac de Peralta, which he received for assaulting one of the *parnassim* in the street:

> Taking into consideration that Isaac de Peralta disobeyed that which the aforesaid *ma'amad* had ordered him, and the fact that Peralta responded with negative words concerning this issue; and not content with this, Peralta dared to go out and look for [members of the *ma'amad*] on the street and insult them. The aforesaid *ma'amad*, considering these things and the importance of the case, decided the following: it is agreed upon unanimously that the aforesaid Isaac de Peralta be excommunicated [*posto em cherem*] because of what he has done. Because he has been declared *menudeh* [a pariah], no one shall talk or deal with him. Only family and other members of his household may talk with him.

After four days Peralta begged forgiveness and paid a fine of sixty guilders, and the *herem* was cancelled. In Spinoza's case, by contrast, there seems to be no hope of reconciliation, no amends that could be made to have the *herem* lifted. Spinoza was out for good.

The obvious question is, why was Spinoza banned with such hostility, such extreme prejudice? Neither the *herem* text nor any document from the period tells us exactly what his "evil opinions and acts [*más opinioins e obras*]" were supposed to have been, nor what "abominable heresies [*horrendas heregias*]" or "monstrous deeds [*ynormes obras*]" he is alleged to have taught and practiced. Spinoza never refers to this period of his life in his extant letters, and thus does not offer his correspondents, or us, any clues about why he was expelled. The whole thing is very mysterious.

Odette Vlessing, a former archivist for Amsterdam's Portuguese-Jewish archives, has argued that Spinoza's *herem* was directly related to his machinations to avoid financial obligations. In March 1656, just four months before the ban, Spinoza initiated drastic steps to relieve himself of debts he had inherited along with the estate of his father. He took advantage of a Dutch law that protected under-aged children who had lost their parents. Since he was a year and a few months shy of his twenty-fifth birthday, he was still legally a minor. Spinoza was thus able to file a petition with the civil authorities and be declared an orphan. The Orphan Masters for the city of Amsterdam then appointed a guardian for him, who successfully argued that he should be discharged from any obligations he might have incurred by initially settling some of his father's debts. According to Vlessing, Spinoza had committed a political sin: his legal maneuver threatened the Jewish community's general reputation for trustworthiness in business affairs — something it counted on heavily in its relations with the Dutch. And it was not only Dutch creditors on his father's estate whose expectations would not be met. Spinoza was also shirking commitments to fellow Portuguese-Jewish merchants. In other words, Spinoza, the son of a one-time *parnas*, was going over the heads of the sitting *parnassim* and putting Dutch law above communal regulations (which stipulated that business disputes should be handled within the community) and Jewish law, and this, as Vlessing sees it, was a very serious offense indeed.

"Michael Spinoza's financial disaster and Baruch Spinoza's appeal for release from his father's estate on the grounds of minority must have shaken the Jewish community," Vlessing argues. She makes a plausible case. Yet the text of Spinoza's *herem* suggests that his offense was more than just a matter of business and financial irregularities or some ordinary violation of Jewish law. The document refers explicitly and dramatically to his "abominable heresies" and "evil opinions." Vlessing insists that "Spinoza was not excommunicated on account of his philosophical ideas." But given the wording of the ban, not to mention its length, its vitriol, its uniqueness, and its finality, it is hard to avoid the conclusion that it was precisely his ideas that occasioned the final and irrevocable ostracism.

Evidence that this is what happened is found in a report that an Augustinian monk, Tomas Solano y Robles, made to the Spanish Inquisition in 1659, when he returned to Madrid after some traveling that had taken him to Amsterdam in late 1658. The Inquisitors were no doubt interested in what was going on among former conversos in northern Europe who had once been within their domain and still had connections with possibly Judaizing families back in Iberia. Brother Tomas told them that in Amsterdam he met Spinoza and another former member of the Sephardic community, a certain Juan de Prado, who were apparently keeping each other company after their respective bans. He claimed that both men told him that they had been observant of Jewish law but "changed their mind," and that they were expelled from the synagogue because of their views on God, the soul, and the law. They had, in the eyes of the congregation, "reached the point of atheism."

Charges of "atheism" are notoriously ambiguous in early modern Europe and rarely provide a clue as to what exactly the subject of the accusation actually believed or said. But if we take as our guide Spinoza's works, it is not very difficult to imagine the kinds of things he must have been thinking — and probably saying — around late 1655 and early 1656, particularly with the help of Brother Tomas' report, as well as the report made to the Inquisition on the following day by Captain Miguel Perez de Maltranilla, another recent visitor to Amsterdam. For all of Spinoza's writings, those he published and those left uncompleted at his death, contain ideas on whose systematic elaboration he was working continuously from the late 1650s onward.

In both the *Ethics,* Spinoza's philosophical masterpiece begun in the early 1660s, and the aborted *Short Treatise on God, Man and His Well-Being,* possibly from as early as 1659 (only three years after the *herem*!) and containing many of the thoughts of the *Ethics* almost fully expressed or in embryonic form, Spinoza basically denies the immortality of the soul. Although he is willing to grant that a part of the human mind — its ideas — is eternal and persists after the death of the body, he believes that there is no such thing as a personal soul that enjoys life in some world to come. Thus, there is nothing to hope for or fear in terms of eternal reward or punishment. Indeed, the notion of God acting as a judge who dispenses either mundane or eternal reward and punishment is based on absurd anthropomorphizing. Ecclesiastics, he claims, have long maintained that "the gods direct all things for the use of men in order to bind men to them and be held by men in the highest honor. So it has happened that each of them has thought up from his own temperament different ways of worshipping God." Ignorance, prejudice, and superstition — not to mention the cynical manipulation of our emotions by priests and preachers — are thus at the basis of organized religion. Finally, Spinoza insists, God is simply the infinite, eternal substance in which all things exist and, as such, is identical with Nature itself. Everything else follows from "God or Nature [*Deus sive Natura*]" with an absolute necessity. The whole notion of a supernatural, providential God is nothing but a pernicious fiction.

Among the primary teachings of the *Theological-Political Treatise*, published to great alarm in 1670 — one overwrought critic called it "a book forged in hell by the devil himself" — is that the Pentateuch, the first five books of the Hebrew Bible, was not in fact written by Moses, as it claims, nor are its precepts literally of divine origin. While there is indeed a "clear divine message" conveyed by the moral teachings found throughout all the prophetic writings, the Bible was really the work of a number of authors and later editors in different historical and political circumstances, and the text we have is the product of a natural process of historical transmission. Spinoza also maintains that if the Jewish people were "elected" in any meaningful sense, it is only a matter of their having achieved, through natural causes, a "temporal physical happiness" and autonomous government during the era of the ancient commonwealth and kingdoms. With God's (Nature's) help, they were able to preserve their sovereignty for an extended period of time and survive as a cohesive political and social unit under their own laws. Yet the notion of the Jews as a "chosen people" has no metaphysical or moral significance; and whatever advantages they did and do happen to enjoy is not necessarily something unique to them. The Jews, Spinoza

225

insists, are neither a morally superior nation nor a people surpassing all others in wisdom.

These were not sentiments that were likely to endear one to the rabbis and lay leaders of a Jewish community in the seventeenth century. And it is all but certain that Spinoza's views regarding God, the soul, the Bible, and the Jewish people that he began to commit to writing just a few years after the *herem* were already fairly developed by 1656. Indeed, Spinoza himself insists, at the heart of his discussion of the Bible in the *Theological-Political Treatise,* that "I write nothing here which I have not thought about long and hard." Moreover, there are the reports of Brother Tomas and Captain Maltranilla. According to their testimonies before the Inquisition, both Spinoza and Prado were claiming in 1658 that the soul was not immortal, that the Law was "not true" and that there was no God except in a "philosophical" sense. In his deposition, Tomas says that

> he knew both Dr. Prado, a physician, whose first name was Juan but whose Jewish name he did not know, who had studied at Alcala, and a certain de Espinosa, who he thinks was a native of one of the villages of Holland, for he had studied at Leiden and was a good philosopher. These two persons had professed the Law of Moses, and the synagogue had expelled and isolated them because they had reached the point of atheism. And they themselves told the witness that they had been circumcised and that they had observed the law of the Jews, and that they had changed their mind because it seemed to them that the said law was not true and that souls died with their bodies and that there is no God except philosophically. And that is why they were expelled from the

synagogue; and, while they regretted the absence of the charity that they used to receive from the synagogue and the communication with other Jews, they were happy to be atheists, since they thought that God exists only philosophically . . . and that souls died with their bodies and that thus they had no need for faith.

If Spinoza was saying these things about God, the soul, and the Law in 1658 — and to strangers! — then the likelihood of his having discussed them two years earlier with members of his own community is quite strong, particularly as that would help to account for the seriousness with which the leaders of the congregation viewed his "heresies" and "opinions." He was a philosophical prodigy and rebel, and he was prodigiously punished for his rebellion. In modern parlance, he was guilty of thought crimes.

All of that is ancient history — or, rather, early modern history. It has been over three hundred and fifty years since Spinoza's ban. By the end of the twentieth century, the Amsterdam Portuguese-Jewish community seemed to have made its peace with its homegrown heretic. Books about him are for sale in the synagogue's shop; they even sell Spinoza finger puppets. Why not try to capitalize on Amsterdam Jewry's most famous son? Members of the community are also eager to learn and talk about Spinoza's life and ideas; after all, he is part of their history, for better or for worse. And yet, at this late date, out of the blue, we now have this letter from the Portuguese congregation's rabbi to a prominent Spinoza scholar essentially banning him from the premises. A second ban to honor the first ban.

Bans, Then and Now

How did this happen?

It began with a very simple, and seemingly innocent, request. On November 22, 2021, the director of Amsterdam's Joods Cultureel Kwartier (Jewish Cultural Quarter, or JCK) conveyed to the board of directors of the Portuguees Israëliti-esche Gemeente a request that he received from a joint Israeli and Dutch television project to visit the synagogue complex and do some filming there, including inside the famed Ets Haim library. The JCK is the non-profit organization that is responsible for the management of a number of sites and institutions of Jewish heritage in the city of Amsterdam. Its portfolio includes the Portuguese synagogue, the Jewish Historical Museum, and the National Holocaust Museum. The film was to be part of Yair Qedar's Israeli television series *Ha-Ivrim* (The Hebrews), which is focused on "Hebrew writers from the seventeenth century to today" and is produced by the Israeli Public Broadcasting Corporation. Professor Melamed, who was not himself personally involved in the request to film inside the synagogue complex, was to be the primary academic consultant for the episode on Spinoza and featured in the film.

According to a message that the *parnassim* later posted (in Dutch) on the internal website for community members, the board had no problem with the request. But a part of the proposal involved an interview with the congregation's rabbinate, and so they passed it on to Rabbi Serfaty *"met positief advies"* — that is, with the recommendation that he approve it. The board was thus stunned by the rabbi's letter to Professor Melamed, which it learned about only when Melamed posted it on social media and it quickly made the rounds of Facebook, the Twitterverse, and the international news media. "The College of Parnassim was not aware of this [letterl in advance and thus was taken by surprise." The board acknowledged the rabbi's right not to participate in any interviews for the film. It also reiterated that the *herem* against Spinoza remains in place, as was reaffirmed in December 2015 by then-Chief Rabbi Pinchas Toledano at a symposium in Amsterdam organized by the journalist Ronit Palache (who hails from an old and distinguished Amsterdam Portuguese-Jewish family) in which arguments pro and con were publicly discussed before an audience of five hundred. "However," the board continued, "it was not necessary for the rabbinate to ratify this again, and it really goes beyond all limits to act on behalf of our community and also to declare someone 'persona non grata.' Moreover, and more importantly, this was not within the purview of the rabbinate."

Thus there reappeared the centuries-old tension between rabbi and *parnassim*, between clergy and lay leadership, over the right to ban people. The board wanted the members of the community to know that "we are not happy with what has happened, because it generates a lot of negative energy and gives a negative image of our community." Meanwhile, they noted, while "the rabbinate [Rabbis Serfaty and Toledano] has apologized for the way it has released the letters, it stands behind their contents. We have given the rabbi a warning, and will make the necessary effort to bring cooperation to the desired level." The board concluded its intramural message by saying that it remains open to considering the filming request, and asked the JCK for more information on the planned documentary.

As for the JCK, its director, Emile Schrijver, was not at all pleased with the rabbi's letter, to say the least. In a November 30 interview with JONET.NL, an independent Dutch Jewish news site, he said that "I find the letter shocking and we strongly distance ourselves from it. The letter is completely unacceptable ... The reactionary position of the rabbi is totally on him ... Free scientific research, free use of resources, free exchange of ideas and so on, should always be possible. You'd hope that in 2021 there would have been no more question about it." In a separate interview with the *Nieuw Israëlitiesch Weekblad,* on November 30, 2021, he called the rabbi's action "outrageous" and "completely dissociates" the JCK from Rabbi Serfaty's views. (The interviews were in Dutch; the translations are my own.)

An even more angry response to Rabbi Serfaty's letter to Professor Melamed came from Israel. Rabbi Nathan Lopes Cardozo is an orthodox rabbi and the dean of the David Cardozo Academy and of the Bet Midrash of Congregation Avraham Avinu in Jerusalem. This is from the open letter (in English) that he published in *The Times of Israel* (November 30, 2021):

> It would seem that you may be ignorant of the fact that the famous former Chief Rabbi of Israel Rabbi Yitzhak HaLevi Herzog of blessed memory (1888-1959) has already stated that the ban was only in force halachically as long as Spinoza was alive. Furthermore, it would seem you are unaware of the story concerning the ban and the many deliberations concerning the real cause of this ban and the very teachings of Spinoza himself ... Your view that the ban on Spinoza's works is still in force clearly indicates that you are not familiar with his writings, and are thus completely incapable of expressing an opinion about his philosophy ... I strongly object to your terming the Professor as a "persona non grata" — an act that is a tremendous insult and *chutzpah.* By banning the professor from the complex of the synagogue, and as such, not

230

even allowing him to join a minyan in our synagogue, you have created an enormous *Chillul Hashem*, desecration of God's name, making Orthodox Judaism a farce in the eyes of the many. You have done all of us, who fight for the honor of Judaism, a great disservice. Shame on you.

Rabbi Cardozo, incidentally, along with myself and several other scholars, was among the panelists at that symposium in 2015 which discussed at great length whether the *herem* against Spinoza should be lifted. He argued strenuously that it should be rescinded.

When Rabbi Toledano quite patiently and eloquently explained at that symposium that he was not going to lift the *herem*, he offered three reasons. First, only the authority that issued the *herem* in 1656 had the right to lift the ban. (And I remember him also saying something like, "Are we today that much wiser than our rabbinic forbears, who at least had first-hand knowledge of Spinoza's offenses?") Second, he claimed that any religious community has the right to police ideas that circulate within it, and that this community at least cannot tolerate people who put the existence of God in doubt and propound other heterodox notions. Third, he insisted that Spinoza had thirty days to retract his views, which he did not do. (As far as I know, there is no historical evidence for this third point.) Toledano could have added that lifting the *herem* against Spinoza would be a meaningless act anyway, since such a ban is primarily a matter of liturgical and social ostracism against an individual, and thus, as Rabbi Cardozo insists, operative only for a living person (although it is true that the *herem* also forbids reading anything Spinoza may have written). What Rabbi Toledano did say toward the end of his remarks at the symposium, however — and this is quite remarkable, given the present affair —that there is no reason why Jews, like anybody, cannot study Spinoza's writings.

Rabbi Toledano, it is worth mentioning, also rejected the request to film within the Amsterdam synagogue, although he did so somewhat more politely:

28 November 2021 / 24 Kislev 5782

Dear Professor Melamed,

This is to let you know that ten professors from all over the world including from Israel came to the symposium which took place on 6 December 2015.

This matter of Spinoza was discussed at length. I myself, as the Chacham [rabbi] of the congregation gave a lecture on this subject and the conclusion was that the cherem which was imposed by our rabbis of the past is to remain.

In view of the above, there is no question of you discussing Spinoza in our complex.

Yours faithfully,

Chacham P. Toledano

One wonders how Rabbi Toledano, or Rabbi Serfaty for that matter, would react were he to catch a member of the congregation "discussing Spinoza in our complex."

As for Rabbi Serfaty's letter, where to begin? Of course, the tone is rude and insulting. (It is interesting to note that in his official profile on the Portuguese-Jewish community's website, Serfaty claims that he "knows how to propose unpredictable solutions through his broad halakhic knowledge and human kindness." Unpredictable? Yes, that seems right. Kindness? One can only wonder.) Serfaty asserted that the *herem* against Spinoza is "in force for all time" and "cannot be rescinded." If, as moral philosophers since Kant say, "ought implies can," anyone with a bit of logic will recognize that "ought not" does not imply "cannot" (although the world would be a much better place if it did). It is up to the rabbis and/or the *parnassim* to decide whether Spinoza's *herem* ought to be lifted; but of course if there is even a question as to whether it ought be lifted, it must be the case that it can be lifted. There is no point in arguing as to whether something should be done if it cannot be done. Moreover, how a mere request to visit the synagogue and do some filming there can be "an assault on our identity and heritage" boggles the sensible mind. One would think that the identity and heritage of a well-established, centuries-old congregation with a rich and celebrated history could survive in the face of such a bid.

Most disturbing of all in this affair is the declaration that Yitzhak Melamed, the Charlotte Bloomberg Professor of Philosophy at Johns Hopkins University — and, it must be added, a Torah-observant orthodox Jew — is now "persona non grata" at the Amsterdam Portuguese-Jewish complex. What does this even mean? Is it a legitimate rabbinic designation? Rabbi Serfaty might be saying that the members of the community should not, and will not, do anything to help Melamed in any endeavor he may undertake regarding the community. My guess, though, is that it is supposed to mean something stronger than this: that Melamed is not welcome to attend the synagogue, make use of the resources of the Ets Haim library, or visit any other facility under their control. Does it, in other words, constitute a new *herem*? The problem is that, once again, among the Amsterdam Sephardim, the right to issue a *herem* belongs only to the *parnassim*. And in this case the *parnassim* have made their view clear. In their online message to the members of the community, they say that "Prof. dr. Melamed is, like every visitor to our complex, welcome regardless of his or her background and/or belief." Similarly, Heide Warncke, the curator of the Ets Haim library, immediately reassured the public that Rabbi Serfaty's letter has no bearing on access to the library, and that its extraordinary resources, along with her invaluable assistance, remain available "to any reputable scholar to do research." Even if Rabbi Serfaty were authorized to issue a "persona non grata" ban, whatever that may be, one cannot help but wonder how it could possibly be justified in this case. The professor's only offense has been to have read and written about Spinoza. But so have a lot of people, including myself, and we have all been graciously and generously welcomed by the Amsterdam Portuguese-Jewish community and granted access to its rich intellectual, cultural, and religious resources. The rabbi's intemperate letter to the professor may have been consistent with his view of his responsibilities to the events of 1656, but it was not in keeping with his pastoral vocation. Everyone — Jew, Gentile, Spinozist, anti-Spinozist, Aristotelian, whatever — should be offended by it.

There is something especially ironic about Serfaty's claim that anything having to do with Spinoza is incompatible with Jewish "ethical tradition." It is true that Spinoza dismisses the ceremonies and laws of Judaism as having any validity for latter-day Jews; since the destruction of the Second Temple, he asserts, these have all lost their *raison d'être*. Yet Spinoza's central argument in the *Theological-Political Treatise* is that theology and philosophy are totally distinct disciplines, and so just as the former should not be allowed to set any limits on the "freedom to philosophize," so the latter represents no threat to religion, or at least to what Spinoza calls "true religion." Philosophy is about truth and knowledge, which are the bailiwick of reason. Theology, on the other hand, is about faith and obedience to God's law. And that law is quite simple: love God and treat other people with justice and charity. All the ceremonies, rites and rules of Judaism — including the 613 commandments of the Torah — have nothing whatsoever to do with true piety. Neither does true religion demand a conception of God as a lawgiver and judge. All of these are merely superstitious practices and doctrines that ecclesiastics have introduced in order to control people's hearts and minds. None of the Bible's authors' descriptions of the cosmos or claims about nature, historical events, or even God should be regarded as philosophically or scientifically informed, as necessarily true propositions. The ancient prophets were not philosophers or scientists or even learned theologians. They were simply morally superior individuals who, because of their superb imaginations, were also gifted storytellers and thus could craft morally inspiring narratives. Therefore, philosophical truths about God, the world, or human nature cannot possibly be a threat to religion, that is, to true piety and its ethical behavior — which happens also to be the ethical imperative of Judaism (and Christianity). As Galileo is reported to have said, the point of the Bible is to tell us how to go to heaven, not how the heavens go.

Thankfully, the Serfaty-Melamed affair seems to have run its course. Professor Melamed was provided with a thoughtful and courteous letter from the chairman of the *ma'amad* of Talmud Torah and the director of JCK, in which they distance themselves from Rabbi Serfaty's action and "regret that a perfectly normal request to visit the premises of the Portuguese Synagogue in order to work on a documentary ... has led to an international uproar." They reiterate that it is the *ma'amad* and not the rabbinate that has "sole authority to declare anyone 'persona non grata' on its premises," confirm "that we will gladly welcome you to visit our premises to work on said documentary" and express their "hope that you will decide to pursue your plans to come to Amsterdam and do your work as requested." They do so, they say, in the name of "academic freedom." To their great credit, the directors of the orthodox Amsterdam Portuguese-Jewish community recognize that we are no longer living in the seventeenth century. As for Rabbi Serfaty, on January 5, 2022, the Dutch newspaper *Trouw* reported that the *ma'amad* has decided that his services will no longer be needed in the Amsterdam Portuguese-Jewish congregation. His contract expired on December 31 and will not be renewed.

236

We do not know whether the seventeenth-century Portuguese-Jewish community's rabbis and governors cut Spinoza off without making a concerted effort to persuade him to repent and return to the congregation's fold. The *herem* document does state that the members of the *ma'amad* "endeavored by various means and promises to turn him from his bad ways." According to an early biographer, Jean Maximilian Lucas (1647–1697) — who, it should be said, is not always to be trusted — Chief Rabbi Saul Levi Mortera, a formidable figure, rushed to the synagogue to see if the reports of the young man's rebellion were true, and then "urged him in a most formidable tone to decide for repentance or for punishment, and vowed that he would excommunicate him if he did not immediately show signs of contrition." Spinoza's alleged response seems to have been calculated impudently to push the rabbi over the edge: "[I] know the gravity of the threat, and in return for the trouble that [you] have taken to teach [me] the Hebrew language, allow [me] to teach [you] how to excommunicate." The rabbi left the synagogue in a fit of rage, "vowing not to come there again except with a thunderbolt in his hand." Spinoza's attitude toward his expulsion is probably best captured in the words attributed to him by Lucas: "All the better; they do not force me to do anything that I would not have done of my own accord if I did not dread scandal. But, since they want it that way, I enter gladly on the path that is opened to me, with the consolation that my departure will be more innocent than was the exodus of the early Hebrews from Egypt."

The path upon which the banished Spinoza embarked, with more innocence than the ancient Israelites, is what we now know as secular liberal modernity. Among the essential values of this modernity — enshrined in the late eighteenth century in the First Amendment of the United States Constitution, in the nineteenth century in John Stuart Mill's *On Liberty*, and in innumerable other works of philosophy and political theory, legal briefs, case law, and even religious texts — is freedom of thought and expression. When, in 2015, Rabbi Toledano said that a religious community has the right to police ideas that circulate within it, one could argue that he had a point. Judaism may thrive on debate, but it is a circumscribed debate. We can live with sectarian congregations setting limits on what opinions they will allow to be openly promulgated among their members, even if it is not in their best interest to do so. The real danger is when such intolerance creeps into the civic arena. This is precisely what seems to be happening in these increasingly illiberal times, when the immediate response to the expression of ideas is often a secular *herem*. People are sanctioned, cancelled, punished, ostracized, and even imprisoned for what they have written or said, and books are banned for their content. And the campaign against "heterodoxy" comes from all sides of the international political spectrum: it occurs in military dictatorships and civilian authoritarian regimes but also within democracies. The threat this poses to the vitality of intellectual life and the health of our societies should not be underestimated.

Tolerating, even encouraging, the free exchange of ideas, especially unpopular ones, can only advance the pursuit of truth and strengthen our common defenses against the lies, misinformation, and prejudices that, in this age of social media, are more dangerous than ever. Such toleration, as Spinoza recognized before anyone else, poses no threat to our political, social, economic, and even religious well-being. This is the great lesson of his *Theological-Political Treatise*. Spinoza began the book just when he feared that the more conservative and intolerant faction within the Dutch Reformed Church was exercising greater influence over Dutch society and threatening the peace and security of what was Europe's most liberal, cosmopolitan, and secular polity. The subtitle of the work — which was banned by the ecclesiastical, civic, and academic authorities — proclaims that its goal is to "show that a republic can grant freedom of philosophizing without harming its peace or piety, and cannot deny it without destroying its peace and piety." And its final chapter closes with this remarkable declaration about freedom of thought and expression:

We conclude that nothing is safer for a republic than that piety and religion should include only the practice of loving-kindness and equity, and that the right of the supreme powers concerning both sacred and secular matters should relate only to actions. For the rest, everyone should be granted the right to think what he wants and to say what he thinks.

Amen.

MORTEN HØI JENSEN

The Fiction That Dare Not Speak Its Name

240 Pity literary biographers. There are few writers less appreciated, there are none more despised. There they sit, with their church bulletins of family trees and their dental records, their interviews with ex-lovers, mad uncles, and discarded children, and go about "reconstructing" the life of someone they never knew, or knew just barely. To George Eliot, biographers were a "disease of English literature," while Auden thought all literary biographies "superfluous and usually in bad taste." Even Ian Hamilton, the intrepid chronicler of Robert Lowell, J. D. Salinger, and Matthew Arnold, thought that there was "some necessary element of sleaze" to the whole enterprise.

And yet biographies of writers continue to excite the reading public's imagination. Last year alone saw big new accounts of the lives of W. G. Sebald, Fernando Pessoa, Philip Roth, Tom Stoppard, D. H. Lawrence, Elizabeth Hardwick, H.G. Wells, Stephen Crane, and Sylvia Plath. The most controversial of these, of course, was Blake Bailey's biography of Roth, which was withdrawn by its publisher just a few weeks after it appeared owing to accusations against Bailey of sexual assault and inappropriate behavior. Even before these accusations were reported, Bailey was criticized by some reviewers for being too sympathetic toward his subject — and for posthumously waging many of Roth's quarrels and vendettas, particularly against ex-wives and lovers. He presumptuously called his book *Philip Roth: The Biography*. *The* biography? As opposed to what?

Whatever privileges Bailey was granted by Roth, his biography will not be the last (it wasn't even the first), nor will it be once and for all definitive. No biography can be. The entire notion of an authorized or definitive or "official" biography is mostly humbug; new information will always come to light, and fresh perspectives will eventually become necessary. (In the case of Roth, a fresh perspective already seems necessary.) That said, a "definitive" biography may serve as a temporary bulwark against the author-industrial complex. Heather Clark's *Red Comet: The Short Life and Blazing Art of Sylvia Plath* is, by my count, the fourteenth biography of Plath, a poet who published just two books before her suicide at the age of thirty, and whose every letter, journal entry, and laundry list has been subjected to forensic analysis by a termitary of critics, scholars, relatives, schemers, and biographers. But to what end, exactly? I have read three of those biographies, as well as several volumes of Plath's letters and journals, and I still don't

241

have the faintest idea who Plath really was. ("For all the drama of her biography, there is a peculiar remoteness about Sylvia Plath," wrote Hardwick.). Each new biographical intervention feels like a paving over of the previous one, adding yet another layer between the reader and the subject.

But perhaps the cases of Roth and Plath are too unusual to be representative. After all, few writers' lives are subject to the kind of bitter posthumous contention in which Plath's family and friends have engaged, and even fewer are embroiled in the criminal accusations against the life-chronicler. On the whole, very little *happens* to writers in the practice of writing, even to those who, like Vladimir Nabokov, Thomas Mann, or Naguib Mahfouz, lived in the thick of history, with all its peril and precariousness. Consider Mann: born four years after the unification of Germany, he lived through the First World War, the Weimar Republic, the Third Reich, the Second World War, and the postwar division of Germany. He was hurled into exile, stripped of his citizenship, put on an arrest warrant for Dachau, and surveilled by the FBI for alleged communist sympathies. In America, his social circle included Albert Einstein, Theodor Adorno, and Franklin Delano Roosevelt, among others. All of which amounts to an exceptionally fascinating life, but it tells us little or nothing about what finally matters: the fiction. In every account of his life, every time he sits down at his desk, whether in Munich, Küsnacht, Princeton, or Los Angeles, Mann disappears from view. We can reconstruct his punctilious routine, we can describe the texture of his desk, we can even name the various brands of cigar that he liked to smoke — but we cannot be present for the moment when the author of *Buddenbrooks, Death in Venice*, and *The Magic Mountain* put pen to paper and chose this word over that word and refined this idea or that idea and generally brought his fictional world to life. Writing is not an activity that can be meaningfully described from the outside. "Surely the writing of a literary life," said Leon Edel, Henry James' celebrated biographer, "would be nothing but a kind of indecent curiosity, and an invasion of privacy, were it not that it seeks always to illuminate the mysterious and magical process of creation." But can this really be done? What is the bridge from the external to the internal?

There are exceptions to the above, of course, when the writer's external circumstances are so extreme that they penetrate more closely to the heart of the mystery of his or her art. Consider Osip Mandelstam, for instance, or the Hungarian poet Miklós Radnóti, composing verse surrounded by the worst totalitarian horrors. Nor do I mean to suggest that one shouldn't try to imagine the act of literary creation, or that it cannot be meaningfully documented in some way. But a straight historiographical method may not be the best way to get at the elusive target. In recent years, for example, there has been a flurry of biographies of individual books, and biographies of individual novels, including *Portrait of a Lady, The Stranger,* and *Les Misérables.* By reversing the role of the writer and the writing, placing a single text at the story's center, these studies liberate the historical and documentarian impulse of literary biography from some of its sleazier and more invasive aspects. It prefers the achievement of the writing to the psychology of the writer, which in many cases would be a welcome reversal.

Still, if the process of creation is precisely what traditional biography cannot illuminate, then what purpose does the genre serve? Is it just a form of higher gossip? Or a way of prolonging our intimacy with an author, as John Updike charitably put it?

The Fiction That Dare Not Speak Its Name

The genre is as old, almost, as the modern novel, and shares its subversive nature. If *Don Quixote*, among many other things, brought fiction down from the chivalric heights to the pedestrian grounds, so literary biography served as a tonic to the genre of biography as a whole, which has always tended toward the exemplary. James Boswell's *Life of Samuel Johnson*, considered by many to be the first modern literary biography, details its subject's appetite for drink, his shabby clothes, his disgusting eating habits. Johnson himself thought it the "business of the biographer to...lead the thoughts into domestic privacies, and display the minute details of daily life."

But what can the daily life of a person whose main occupation consists of sitting at home tell us? A writer's life, truthfully told, would be unremittingly, unbelievably boring. (At least those writers who have the historical privilege of a secure and peaceful life.) It would be a catalog of all the possible ways of describing everyday banalities: scratching one's head, gazing out the window, tapping an impatient finger against a desk. (For excitement, perhaps posting a letter, or emptying the dishwasher.) A writer lives on paper, but on paper a writer's life resembles nothing so much as a failure to live. To circumvent this problem, most biographers tend to put the process in reverse: since they cannot find much to say about the writer's work from the dailyness of the life, they instead mine the work for clues about the life. They frantically insist on what is incriminatingly known as the biographical fallacy: the connection between life and art. "They have to," as Martin Amis once put it, a little simplistically, in a review of a biography of Philip Larkin. "Or what are they about? What the hell are they doing day after day, year after year... if the life doesn't somehow account for the art?"

This is what gives many literary biographies their reductive, psychologizing, and prurient nature. Childhood trauma, sexual repression, marital failure: complex fictional worlds are reduced to the graspable symptoms of underlying conditions, and the author is stripped of his mystery and his ability in some way to transcend his conditions and become more than the totality of his circumstances. As late as 1911, an essay by Frederick Graves in *The Westminster Review* dismissed literary biographers as rakers: "No degree of eminence, no feeling of compassion, may appeal, for the greater the man in the halls of fame, the more touching his struggles on the slopes of Parnassus, the busier are the rakers upon the ashes of his past." But by then it was already too late: Lytton Strachey's reputation-puncturing *Eminent Victorians* was published in 1918, freeing all future biographers from the chains of decorum and respect. In his preface, Strachey said that it is not the business of the biographer to be complimentary but to "lay bare the facts of the case, as he understands them." He concluded the preface to his exercise in genre subversion by quoting the French economist Charles Dunoyer: *"Je n'impose rien; je ne propose rien: j'expose."*

In his lively book on the subject, *The Impossible Craft,* the late Scott Donaldson, a career biographer of Cheever, Hemingway, Fitzgerald, and others, wrote that with biography there is a time before Freud and a time after Freud. (Lytton Strachey's brother and sister-in-law, James and Alix Strachey, were Freud's authorized English translators.) As theories of psychoanalysis began to pervade the broader culture, artistic achievements were regarded as clinical documents — as the records of sublimated sex drives or compensations for some general inadequacy. Thus, Robert Louis Stevenson's life is read in the light of his relationship to his mother, or Thomas Mann's fictional works as a sublimation of his homoerotic desires. And so on. In other words, the mystery of literary creation is trivialized by being rendered familiar, comprehensible, scrutable. (It is worth pointing out that Freud himself remained skeptical of this biographical approach, and in 1936 turned down Arnold Zweig's offer to serve as his biographer, remarking that "to be a biographer, you must tie yourself up in lies, concealments, hypocrisies, false colorings, and even in hiding a lack of understanding.")

And yet we should keep in mind that the notion of the "biographical fallacy" was introduced by exponents of New Criticism in the 1930s and 1940s — by radical formalists with no interest in the connections between literature and life. Espousing the primacy and the autonomy of the text, New Critics repudiated the idea that a writer's life could in any way be reconstructed or inferred from a piece of writing. There is a cautionary grain of truth in their insistence on reading art as art, on the independent power of the imagination; but as Edel sensibly pointed out, "if a work cannot be redissolved into a life, it can offer us something of the — shall we say? — *texture* of that life." Some of the great nineteenth-century critics, such as Georg Brandes and Charles Sainte-Beuve, were gluttons of life; their essays are fattened with anecdote, detail, incident, gossip. True, their critical judgments were not always sound — Sainte-Beuve in particular was almost impressively wrong about all the writers who mattered — but they wrote with an attractively novelistic ravenousness.

Perhaps they also wrote with a certain innocence, a charming naivete that could not be sustained into the twentieth century. Certainly the attitude toward literary texts and their authors became more interrogative, more suspicious, even accusatory. At its worst, the post-Freudian psychobiography degenerated into a dismal rap sheet of cruelties, failures, traumas, and offenses. Lo and behold, behind a masterpiece there stands a mere mortal! And a rather repugnant one at that. I have always found James Atlas' account of his decision not to write a biography of Edmund Wilson, for instance, a little comical. In the introduction to his biography of Saul Bellow, Atlas recounts signing a contract for a Wilson book only to discover, five years later, that he had a "toxic response" to Wilson's character: "The bullying proclamations, the tedious self-revelations, the drinking and philandering — in the end, he just didn't appeal to me as a subject to whose life and work I was willing to apprentice myself for the better part of a decade." It is an odd admission: as if Atlas thought his task was to write the biography of a philanderer and alcoholic rather than of an uncommonly brilliant and prolific literary critic. I do not mean that the unsavory aspects of Wilson's life and character should be excised from an account of his life; only that to be appalled by the realization that a writer whose work you admire was, in his or her private life, disappointingly and fallibly human — well, why on earth are you reading literature if not to be baffled by humanity? (Atlas went ahead and wrote a nasty biography of Bellow, whom he clearly disdained.)

All writers lead double lives: one on the page, one off. And no account or portrait of a writer's life will resolve this fissure. There will always be a scandalizing disproportion between the human messiness of a writer's life and the size, the scope, and the opacity of their fictional work. Partly this has to do, I think, with a general epistemological uncertainty. One of the sources of human tragedy is that we cannot ever truly and definitively know anyone, not other people and not even ourselves. We must always be approximating and interpreting. Philosophers call this the problem of other minds — and what is literature, if not the creation, and the interpretation, of other minds? How, then, should we presume to know someone whose life consists of living vicariously through fictional invitations? "My own view," Valéry observed in an essay on Descartes, "is that we cannot really circumscribe a man's life, imprison him in his ideas and his actions, reduce him to what he appeared to be and, so to speak, lay siege to him in his works. We are much more (and sometimes much less) than we have done."

A small confession: I am a one-time literary biographer. My subject, fortunately, was little known, long dead, and largely forgotten, thereby all but ensuring that my book would be hermetically sealed from public interest. But in the three years I spent writing it (and in subsequent work of a related nature), I have come to sympathize with an idea of Roland Barthes', the truth of which I see no point in denying: literary biography is fiction that dare not speak its name.

The subject of my biography was Jens Peter Jacobsen, an influential Danish novelist and botanist who died of pulmonary tuberculosis in 1885 at the age of thirty-eight. Though his great novel *Niels Lyhne* would eventually become, as Stefan Zweig put it, the *Young Werther* of its time, Jacobsen produced only a few hundred pages of writing and virtually nothing in the way of diaries or letters. My task, then, was both remarkably straightforward and virtually impossible: I had to imagine being a young man whom I had never known, in a time in which I had never lived, using only whatever scraps of biographical material he left behind, filling in the gaps with the recollections of his contemporaries.

Beyond that, I had only two novels, six stories, and a few dozen poems to work with.

Where possible, I stuck to the facts. The fiction that dare not speak its name is not entirely fiction: there are facts and they matter. But sometimes the facts are few or controversial. If I came across an anecdote about Jacobsen that I suspected of being apocryphal, or one that I could not verify — well, if it suited my purposes, I naturally decided to include it. Why not? Any portrait of another human being, especially one about whom so little is known, will require an element of fiction beyond that afforded by the written record. And during the writing, adherence to the real, the actual, is gradually augmented by adherence to the imagined, the inferred, the supposed, to your educated but imperfect impression of what this or that person was like. I found it both daunting and emancipating to realize, a year or so into the writing of the book, that my portrait of Jacobsen would inevitably be equal parts Jacobsen and Jensen. (As if to emphasize this point, a flyer advertising one of my readings erroneously identified me as "Morten Peter Jacobsen.")

Let me give another example. In 2000, a minor controversy flickered in Denmark when the Kierkegaard scholar Peter Tudvad, in a blizzard of newspaper articles, began a sustained and systematic assault on his colleague Joakim Garff's acclaimed and bestselling biography of Kierkegaard, called *SAK* for its subject's initials. In an essay in the Danish literary journal *Faklen* entitled "*SAK* - An Unscholarly Biography of Kierkegaard," Tudvad accused the book's author of being so insufficiently critical of his sources that it was "impossible to distinguish systematically between historical truth and literary fiction." One of the supposed infractions that Tudvad pounced upon involved the matter of Kierkegard's servant, Anders Westergaard. In Garff's biography, Kierkegaard was accompanied by Westergarrd on his trip to Jutland on July 17, 1840, but as Tudvad painstakingly expends five paragraphs demonstrating, this was impossible, because Westergaard was not hired by Kierkegaard until 1844. What's more, Garff mistakenly describes Westergaard as being two years older than Kierkegaard, when in fact he was four years younger. An outrage! Tudvad continues:

> There are many other errors in Garff's chapter on the Jutland trip, errors particularly well suited to strengthen the view of Kierkegaard as a dandy. He is described by Garff, for example, as installing himself immediately upon his arrival in Århus in the city's best hotel, even though we know nothing of where Kierkegaard stayed that first night. Similarly, Garff presents Kierkegaard, the resident of Copenhagen, as offended by the amount of bovine excrement in the streets of Århus, even though he must have been accustomed to maneuvering his way through such excrement since Copenhagen had three times as many cows then within its city walls as did Århus.

His extreme pedantry no doubt performs a certain scholarly service, but really what Tudvad is revealing is simply that his image of Kierkegaard is at odds with Garff's. Tudvad does not agree with Garff that Kierkegaard was a dandy — but so what? That is a difference of interpretation, not scholarly fact. In other words, Tudvad is himself inferring things from his imagination, the very crime for which he arraigns Garff.

In general, Tudvad treats literary biography as a kind of science, or at best an art form that demands overwhelming empirical rigor. He accuses Garff of telling a story at the expense of a "trustworthy biography." But what kind of biography could deserve to be called completely trustworthy? "Biographers aren't stenographers," the biographer and critic Ruth Franklin observed recently, "we're more akin to novelists, constructing a narrative of a person's life and making editorial choices at every turn." A biography, if it is to be more than just a collection of evidentiary material, must necessarily tell a story, and a story distinguishes itself by what it leaves out as much as by what it includes. To suppose that rigorous scholarship could ever be sufficient basis for the portrayal of a life seems to me a ludicrous positivistic presumption.

Obviously — well, I hope it is obvious — I don't mean to diminish the necessary, the indispensable, the fundamental role that history and recorded fact serve in any account of a writer's life. Without it, biographies of Shakespeare and Cervantes, writers about whom we know very little, would almost be inconceivable. When Clarence Brown wrote his great life of Mandelstam, the excavation of basic facts out of the obscurity of the poet's exile, the establishment of the poet's whereabouts in any given month or year in the Stalinist hell, was an even greater accomplishment than his readings of the poems. And even if we cannot look over Joyce's shoulder as he wrote *Ulysses* or *Finnegan's Wake*, our understanding of his life and his work have no doubt been improved by the colossal achievement of Richard Ellmann, his best biographer.

The crucial point is that although we can reconstruct much, if not most, of a writer's life, in terms of events and incidents in the world, we cannot reconstruct the writer's inner life. The vagaries of Virginia Woolf's mental health, Thomas Mann's feelings toward his children, the precise nature of Henry James' sexuality — these are questions to

The Fiction That Dare Not Speak Its Name

which there will always be different answers. There is nothing relativistic about this; it is the very nature of humanistic understanding. The facts are the anchor but interpretation is the sea, and the sea is seldom still.

Perhaps the question of fiction in biography can be illuminated by the question of biography in fiction. Based on what I have written above, I ought to be gratefully receptive to what John Mullan calls "biographical fiction," and what Anthony Domestico refers to as "literary fanfic." Here the fictional element in the account of a real author takes center stage, and a proper novelist, unshackled by fealty to the clang and whir of biographical machinery, imagines a fellow writer into being from the ground up. Tolstoy, Zelda Fitzgerald, Vanessa Bell, and Virginia Woolf are just a few of the increasing number of writers who have had novels made out of them. Possibly the best-known example of this peculiar genre is Colm Tóibín's *The Master*, a much-lauded and award-cosseted portrait of Henry James.

Any reader would sympathize with the desire to imagine one's favorite writers into being, especially with the solvent of fiction, whereby the novelist is free to go where we biographers generally fear to tread. Imagine what I might have done with — or to — Jens Peter Jacobsen had I been gifted with a talent for fiction and the artistic daring required to pursue him off-piste. Would I have permitted him a brief romantic dalliance? A passionate exchange with a literary ally? Or perhaps a tearful goodbye with his friends in Copenhagen, before he returned home to his parents in Thisted to die? And all the while I would insist that, no matter how fanciful my inventions, I was still writing about the actual Jens Peter Jacobsen.

The problem with most biographical fiction is that it is too anxiously tempted toward biography and thus away from fiction. Ironically, therefore, it suffers from a paucity of imagination. It is intimidated by fact, and it battens off the allure of facticity. With so much of the scaffolding already done, the enterprising bio-novelist is free to acquit himself by merely applying a little fictional adhesive to the preassembled bits of written record. Tóibín's second foray into the genre, *The Magician*, a novel about the life of Thomas Mann, reads less like a novel than a diligently paraphrased biography. Here is a passage from about a third-way into the novel, just as the First World War gets underway and Thomas and Heinrich Mann, brothers and bitter rivals, find themselves on opposite sides of the conflict:

> While Heinrich developed a following among young, left-wing activists, Thomas found himself the object of casual deprecation even among those who had been his avid readers. Since much opinion was censored, it was difficult to write openly about the war. Offering views in print, instead, on the relative merits of the Mann brothers came to be an indirect, but powerful, way for writers and journalists to make their position on the war clear.

This sentence could be lifted and seamlessly dropped into virtually any biography or biographical essay about Mann, unchanged even in tone. Nothing distinguishes it as an exertion of the imagination. Here is another example:

> Late in 1915, Heinrich published an essay invoking Zola as a novelist who had, during the Dreyfus case, attempted to alert his fellow countrymen to a wrong that was being committed... As the war waged, Thomas continued to

monitor Heinrich's articles. His brother, he saw, did not often write directly about the conflict. Instead, he shared his views on the French Second Empire, leaving enough space for his readers to understand the connections between France then and Germany now.

And here is Ronald Hayman, from his biography of Mann, which Tóibín reviewed in the *London Review of Books* in 1995:

> Now, unable to criticize either Germany or complaisant intellectuals, Heinrich had found a way of breaking the awkward silence he'd kept since August 1914 by commenting obliquely on the current situation. Attacking France's Second Empire as a state that had come into existence through violence, he praised Zola for realizing that it was disintegrating and for championing Dreyfus, the Jewish officer who'd been unjustly accused of treason.

Tóibín's passage has the linguistic flatness of information, which is much more egregious in a novel than in a biography. When he was typing such paragraphs, and the novel is full of them, what did he think he was doing?

The Magician is one of the most anxious and perfunctory novels that I have ever read. It is nothing but protracted literary piety, or very long-form book chat. It is so unpersuaded by its own claim to being a work of fiction that it dare not loosen its grip from the sturdy handrail of biography. And so it proceeds in meek chronological order, dutifully integrating little facts into the colorless edifice of its prose, and goes exactly, literally, where you expect it to go. Why is this interesting? And when Toibin shakes himself loose from his prosaicness and tries to take flight, things get worse and one longs for a return to austerity of the factual. The few flights of fancy that Tóibín allows himself — most notably, the unlikely idea that Mann acted on or consummated his homosexual desires, a fantasy that has become the hot cliché of contemporary Mann worship — more closely resemble failures of imagination than feats thereof. They seem more like examples of wishful thinking. Is Mann being enlisted in the cause? Was this novel about Mann conceived as a contribution to gay literature?

Perhaps biographical novels are, in essence, little more than minor instances of historical fiction, the perfect middlebrow entertainment. The satisfactions of historical fiction are vicarious and voyeuristic, which is why so many historical novels eventually become adolescent fare. One of the most astute diagnosticians of the historical novel was Henry James, who in 1901 wrote to the historical novelist Sarah Orne Jewett:

> The "historic" novel is, for me, condemned, even in cases of labour as delicate as yours, to a fatal *cheapness*, for the simple reason that the difficulty of the job is inordinate & that a mere *escamotage*, in the interest of ease, & of the abysmal public *naïveté*, becomes inevitable. You may multiply the little facts that can be got from pictures & documents, relics & prints, as much as you like — *the* real thing is almost impossible to do, & in its absence the whole effect is as nought; I mean the invention, the representation of the old *consciousness*, the soul, the sense, the horizon, the vision of individuals in whose minds half the things that make ours, that make the modern world, were non-existent. You have to think with your modern apparatus a man, a woman — or rather fifty —

whose own thinking was intensely — otherwise condi-
tioned, you have to simplify back by an amazing tour de
force — & even then it's all humbug.

James is here describing what we have come to call kitsch.
And some of the same "cheapness" and "naivete" impairs most
biographical fiction. Like biopics, they seem like projections of
our own cultural moment grafted onto the past.

To read a work of biographical fiction is to read a novel
that desperately, harassingly, wants to assure you that it is
not just a novel, that it is more than a novel. But it is less
than a novel, and except for reasons of commerce it has
rarely anything to commend it. (The dialogue is usually the
fictional equivalent of Romans or Nazis speaking in English
or American accents). And as is the case with *The Magician*,
there is usually an acknowledgments section to undo the
spell, like the long unspooling of credits at the end of a movie.
These acknowledgements are the final insult, because there
is something rather peacock-ish about them. Research is
nothing new in fiction; but it is fatal for fiction to recommend
itself for its research.

256

Of course it is possible to write imaginatively about other
writers, only it requires a more oblique, sidelong approach.
Lisa Halliday's *Assymetry*, a novel partly based on its author's
affair with Philip Roth, is a bold exploration of fiction's ability
to conjure the consciousness of others. Jose Saramago's novel
The Year of the Death of Ricardo Reis, based on the last year of
Fernando Pessoa's life, is a metafictional inquiry into narra-
tive and selfhood. In *The Messiah of Stockholm*, Cynthia Ozick

explored the legacy of the Polish Jewish writer Bruno Schulz in the farcical yet finely moving scenario of a middling Swedish literary critic convinced that he is Schulz's son.

Another recent example is *Last Words on Earth*, a first novel by the Spanish writer Javier Serena, which tells the story of a Peruvian author — "I'll call him Ricardo, Ricardo Funes, although that isn't his real name, or last" — who toils away in passionate obscurity in a coastal town north of Barcelona, achieving literary acclaim only to die prematurely of a lung disease. Funes, quite obviously, is modelled on the Chilean poet and novelist Roberto Bolaño, who spent the last decades of his life in Blanes, a Catalan beach town north of Barcelona, and like Funes died just as he began tasting the fruits of literary fame. To anyone familiar with Bolaño's life and work, the similarities are almost comically obvious (and just in case, there is the back matter and promotional text to remind us) — so obvious, in fact, that some reviewers have wondered why Serena did not simply go ahead and call his fictional creation by his proper name.

But this seems to me to miss the point. Bolaño was an intensely self-mythologizing writer; several details of his biography, such as the idea that he was imprisoned in Chile after Pinochet's coup against Allende, or that he spent time with the guerrillas of the Farabundo Martí National Liberation Front in El Salvador, are likely apocryphal. His fictional universe, connected and constructed across several novels, novellas, and short stories in which characters appear and reappear, is steeped in literary mystery and mythmaking. At least one of Bolaño's recurring characters, the writer Arturo Belano, is a fictional self-portrait. In the novel *The Savage Detectives*, Belano is described as having been involved with a rebellious literary group in Mexico City in the 1970s called the Visceral Realists, and Bolaño was himself part of such a group in the same city at the same time, called the Infrarealists. In *Last Words on Earth*, Serena has Ricardo Funes belong to a radical literary movement in Mexico City in the 1970s called *negacionismo*.

For readers who look to the novel for a deeper and less self-regarding relationship to reality, all this may seem like a Borgesian rabbit hole. In Bolano's case, however, it may be said that he brought it on himself. Serena's novel succeeds because it knows that a writer whose life was as soaked in fiction and self-mythology as Bolaño's deserves to be appropriated by a rival fiction rather than be detained by biographical fidelity. Otherwise, the novelist becomes hostage to a panoply of fictions not of his invention, and thus surrenders some crucial measure of his artistic freedom. Still, one must wonder whether all these metafictional devices and tricks should suffice to protect a writer from an empirical and critical account of the facts of his life and his style. If biography is fiction and bio-fiction is fiction, then this is yet another case of the widespread contemporary abandonment of the scruple about veracity.

Biographical fiction, at least in its more literalist mode, is a gratuitous genre, like the novelization of a film. Biography is always already fiction, at least in part, because it involves imagining one's way into a life lived primarily in the imagination. (This is what distinguishes the biography of a writer from, say, the biography of a politician, where the achievements for which they become known are so much more public.) What's more, being fictional, biographical fiction is often very bad at the necessary nonfictional elements of biography. In Tóibín's *The Magician*, the fascinating and formative years of the First World War, when Thomas Mann cheered the German cause and wrote his *Reflections of a Nonpolitical Man*, which over time became a record of his dramatic intellectual evolution, are dispensed with almost in passing, despite its being, as Mann's biographer Hermann Kürzke has put it, one of the "great riddles a biography must solve."

Too self-conscious to be wholly fictional, too fictional to be sufficiently factual— no, the biographical novel is a superfluous endeavor, a bourgeois indulgence. We are stuck, in other words, with old-fashioned literary biography, warts and all. But perhaps, by virtue of leaving so much space for the imaginative, for the fictional, biographies of writers may be in some strange way the most truthful form of biography there is. Like writers, most people lead double lives, too: one in their imagination and one out there in the world. As William Dubin, the title character of Bernard Malamud's *Dubin's Lives*, a novel about a biographer writing the life of D. H. Lawrence, observes, "There is no life that can be recaptured wholly."

259

CLARA COLLIER

Women With Whips

Name a classic Western of the 1950s starring a great actress of the 1930s. She should play a woman of power and influence, maybe with a little bit of a dominatrix vibe. (When critics talk about the film, they will probably call it "psychosexual".) It is highly stylized. Whatever happens in it, it doesn't take place in the West of the United States sometime between the 1860s and the 1890s, but in the West of Hollywood movies, and it wants you to know that it knows it. Deep down, it is all about sex and violence. Horsewhips feature prominently. And the French New Wave was obsessed with it.

Three movies spring to mind: Fritz Lang's *Rancho Notorious,* from 1952, with Marlene Dietrich; Nicholas Ray's *Johnny Guitar,* from 1954, with Joan Crawford; and Samuel Fuller's *Forty Guns,* from 1957, with Barbara Stanwyck. That might not be quite enough to constitute a microgenre, but it is remarkable that three such films exist at all. Not that it's a coincidence: Ray and Fuller both revered Lang, and both certainly had *Rancho Notorious* in mind when making their own movies. And all three drew on trends that reflected the growing discomfort of the post-war Western: Western noirs, which paint the wide-open range with chiaroscuro shadows, and psychological Westerns, which explored how pioneer virtues such as freedom and self-reliance sour into obsessive greed, lust for power, or rancid cruelty. The post-war years even saw an uptick in films where women owned land and property — Veronica Lake in *Ramrod,* Agnes Moorehead in *Station West,* Ruth Roman in *The Far Country,* Barbara Stanwyck in any of half a dozen roles.

The films in question here are doing something stranger and more specific. More than any other entries in the genre (including the others starring Stanwyck), they are interested in their own relationship with the past. Careers such as the ones Crawford, Stanwyck, and Dietrich enjoyed were incredibly rare, even in an era when stars had the full weight of the studio system behind them. (Bette Davis and Katherine Hepburn are the only other examples.) All three started acting in the silent era or very soon after the introduction of sound. They had been stars as long as the medium of film had existed. Their way of acting helped to define what female stardom meant — and by the 1950s it was on the way out. They didn't do naturalism, like the up-and-coming graduates of the Actor's Studio. They were not interested in representing the concerns of young people in a decade that was increasingly concerned with youth. Hollywood did not know quite what to do with them. The fear that a changing, civilizing West would have no place for the people who first settled it is a common preoccupation of the darker post-war westerns, and it is common thread in all three films. But nothing as simplistic as actresses playing themselves is taking place here. Like all great stars of their generation, they were able to embody a distinct persona that followed them from role to role — and in each case, that persona is the skeleton around which the rest of the film is built.

An interviewer, discussing *Rancho Notorious*, once asked Fritz Lang if he watched many Westerns. "Yes," he said. "I like Westerns. They have an ethic that is very simple and very necessary. It is an ethic which one doesn't see now because critics are too sophisticated. They want to ignore that it is necessary to really love a woman and to fight for her." Remarks like these make me wonder if Lang and I are talking about the same movie. There is a simple ethic at the core of *Rancho Notorious*, but the love of a woman is a transparent pretext. The chorus of the film's central ballad says it all: this is a story of *hatred, murder*, and *revenge*.

We open on a sleepy little town in Wyoming as mild-mannered cattle-hand Vern Haskell (Arthur Kennedy) gives his fiancée a diamond brooch. In short order, she is brutally raped and murdered. The next few years pass by in a couple of on-screen minutes as Vern scours the West for her killer. He only has one clue: the name "Chuck-a-Luck." Eventually he learns that Chuck-a-luck is a ranch belonging to retired show-girl Altar Keane (Marlene Dietrich). Vern gets himself thrown in Jail with Frenchy (Mel Ferrer), Altar's lover, and when the two break out Frenchy brings him to the ranch, a hideout for a rotating cast of aging outlaws. Altar is there, wearing Vern's dead fiancée's brooch. He tries to seduce her to learn the name of the man who gave it to her and, remarkably, succeeds. The whole thing ends in a gunfight where Altar dies protecting Frenchy and Vern gets his man, far too late for it to make any difference.

Marlene Dietrich played a lot of showgirls in her day, on a spectrum from poisonous (*The Blue Angel*) to noble (*Blonde Venus*). Somewhere in the middle is the role of Frenchie in *Destry Rides Again,* from 1939, another western where her character ultimately dies to protect the man she loves. *Rancho Notorious* is full of nods to her earlier roles — Frenchy's name, of course, and the flashbacks to Altar in her performing days, riding patrons like horses while wearing eye-popping quantities of fringe. The whole film is fixated on Altar's past, and by extension Dietrich's. There's a scene where she sings the frontier ballad "Black Jack Davy" with her unmistakable throaty Teutonic monotone. We are faced with a strange, layered kind of nostalgia — for the old West, the golden age of Hollywood, and the bacchanals in Weimar cabarets where it always seems that her characters really belonged.

Under Lang's direction, all of it seems to have gone sour. Vern is one of the most comprehensively nasty protagonists to swagger down the main street of Republic Studios' western set. He lies and manipulates, seduces Altar and coldly reveals his contempt when he finally has what he wants. Kennedy gives him a breathtakingly malicious sneer as he lays into it. One might almost suspect that he is enjoying it, if only he were capable of joy. I have never understood what Altar is meant to see in Vern that she doesn't see in Ferrer's gentlemanly

Frenchy, except youth. "I wish you'd go away," she tells him, "and come back ten years ago." Not that it would have made a difference. No one in a Lang movie can escape their fate.

The first thing everyone remembers about *Johnny Guitar* is the colors: teal, turquoise, and deep earthy browns, punctuated by the occasional violent pink dress or the scarlet of Joan Crawford's lipstick. When critics talk about this film, which is often just plain bizarre, they like to use words like "operatic" or "phantasmagoric," and it is easy to see why: the palette would be right at home in *Tales of Hoffman*, or more appropriately a Douglas Sirk melodrama. In fact, *Johnny Guitar* is really a Western melodrama, the way *Rancho Notorious* is a Western noir. The plot, such as it is, exists to push outsized characters into outsized confrontations — and nobody does outsized like Crawford.

Here she plays Vienna, the owner of a cathedralesque saloon, which is certainly one of the hands-down stranger spaces in the whole Western genre. Instead of the traditional low ceilings and smoke stains, it has a vaulting A-frame roof, bright white walls, and a weird rock-lined dais with an out-of-place piano. The whole effect is very '70s for a movie made in 1954. Mostly, it looks like a twisted stage. Characters are always emerging from the wings and presenting themselves in strikingly arranged groups. Truffaut nailed it in his famous review of the film:

> *Johnny Guitar* is a phony Western, but not an "intellectual" one. It is dreamed, a fairy tale, a hallucinatory Western.... *Johnny Guitar* was "made" rather hastily, out

of very long scenes that were cut up into ten segments. The editing is jerky, but what interests us is something else: for example, an extraordinarily beautiful placement of individuals in a certain setting. (The members of the patrol at Vienna's, for example, arrange themselves in the V of migratory birds.) ... *Johnny Guitar* is the *Beauty and the Beast* of Westerns, a Western dream. The cowboys vanish and die with the grace of ballerinas.

That's the other thing everyone remembers about *Johnny Guitar*: it's the men who flutter and leap and die like dancers. One of the central male characters is an outlaw called the Dancin' Kid. The other is the titular Johnny Guitar, the dopily handsome traveling musician played by Sterling Hayden. Vienna has hired him to play at her saloon, but it is obvious that more is going on. Johnny Guitar is actually the renowned gunslinger Johnny Logan, and Vienna's former lover. She left him because she wanted to settle down and build something — and she has. Her land stands in the way of the new railroad route, and when it is built she stands to make a killing. Meanwhile she is locked in a sexually charged feud with Emma Smalls, played with unforgettable derangement by Mercedes McCambridge. (Crawford wanted Bette Davis for the part, which would have made an interesting prequel to *Whatever Happened to Baby Jane?*)

We meet Emma when she bursts into Vienna's place with a posse and her brother's corpse, trying to pin the murder on the Dancin' Kid and his gang. McCambridge plays Emma as a seething mass of repression and rage, a sharp contrast to Crawford's cuttingly precise performance. In Vienna's first appearance, in trousers and a to-die-for teal bolo tie, her acting is concentrated in the hips and shoulders. The way she propels herself through space is square and deliberate and, yes, very masculine. Later, when she swans down a staircase to confront Emma, it's all in the face. Each perfect individual movement of her eyes, her eyebrows, or her lips telegraphs a new shift from anger to contempt to defiance. This is *not* naturalistic acting. Crawford didn't do naturalistic acting. It is instead a master class in emoting for an audience. We know exactly what she thinks and how she feels and what kind of person she is: independent and hard.

In contrast, Sterling Hayden looks and acts like a golden retriever. He is gentle and relaxed and a little bit droopy — Sterling Hayden! — especially in his scenes with Vienna. There is plenty of threatened masculinity in this film, but it comes mostly in response to his softness, not her hardness. At one point one of Vienna's bartenders remarks that "I've never seen a woman who was more a man ...she thinks like one, acts like one, and sometimes makes me feel like I'm not." But still he is happy to work for her. When Johnny refuses to play a song for the Dancin' Kid, it is a different story: the Kid is practically hysterical that this man who doesn't even carry a gun will not rise to his bait. Being a man in his mind is not just about the willingness to use violence; it is about living in a world where violence is the thing that gets you what you want. And beneath the pacifist persona, Johnny is also fighting the same gravitational pull of violence. The first time he gets his hands on a gun, we can see him sweat and tremble with the stress of keeping himself from pulling the trigger. Hayden makes the pull towards violence look like a real physical illness.

This ethic of violence, its normative status in this contrived world, is most fully embodied not by any of the male characters but by Emma. Once again, the girls are butcher than the boys. We are told that Emma lusts after the Kid, even

266

as she agitates to have him lynched. A minor character remarks that "he makes her feel like a woman — and that terrifies her." Emma has repressed her own desires so violently that her personality has collapsed into a monotonic rage. Ray isn't exactly subtle when he hints at the possibility that one of the objects of her obsessive desiring might be Vienna.

In the end there is a climactic ambush, Emma is killed, Vienna and Johnny kiss under a virulently green waterfall, and shooting solves everyone's problems. If you want thematic consistency, don't look for it in *Johnny Guitar*. Instead, there is the fluid succession of gorgeous individual scenes, like the truly oneiric scene in which Vienna puts on a poofy white organza gown and sits down to play the grand piano while a posse comes to arrest her, or the one in which she flees her burning saloon through an abandoned mineshaft and emerges by a turquoise lake. When Truffaut called it the *Beauty and the Beast* of Westerns, he meant that Vienna was the beast — and she can be beauty when she wants to be. (Sterling Hayden's beast is there, too, waiting to be let out.) Finally the film is a fairy tale. It doesn't have to make sense.

Unlike Dietrich and Crawford, Barbara Stanwyck had a long history with Westerns, which were probably her favorite genre. Her career spanned from studio programmers such as *Annie Oakley* and *Union Pacific* in the 1930s through genre-busting 1950s psychological westerns such as *The Furies* and *Forty Guns,* ending with the television series *The Big Valley* in the late 1960s. By that point in her career Stanwyck had perfected the steely, ambitious landed frontierswoman — she had played versions of the ranching aristocrat role in *The Violent Men, The Maverick*

Queen, and the aptly named *Cattle Queen of Montana.* I have to imagine that she felt a natural connection to the part. She really did own a ranch, rode horses daily, and did her own stunts well into middle age. There is a famous scene in *Forty Guns* (there are many famous scenes in *Forty Guns*) where Stanwyck's character is dragged behind a horse in a tornado. She did it herself — she was forty-nine at the time — and when Fuller wasn't happy with the take she did it again. Twice. Stanwyck was as steely as they come; her natural toughness was an essential part of her on-screen persona.

You know that you are watching a Fuller movie when your jaw hits the floor between the thirty-second and two minute marks, and *Forty Guns* is no exception. It opens with a tracking bird's-eye view of vast, silent ranchland with a flyspeck of a wagon rolling down the dirt road. As the camera shifts to a low-angle view of the wagon, with a man on the driver's bench, he sees something that we do not yet see and calls a halt. At that moment an endless-looking line of men on horseback cuts across the empty landscape. We see the horses' legs — the dust they kick up — the three men on the wagon, gawping, as the line of riders parts and curves around them — and finally the woman at their head, dressed in black and riding a white stallion. She looks positively mythological. And then they're gone, cutting across the empty landscape in a clean, brutal, diagonal slash. From the beginning, the bones of the film are on display: Fuller's penchant for odd framings and ambitious compositions and slightly queasy low-angle shots, the gothic visual austerity amid the photographic grandeur, and the fact that none of us know what to make of Jessica Drummond, the Stanwyck character, who runs her ranch and the rest of Cochise County, Arizona backed up by forty hired guns.

The man in the wagon is Griff Bonnel (Barry Sullivan), a gunslinger-turned-lawman who has come to Cochise with a warrant to bring in one of Jessica's men for mail robbery. It is quickly obvious that Jessica is the real mastermind behind the operation. Her men are responsible for tax collecting in Cochise. In exchange, the government turns a blind eye when she skims the profits. Her younger brother, Brockie, terrorizes the nearby town of Tombstone with equal impunity. Not that any of this presents an obstacle to the developing romance between Jessica and Griff. We can tell Jessica is interested the moment they meet, when Griff shows up at her mansion to arrest her deputy hours after pistol-whipping Brockie unconscious in the town square. Jessica is not the kind of woman to let such trivialities stop her from getting what she wants.

It's about sex, of course. Jessica and Griff's early flirtation is full of Fuller's characteristic tabloid vulgarity. (At one point, Jessica asks to feel Griff's "pistol." He warns her off: "It might go off in your face." "I'll take a chance," she leers back.) But for all the heat, there is something unexpectedly adult about their relationship. It surfaces in the quiet moments between shootouts and showdowns — when Griff casually unburdens his guilt about his past as a hired killer, or in the extraordinary scene where the two of them are trapped in an abandoned shack by a freak tornado.

Stanwyck had a gift for balancing icy control with remarkable tenderness. The gentleness in her little gestures — the way she holds Griff's hand or bends down to kiss his knuckles — stands out in this movie full of cavernous Cinemascope shots and heightened performances. While the storm rages, Jessica explains that the shack is where she was born, where she delivered Brockie, and where their mother died in childbirth. Griff comes to Cochise with his own younger brothers in tow: responsible Wes, his right-hand man, and callow Chico, who is being reluctantly packed off to California to work their parents' farm. They have both acted as parents to their siblings, made a name for themselves in the unforgiving frontier, done terrible things and made their peace with it. And they both represent a way of life that is dying.

"There's a new era coming, Chico," Griff tells his youngest brother. "My way of living is on the way out." Jessica tells him the same thing when she asks him to settle down with her: "This is the last stop, Griff. The frontier is finished." And her sweetheart deal with Uncle Sam can't last forever. They are both essentially melancholy characters, living with one foot in the past, reluctantly dragging themselves towards an uncertain future. This is not what draws them together (that would, again, be the sex), but I think it explains how quickly and easily they fall into intimacy. For the few days that the romance lasts, it feels more real and solid than anything else in Fuller's self-consciously artificial landscape.

The past is always close to the surface in *Forty Guns*. When Jessica finishes her story, Griff asks her if she has kept the old shack as a shrine. Her response is a summation of her character, and of almost every character Stanwyck ever played: "No. Just a reminder not to let go of anything." Those words, and the way she says them — quietly, firmly, not to him but to herself — would be equally at home with the scrappy Depression-era gangster's molls and working girls that she played in the early 1930s or her femme fatales of the 1940s. In that moment, she could be Lily Powers from *Baby Face,* with her ruthless pursuit of wealth, Stella from *Stella Dallas,* singlemindedly clawing out a place in society for her daughter, Phyllis Dietrichson in *Double Indemnity,* or Vance Jeffords in *The Furies* — all very different women, representing a fraction of Stanwyck's range, but built around the same hard core. Stanwyck excelled at portraying women who wanted

270

things, who would stop at nothing to get them, and who, once they had them, knew how to hang on for dear life.

In the end, Jessica does let go of her empire. The film shifts into serious mode about two-thirds of the way through. Jessica and Griff are talking in her parlor when they are interrupted by gunfire. The shots came from one of Jessica's deputies, Ned, who proceeds to confess his love for her with painful, halting sincerity. Fuller frames the scene with a stunning triangular shot, from Jessica to Ned to Griff, each facing each other but isolated on the huge cinemascope screen. Ned leaves. And then Jessica crumples, confessing her love and her willingness to leave everything for Griff. A chair topples in another room. They go running. Ned, of course, has hung himself. It is not unusual for Stanwyck's self-made women to give it all up for love, but what we see here is different. In the hands of a different director, her sacrifice would lead straight to death or redemption. Fuller, being Fuller, cuts straight from Ned's swinging body to a raucous communal bath scene. Once the moment is interrupted, it's gone — there is no quick resolution here. Stanwyck is playing her real age here, and she is old enough that moments which might seem life-defining to a younger woman sometimes just pass.

Griff's brother Wes falls for the daughter of the town gunsmith, and Brockie shoots him dead outside the church on the day of their wedding. For this he is going to hang — Jessica cannot fix this and she wouldn't if she could. But when Griff arrives at the jail, Brockie breaks out, grabs Jessica as a human shield, and drags her into the street. Griff pulls out his gun and, for the first time since turning white-hat, shoots to kill — right through Jessica. Brockie dies. Jessica, improbably, survives. In the final shot of the film, we see her running after Griff's wagon while the town balladeer croons that this high-riding woman with a whip is only a woman after all. He stops to let her on, and they ride off together for California.

It is too facile to mistake an ending like that for an attempt to turn the film into a battle of the sexes. That misses the point. When Jessica and Griff are pushed apart, it is not by his masculinity, injured or otherwise. They both have deeper, earlier obligations. And in any case the movie was never meant to end that way. As an independent producer, Fuller was able to get around the most officious forms of studio meddling, but his distributors at 20th Century Fox had one absolute requirement: Jessica had to live. Fuller hated the studio-mandated ending, and would complain about it in interviews years later:

> Zanuck said she must not die. "We've been making pictures for years, and the hero does not kill the heroine. You've seen *High Noon*. At a very vital moment, Kelly pushes the guy away, and that's when Cooper shoots him." Now how can [Stanwyck] push the guy away? He's holding her with an iron grip. That man [Barry Sullivan] hasn't used a gun in ten years. When he picks up a gun, it's to kill. If that was his mother shielding that guy, he'd kill her because he has a gun and doesn't want to use a gun. [Sullivan] said, "Wait a minute, you cannot kill the heroine. I like the picture, but you cannot shoot her." I said, "He's not himself. He's a gun."

In a movie full of deliberately strange performances, Barry Sullivan's is hands-down the weirdest. With his hyper-stressed, staccato delivery and exaggerated physical movements, he almost looks like a parody of a Western marshal. There's none of Sterling Hayden's gentle, deliberate trembling when he gets his hands on a gun. Sullivan is a square-jawed cliché up until the moment he shoots through his love interest to kill her brother.

So let us imagine Griff riding off into the sunset alone. Where does that leave us? And, more importantly, where does that leave Barbara Stanwyck? In an essay in *Cahiers du Cinéma*, Claude Chabrol claimed that Jessica is just like a Fuller man. I don't quite agree, but she is certainly not defined by sex — no Nicholas Ray-style hallucinatory meditations on femininity here. If anything, it is the weird, schematic Griff who is flattened into a sketch of Western masculinity. And in his final shootout, he is flattened even further: he's not a man, Fuller reminds us, "he's a gun." It is interesting to compare the ending of *Forty Guns* to that of *Johnny Guitar*. For all its grotesquerie, *Johnny Guitar* is much more interested in the dehumanizing potential of violence, but it is *Forty Guns* that follows through. Whether or not Jessica survives, there is nothing redemptive or freeing about the moment when Griff shoots her. In the end this is a tragedy, and most centrally her tragedy. Stanwyck's performance anchors the film, and Jessica is the most human character in it. It was the actress' last major role.

There is a certain glib reading of all of these films, according to which their decision to portray women in positions of power speaks to a very 1950s anxiety about male weakness. This phenomenon had a number of causes: World War II and the rise of women in the workforce, the Kinsey Report, the fear of being outed as either gay or a communist or both. There is definitely a crisis of masculinity brewing in *Johnny Guitar* (Ray had issues), but overall I tend to think that it's beside the point. Gender is not a zero-sum game. Even in *Johnny Guitar*, male weakness is not a result of female strength. In these films

Dietrich, Crawford, and Stanwyck are in their late forties or early fifties, they mostly wear men's clothes, and they are as unapologetically sexy as they have ever been in their lives. It is a joy to behold. No one should be so silly as to suggest that there is something emasculating about being attracted to them.

Ironically, the blend of masculinity and femininity that looks so transgressive in the 1950s was par for the course in the 1930s. Dietrich and Crawford and Stanwyck are doing here what they have always done. On-screen couples back then were more fluid. Think of Crawford and Clark Gable, of Stanwyck and Henry Fonda or Gary Cooper, of Dietrich and anyone, of Katharine Hepburn and Cary Grant — there is a constant exchange of hardness and softness, masculinity and femininity. And its spirit is playful. The closing of American society in the 1950s meant a loss of that playfulness, especially in big-budget Hollywood productions, which are veritable documents of sexual anxiety. When it survived, it was on the margins of popular genres — mainly westerns and noirs, which encompassed the decades' most innovative film-making.

In the end, westerns provided the best canvas for mid-century American filmmakers who wanted to play with, and explore, gender and genre. (Noir, by contrast, tends towards a more Manichean view of women specifically and society generally). The 1950s also saw the height of psychoanalytic influence on American film, and the West represented the country's collective unconscious. It was the place to identify and work through unacknowledged impulses, to reimagine the archetypes that define the social contract and the customs of ordinary life. And it was gradually being fenced in.

HELEN VENDLER

Art Against Stereotype

England

with its baby rivers and little towns, each with its abbey
    or its cathedral,
  with voices—one voice perhaps, echoing through
    the transept—the
criterion of suitability and convenience: and Italy with
  its equal
    shores—contriving an epicureanism from which the
    grossness has been

extracted: and Greece with its goats and its gourds, the
    nest of modified illusions:
  and France, the "chrysalis of the nocturnal butterfly," in

whose products, mystery of construction diverts one
　　　　from what was originally one's
　　　object—substance at the core: and the East with its snails,
　　　　its emotional

shorthand and jade cockroaches, its rock crystal and
　　　　its imperturbability,
　　　all of museum quality: and America where there
is the little old ramshackle victoria in the south,
　　　　where cigars are smoked on the
　　　　street in the north; where there are no proofreaders,
　　　　no silkworms, no digressions;

the wild man's land; grass-less, links-less, language-less
　　　　country in which letters are written
　　　not in Spanish not in Greek, not in Latin, not in shorthand
but in plain American which cats and dogs can read!
　　　　the letter "a" in psalm and calm when
　　　　pronounced with the sound of "a" in candle, is very
　　　　noticeable but

why should continents of misapprehension have to
　　　　be accounted for by the
　　　fact? Does it follow that because there are poisonous
　　　　toadstools
which resemble mushrooms, both are dangerous? In the
　　　　case of mettlesomeness which may be
　　　　mistaken for appetite, of heat which may appear to
　　　　be haste, no con-

clusions may be drawn. To have misapprehended the matter,
　　　　is to have confessed

Liberties

that one has not looked far enough. The sublimated wisdom
of China, Egyptian discernment, the cataclysmic torrent
        of emotion compressed
    in the verbs of the Hebrew language, the books of
        the man who is able

to say, "I envy nobody but him and him only, who catches
        more fish than
    I do,"—the flower and fruit of all that noted superi-
ority—should one not have stumbled upon it in America,
        must one imagine
    that it is not there? It has never been confined to
        one locality.

by Marianne Moore

Poems responding to prejudice, ordinarily uttered by the
oppressed, are variously angry, depressed, or revolution-
ary in sentiment. Only rarely are they humorous or ironic.
Yet examples of poems resisting prejudice through wit and
comedy turn up in such twentieth-century poets as Marianne
Moore, D.H. Lawrence, and Allen Ginsberg. Comedy, for
obvious reasons, is more available to writers not themselves
among the most heavily oppressed; although they may belong
to oppressed populations (women, the Welsh, homosexuals),
they have usually become — through innate genius, childhood
wealth, or admission to elite education — socially equal (or
superior) to their earlier oppressors.

Marianne Moore, for example, was born to the daughter of
a well-off Presbyterian minister, but also to a psychotic father
confined in an asylum. She and her mother were relatively
impoverished after her grandfather's death when she was seven.

Yet she was educated at Bryn Mawr, and became after college a teacher "of English and business subjects" (at one of the now-infamous boarding schools for "Indians"), a librarian, and the editor of an avant-garde journal. She also had the luck of having her poems brought to the attention of T.S. Eliot in England through the influence of her poet-friend Hilda Doolittle (whose wealthy lover, Winifred Ellerman, paid for the original publication of Moore's poems in England without Moore's knowledge or consent).

Although Moore was trained in college to recognize social prejudice — she enthusiastically attended lectures by visiting feminists at Bryn Mawr and took an interest in the Suffragist movement — she was also, I think, brought up by her mother (who eventually took a lesbian lover) to feel indignant at the common private prejudice against those who, like herself later, resisted the usual social program of female life. (Emily Dickinson, even more eccentric than Moore, had implicitly described herself to Thomas Wentworth Higginson as of a different species from conventional women: "the only kangaroo among the beauty.") When Moore visited England in 1911 with her mother, she was nettled by the persistent prejudice there against all things American; and in 1920, in a poem mischievously titled "England," she could afford (because of her maternal family and her upper-class education) to choose satire rather than resentment as her initial weapon against hostile English judgments of things American. In between a scanty overture on England and a coda on America, Moore recites common stereotypes of Italy, Greece, France, and "the East" before coming to a defiant conclusion which not only counters English prejudice against America, but also confesses to her own previously unconscious use of superficial stereotypes.

Moore's chief precursors in asserting America's right to contest the Old World's supposed excellence were Whitman and Dickinson. In 1871, by invitation, Whitman recited "Song of the Exposition" at the fortieth National Industrial Exposition in New York City, sponsored to display the newest products of agriculture and machinery. In the poem, he blithely disdained the assumed superiority of the European classics, flippantly declaring to the Muse that she has exhausted the literary materials of the past. Urging her to join him in the New World, he is irresistibly persuasive:

> Come Muse migrate from Greece and Ionia,
> Cross out please those immensely overpaid accounts,
> That matter of Troy and Achilles' wrath, and Aeneas',
>   Odysseus' wanderings,
> Placard "Removed" and "To Let" on the rocks of your
>   snowy Parnassus, . . .
> For know a better, fresher, busier sphere, a wide, untried
>   domain awaits, demands you.

Predicting the Muse's smiling response to his call, he announces to his fellow citizens her choice of location for her new American shrine:

> Bluff'd not a bit by drain-pipe, gasometers, artificial
>   fertilizers,
> Smiling and pleas'd with palpable intent to stay,
> She's here, install'd amid the kitchen ware!

Dickinson, for her part, mocked the adoption by New England women of English manners and complacent class-consciousness, reproaching her contemporaries' supposed

"Convictions" as ones composed of "dimity" (a light summer cotton dress-fabric) and their Christianity as one that would haughtily recoil from St. Peter himself as a mere "Fisherman":

Such Dimity Convictions -
A Horror so refined
Of freckled Human Nature -
Of Deity - Ashamed -

It's such a common - Glory -
A Fisherman's - Degree –

Most nineteenth-century American poets — contemporaries of the scandalous Whitman and the unknown Dickinson — had tended to imitate beloved English models (while substituting American heroes or locales for English ones). Longfellow, Bryant, Whittier, and Lowell wrote in all the conventional genres: accomplished ballads, seasonal observations, philosophical reflections, elegies, love lyrics, satires, hymns. But Whitman and Dickinson — already social exiles but superbly self-educated — broke the Anglophone molds of subject and form, and so did the subsequent American modernists, Moore among them.

Conscious of herself as a misfit, Moore deliberately wrote poems about misfits, sometimes exotic untamed animals (an ostrich, a giraffe) and sometimes handicapped vegetables (a carrot thwarted of its genetic shape by natural obstructions, a strawberry distorted in shape by a struggle in growth). The most piercing — because the most personal — of her misfits is a tree. "The Monkey Puzzler," which appeared in 1924 in her first American publication, the vividly original *Observations,* describes a bizarre species of Chilean pine putting forth spiky branches which, instead of spreading out, curl back on themselves. Perhaps owing to her own Irish forebears — "I'm troubled, I'm dissatisfied, I'm Irish" — Moore was drawn to the half-Irish, half-Greek [Patrick] Lafcadio Hearn, another misfit in both Dublin and the United States, who eventually took Japan as his country. Moore quotes his praise of the monkey-puzzle tree's peculiar aesthetic appeal:

> This porcupine-quilled, infinitely complicated starkness —
> this is beauty — "a certain proportion in the skeleton
>   which gives the best results."

But praise does not solve the questions that a naturalist would ask of the monkey-puzzle tree: How did it come to originate in Chile? And how was it genetically compelled into its strange distortions? One cannot answer such questions, any more than one can account for nature's casting an idiosyncratic human child of linguistic genius into a strained Missouri ecclesiastical environment. Moore, knowing her own eccentricity, closes her impersonal third-person portrait of the monkey-puzzle tree with a human first person "we" — a strikingly pained but accurate self-recognition. At the last moment she discovers a new verb ("prove") of self-justification:

> One is at a loss, however, to know why it should be here
> in this morose part of the earth —
> to account for its origin at all;
> but we prove, we do not explain our birth.

How did a Missouri girl born of a domineering mother and a psychotic engineer-father (whom she never knew) become a poet? Why in her adult life did she remain unmarried, living (except for her four years at Bryn Mawr) in rented apartments with her mother, sharing her bed until she was fifty-nine, and later buried with her under a joint tombstone? Her sole testimony to her individual existence was the poetry that she generated: "we prove, we do not explain, our birth." The climactic "prove" (from the Latin *probare,* "to test") shines out in all its plural meanings: we prove our life has a purpose; we test the value of our birth; we dare to exhibit to others our strangeness-from-birth; we claim a right to our birth-identity by the proof of its creations.

Many of Moore's poems are about such oddities as the monkey-puzzle tree. For her, such strange things derive their intrinsic value from their creation by God. Brought up through her seventh year in the house of her Presbyterian minister-grandfather, daughter to her religious mother, and sister to her Presbyterian minister-brother, Moore (with and like her mother) remained a church-going Christian. Myth and nature appear in her poetry as rich sources of the eccentric: unicorns, dragons, pangolins, the plumet basilisk, the jerboa, the octopus, the porcupine — these caught her eye, all of them animals never domesticated. In "Black Earth," a glorious self-portrait where she speaks in the first person as an elephant in the wild, she is represented as entirely free. She remained psychologically undomesticated herself, in spite of her never-terminated maternal connection and the strong family ties generating countless interwoven letters among her mother, her brother, and herself, in which each went by the name of an ungendered and undomesticated animal: "Rat" was Marianne, "Mole" was her mother Mary (sometimes called by other animal names such as "Fawn" or "Cub"), and "Badger" was her elder brother John. The family group seemed to others essentially impenetrable. Mary, who had become an English teacher, set the linguistic standard which her daughter — though always deferring to the example of her mother — far surpassed.

A restless reader both in conventional subjects (literature, history, mythology, art) and in odd corners of exotica (the outliers of the animal kingdom, anthropology, couturier fashions, geography), Moore dared to envisage an audience as extravagantly informed as herself. Her stanzas elaborate themselves by inlaid bits and pieces, relics of the intellectual accumulation of a lifelong collector of the remote and the strange. In almost every poem, ecological and historical and aesthetic details crowd together in what seems a forbidding hedge between her pages and any ill-read reader. She understands, from her new acquaintance with England, that the English regard America as a misfit among countries, a savage land alien to Anglo-European "civilization," with "inferior" mores and manners. In "England," she will comically teach our transatlantic relatives otherwise.

"England" — its title spilling over into its descriptions — seems to begin innocently enough, with touristic stereotypes of England's geography and its Christianity:

England

with its baby rivers and little towns, each with its abbey
    or its cathedral,
with voices — one voice perhaps, echoing through
    the transept — the
criterion of suitability and convenience:

This description seems initially bland enough to be included in a travel brochure, but Moore's first insidious gesture — voiced by a critical sensibility foreign to England — is to slip in the tiny adjective "baby." Who would call English streams — the Thames, the Wye — "baby" rivers, except someone who knew the broad Mississippi or another "giant" river of the Americas? Who, except one who had taken the measure of New York or Chicago, would see all English towns as "little" and tediously identical in their monocultural Christianity except that one has an abbey, another a cathedral? Who — knowing choral possibilities — would limit a cathedral transept to "one voice perhaps," the most minimal musical requirement? And who, familiar with the mighty ambitions of European Christian music, would regard the anorexic English criterion of "suitability and convenience" as sufficient for a whole country? It is an American voice, with its own contempt for a declining England of limited ambition, that utters these opening lines, but it has concealed itself within an apparent banality. Moore's opening strategy is to muffle her own indictment of English prejudice in apparently inoffensive language, but her satire will eventually mount into a climactic parody of England's shallow judgments.

Having disposed of its titular subject — England — in three lines, the commenting voice of the poem, without a stanza break, proceeds to instance — still in travelogue-form, but becoming more and more ignorant — aspects of other cultures of Europe and the far East. Italy is disparagingly said to have "contrived" an over-aesthetic epicureanism by "extracting" the "grossness" from its original recipes, timidly denaturing the typical offerings of its own indigenous cuisine. (Does this indictment for "grossness" bear examination?) Greece — the site, after all, of the Parthenon — displays visually to this voice, which is hostile to grand artifice, nothing but its alliterating rural "goats and gourds." These are quickly enough swept out of sight, but the philosophy of Greece is less easily ignored: the voice knows that Greece has recognized the vexing problem of illusions (Plato), but it has modified those illusions into a stunted realism (Aristotle) that so diminishes them in size that they fit into a single containing nest.

With France, a distrusted sophistication is said (in a conventional stereotype) to obscure practical function. One goes to a couturier in search of substance — a warm coat, perhaps — only to find that the cunning systems of French tailoring are more intriguing than the garment itself. The Paris couturier Erté has devised an evening gown so artfully cocooning the wearer (and here the poem quotes his hyperbolic French metaphor) that it becomes a chrysalis from which the buyer's body will emerge as a butterfly. Yes, the voice grants, fashion's inventions are "mysteries of construction," but the ingenuity of the craft diverts one from something surely more worthy: "substance at the core." Just as Moore does not bring the first four-line stanza to a close in England (suggesting that the country does not merit a whole stanza) but extends it into Italy's originally "gross" cuisine, so she does not close her second stanza within Europe, intimating that like England and Italy, Greece and France are rapidly shrinking in significance.

Instead the embodied voice runs on to the baffling culture of the East, reciting Western stereotypes of "the mysterious East" as superficial as those that England holds with respect to America. Some source must have informed Moore that "Chinese mystery snails" are so called because unlike snails from other countries, they give birth to live young. No less mysterious is the multi-stroke ideogram of

285

classical Chinese, which Moore — allowing her own voice to intervene — excitedly names "emotional shorthand," remarkable for its visual compression of semantic meaning. (The word "shorthand" brings the poem into Moore's own modernity, revealing the contemporary writer 's envy of such condensed, if inimitable, poetic means.) Conventional stereotypes return, as the East is said to offer repellent non-Western notions of what a precious jade artwork might represent — a cockroach — and its equally strange calm, its "imperturbability." (Moore imagines that her reader knows this stereotype of the Chinese character: the Oxford English Dictionary illustrates "imperturbability" with a quotation remarking on "the amazing stolidity and imperturbability of the Chinese in the face of all changes and disasters.") The voice becomes intellectually abstract as it summarizes its preceding inventory of Asian artworks: they are "all of museum quality," that is, removed in time and therefore only partly intelligible to foreign speculation on what fundamental aesthetic could prompt an object such as the jade cockroach.

So far, the poem — after beginning with Moore's satire on "baby" rivers, has continued with a list of common stereotypes for even the most ancient and revered cultures — the Greek, the Chinese. But suddenly (and before we quite realize it) the voice reverts to one Moore might have heard during her visit to England: that of a critical English observer being as dismissive of American phenomena as she (and other Americans) have been of trivially noted foreign peculiarities. As Moore "channels" the voice of this supercilious critic, citing a throng of English stereotypes of America's ignorant barbarity, she glances from particular regions to the deplorable whole to offer indisputable evidence of British prejudice. Both the American South and the American North, says the English aesthete, display untended objects and objectionable customs: the South exhibits a ramshackle version of a normally attractive English light carriage (named after Queen Victoria), and the North discloses, shockingly, men actually smoking cigars on the streets. But those are only the beginning of the expanding English list of American deficiencies (petrifying into generalized stereotypes). Horror of horrors, in America, with its error-spotted newspapers, there are no proofreaders! Aware of the aristocratic silks of the Far East, the "English" voice reproaches America for having no silkworms, and — recalling the leisurely prose of English essayists — the voice finds the curt practical discourse of America lacking in elegance. It has no digressions!

Other American defects are marked by implicit comparison with England: this is "a wild man's land" because it doesn't turn its prairies into beautiful English lawns; and still less is it conceivable that a culture should not have installed golf-courses. America in 1920 is "links-less." And in synchrony with its uncultivated wildness of landscape, barren America is "language-less." Its inhabitants know no foreign tongues: its letters are written not in Spanish (even with the country's Mexican border), and certainly not in Greek or in Latin, because its population has not had the advantage of aristocratic English schooling. In fact, its letters do not rise even to the scribal vocabulary of shorthand, but — and here the English voice reaches its disbelieving climax — Americans write letters "in plain American that cats and dogs can read!" This is very funny, but in its reporting of English snobbery all too convincing in its taxonomic categorizing of sublit-

287

erate Americans into "inferior" animal species — language-less cats and dogs. And not only do the English deem our written language elementary, they also reject our pronunciation as incorrect, denigrating the American flat "a" in "psalm" and "calm" in implicit praise of the open British "ah" which they (irrationally) find more suitable.

There ends Moore's sardonic parody of the way in which the English tourist isolates, misapprehends, and scorns various observed American features. Very well, says Moore, now not in the disguised voice of her subversive opening, nor in the imitative-of-stereotypes voice ranging through foreign territories, nor in the parodic voice of her British mockery, but in a didactic postcolonial voice we recognize as her own — very well, but upon such slender individual phenomena is it legitimate for the English to establish "continents of misapprehension"? She poses rapid questions of rebuttal: Why should a single difference of pronunciation justify the condemnation of a whole nation? Is there any logic to finding harmless mushrooms dangerous just because there exist poisonous toadstools? Is it reasonable to conclude that Americans possess a crass business appetite just because they are mettlesome, or to argue that they are hasty (say, in drawing conclusions) just because they are heated (say, in argument)?

There the questions break off. Moore knows how embarrassing it is, if you have been proud of your own precision, to discover that you have misapprehended something; it shames you to realize that you have not studied the object of your curiosity with sufficient attention. In contrast with the entertaining sequence of her travelogue-of-stereotypes, her parody of the British tourist-in-America, and her rapid questions, Moore couches in a single dry and damning sentence her own redeeming confession of past prejudice:

To have misapprehended the matter, is to have confessed that one has not looked far enough.

Indicting general prejudice (found world-wide and not least in herself) and admitting general fallibility, the poet asks by implication whether we Americans have tried to see an England larger than the one displaying only unimpressive rivers and thin threads of liturgical sound? Have the English tried to see us beyond our different pronunciation, our absence of enthusiasm for golf, our frequency of typographical errors, and our lack of acquaintance with foreign languages?

Another list follows, the very opposite of the initial intemperate list of superficial remarks from English observers and the ignorant stereotypes we ourselves might use in describing foreign countries in Europe or Asia. Moore's last list is a heterogeneous one, offering examples of what she calls "notable superiority." These — based on her own study and the learning of scholars — range from the wisdom of China (a contrast to citing its jade cockroaches) to the "discernment" of Egypt (harbinger of Western literacy), to the unsurpassed torrent of emotion in Hebrew verbs (more valuable than shorthand), to the nonchalance of the Compleat Angler (in Moore's excerpt from Walton beginning "I envy no man"). Such "notable superiority," Moore claims, bears flowers which will generate the eventual fruit of a country's cultural cornucopia. Addressing those who dismiss her cherished America, Moore asks a single logical question: If one hasn't yet "stumbled across" examples of such superiority in America, does it follow that it does not exist here? (The absurdity of generalizing from absence of evidence to evidence of absence is self-evident.) She appends an uninsistent truth: that such notable superiority "has never been confined to one locality." This irrefutable rebuke — superbly understated — disposes not only of the contemptuous English observer who prompted the poem, but also of Americans invoking petrified stereotypes of other cultures.

If, having followed Moore's argument and filled in all that is implied within it, we ask what kind of a poem "England" is, from what notion of poetry it must issue, we see that for Moore poetry must be heterogeneous to be interesting: it must admit learning, argument, allusion, inference, and conclusions, but it also must permit fantasy, comedy, satire, mockery, and uncircumscribed linguistic possibility. Jokes about literate cats and dogs are allowed to occupy the same art-space as Chinese snails and Chinese wisdom. The Compleat Angler's unworldly admiration for a fellow-fisherman can coexist with scholarly admiration of the "torrent of emotion" in the verbs of a non-English, non-European, non-Chinese language — Hebrew; the intellectual wit of calling individual ideograms "emotional shorthand" may be harbored next to a down-to-earth example of the trivial sonic phenomenon of the flat American "a" in "psalm." Moore's readers — warned by her deceptive touristic subterfuge that what seems a tender picture of rural England can evolve into a freewheeling farce on English snobbery, and develop in turn into an indictment of all human prejudice — discover at the same moment, on another plane, that a succession of equal four-line stanzas — even if they do not scan, even if they do not rhyme — can formally identify the object on the page as a poem. Unlike the primary aim of prose, which is logical exposition, the object of verse — defined as such by its formal patterning — is chiefly a display of the imagination delighting in its own activity.

In any writer, the drive to create dazzling play in the chosen medium is often accompanied, often somewhat later in the process of creation, by an equal need to fill a lack in the surrounding historical, ethical, or cognitive context. What, in the artist's view, does the contemporary world need to hear or to see? Along with aesthetic joy, a poem must offer, said Horace, something of use to the reader. At their best, Moore's crisp intuitions of fallible human nature, as they discover a moving analogy from her zoo of undomesticated animals, arrive at precisely such a seamless junction of wisdom and delight. Just as Moore was drawn to translate the fables of La Fontaine in which a beast-fable is followed by a moral, so she could rarely resist, within her exhibits of rarity or oddity, a kernel of philosophical epigram: "It has never been confined to one locality"; "we prove, we do not explain our birth."

Unmarried — and jesting, in her long poem "Marriage," that marriage takes "all one's criminal ingenuity to avoid" — Moore was, after her mother died, for the first time alone. Missing her mother and her deceased contemporaries, Moore made friends with the larger American world, writing poems about sports figures, including Muhammed Ali, jockeys, and baseball players. She wore, when she left her Brooklyn apartment for the city, an eccentric ensemble of a black tricorn hat and black cape. (Her first cape, in youth, was sewn by her mother, and wearing one as her distinguishing garment must have kept her mother's presence nearby.) She became something of a public pet, genially throwing out the first pitch to open the baseball season. In those later years, the conspicuous old woman photographed by the newspapers seems far from the young poet praised by Eliot or the dauntless editor of *The Dial*, which gave her, with its office, a five-year daily base among New York writers. Wallace Stevens and William Carlos

Williams found her an enchanting companion. "All great men," said Yeats, "are owls, scarecrows, by the time their fame has come." That may be true of great women, too.

Moore created a powerful and influential style, an inimitable one — although Auden and others imitated her use of syllables, instead of accents, to determine line-lengths; and Elizabeth Bishop, James Merrill, and Amy Clampitt were indebted to her rendition of the visual world and her unpredictable montages and collages of surface terrain. Later poets have both softened and sweetened her bristly or spiny poetic, smoothed her ungainly ostrich-gait. It still takes work to internalize a Moore poem — to look up its unfamiliar allusions to Erté or Chinese snails, to comb through its intricate syntax, to deduce which philosophical or psycholog-ical problem has generated its tight-knit emblem-illustrations. But after gaining a footing in Moore's irregular territory, one can arrive at a relish for the very oddities that originally seemed obstacles. The maze once entered and its center attained, one luxuriates in the sound-world of an apparently effortless chamber music.

And precisely because most protest-poems are by their content alone made unrelievedly earnest, a reader can be charmed by a poet's decision to choose the weapon of wit. The American Moore was not the only writer to feel the lash of British dismissal: the Irish, the Australian, the Welsh, the Caribbean writer felt it, too. The best parody of the maliciously patronizing English manner is D. H. Lawrence's corrosive poem on English hypocrisy, "The English are So Nice!" (Lawrence was Welsh, and his father was a miner: he was well acquainted with English condescension.) I quote his poem here only as an example of a protest-poem which, although resembling Moore's in intensity and comic bitterness, abandons the allusive for the apparently artless. After its deceptive opening lines with their third-person description of the English as "awfully nice," Lawrence's poem quickly devolves into a rendition of the truly awful sentiments of prejudice as they appear in bourgeois conversation. What that "niceness" conveys, its scorpion-sting — as experienced by the hapless human object of its aggression — appears as early as the sixth line and stings its object fatally in its lethal xenophobic conclusion:

The English are so nice
so awfully nice
they are the nicest people in the world.

And what's more, they're very nice about being nice
about your being nice as well!
If you're not nice they soon make you feel it.

Americans and French and Germans and so on
they're all very well
but they're not really nice, you know.
They're not nice in our sense of the word, are they now?

That's why one doesn't have to take them seriously.
We must be nice to them, of course,
of course, naturally —
but it doesn't really matter what you say to them,
they don't really understand — you can just say anything
        to them:
be nice you know, just be nice
but you must never take them seriously, they wouldn't
        understand.

Art Against Stereotype

Just be nice, you know! oh, fairly nice,
not too nice of course, they take advantage —
but nice enough, just nice enough
to let them feel they're not quite as nice as they might be.

The social convention of covering all possible situations with the "unobjectionable" word *nice* wears so thin, even to the ears of its English utterer, that the poem eventually slips into the openly prejudiced "not *really* nice," the disdainful "they wouldn't understand," and finally into the spiteful and fearful "they take advantage —."

Lawrence, the master of eloquence, exposes by apparently artless mimicry the appalling verbal poverty of the English middle class as they scorn and fear all foreigners, even English-speaking ones. Masquerading as one of the insular English, he betters them at their own game, while Moore, exhibiting foreign stereotypes of other cultures, shames American provinciality as well as English snobbery. Both poets, with their wit, hit their mark.

Any young woman scholar of my era encountered prejudiced male teachers and colleagues, but along with the prejudiced I encountered the kind and the just. Lyric poets writing protest poems risk simplifying the world into a melodrama of the good and the evil, thereby rendering their representations unreal. (It is of course an equally coarse assertion that claims that there were "very fine people on both sides.") Pure parody such as Lawrence's "The English Are So Nice" is by its very genre not obligated to justice of representation: justice is immediately perceived as the opposite of the parodic. But lyric poets of protest are obliged to incriminate themselves if their remarks about others' faults are to be believed. Moore redeems "England," in the end, by including in it a genuine — if impersonally put — confession of her own past stereotyping of the foreign. Unlike the believable poets, the prejudiced ones never include themselves among the sinners.

A Gift from Heaven

What makes you think
I can live in a room
from which you have removed
– admittedly with considerable tact –
one of the four walls?
I agree, the view has really improved
(not that you can see the Arno and the Ponte Vecchio
in the distance)
but is the (let's call it) "radical renovation"
sufficient for us to return,
in better spirits,
to the first act of the play?
And the four-syllable word on the wine label
and the meat in plum sauce
and the candles that (supposedly) repel mosquitos,
what exactly do they mean?
And the young waiter
with the thick accent,
out of which Russian novel
did he leap?
And the fact that Adorno,
as you tell me knowingly,
dined in Los Angeles
with Greta Garbo in 1944
and his dog Ali Baba (what a name!)
pissed on her book,

how does that alter the facts?
Can you hear the rustling of the leaves
and the voices of the children
going down our street
on their skateboards?
Do you realize that the message they are bringing
belongs to a future
you never imagined?

Close your eyes for a while.
It is often better
to look reality in the face
without trying to calculate
the number of minutes until the sun sets.
Besides, at this moment
the question is not
the specific sunset
but the gift we have been given.

"Lost years," did you say?
Don't be melodramatic.
Is there any paradise
that at the end of the dream
is not lost?

Blake in Paradise

Biographers and scholars agree:
he was mad.
But does it matter
whether he really used to see
angels dancing
in the trees in his garden,
or would spend long evening hours conversing
with Isaiah and Ezekiel?
Isn't it enough that that he left us
"Proverbs of Hell" and "Jerusalem"?

Shortly before closing his eyes
he asked for a piece of paper and a pencil
so that he could sketch for the last time
the face of his beloved Catherine.
Beneath her portrait
he noted with a trembling hand:
"I am certain He exists,
since You exist."

Delirious Passion

Each morning when you go out on the balcony
to enjoy your first coffee of the day
you face the same intolerable backdrop:
Delos reposing nonchalantly
in precisely the same place you left it yesterday.

How much you wish that nature,
just for once, would cast off for a while
its earnest attire
and, like a mischievous girl,
astonish you with her coquetry
by sending the sacred island
to the bottom of the sea –
so that your gaze would at last
reach the horizon
without tripping over some barren piece of land.

But she would disapprove
of such a *dramatische* development.
At night she reads Hölderlin in German,
memorizing all those Olympian verses
and believing that she wanders arm-in-arm
with Apollo himself
through the ruins of his temple.

How can you pick a quarrel with a god,
a hunk of a lover
who knows what secrets
a woman hides in her heart,
what she desires when she lies down naked in bed
and – let me not forget! –
who permanently holds a lyre in his hand?

If I were you
I would change islands,
or houses,
or at least balconies.

Still, Hölderlin is the last person to blame.
He went mad long before you,
and at least he signed his works
as Scardanelli
and not as Héloïse and Abelard.

Poetic License

For Anne Carson

In the second book of the *Iliad*, he calls him a mighty king:
λάσιον κῆρ – in Rieu's prose:
"Pylaemenes of the shaggy breast led the Paphlagonians".
In the Fifth Book, he decides to have him killed –
without too much fuss, in just two lines:
"the great spearman Menelaus son of Atreus struck him
       with a javelin,
which landed on his collar bone".
In the Thirteenth Book, however, he changes his mind,
and describes in a moving scene the death of Pylaemenes' son:
"Meriones shot at him with a bronze-headed arrow
and hit him on the right buttock. The arrow went clean
through his bladder and came out under the bone.
Harpalion collapsed forthwith, gasped out his life in the
       arms of his friends,
and lay stretched on the ground like a worm,
while the dark blood poured out of him and soaked the earth,"
and then has his weeping father
drive him on a chariot,
together with the other Paphlagonians, back to Troy,
"leaving his son's death unavenged".
In this episode he skips the usual phrase:
"Then night descended on his eyes".

It's his work after all.
It's not like he's accountable to anyone else.
He's the one that decides who lives, who dies.

Who should be resurrected.

*

When later he heard about Lazarus
he permitted himself a smile of satisfaction
at being some centuries ahead
in the art of funerary management.

302

Cycladic Idyll

Lower your eyes.
When beauty
invades your life with such force,
it can destroy you.
The two ants hurrying along
next to the soles of your feet
are burying their summer dreams
deep in the ground.
The load they are carrying
will not crush them.
They have measured their strength accurately.

Your shadow melts into the shade of the tree.
Black on black.
Guilt that must remain in the dark,
so as to go on defining you.
But the glare of those fragments
may still hold you.
You have no need of adjectives,
of devious subterfuge.
Every question is a desire.
Every answer (you know by now) is a loss.
Stay where you are standing.
In a while it will overtake you.
The clouds do not ask where,
they just continue on their way.

Translated by Peter Mackridge

CELESTE MARCUS

The Beehive

The ambition that burned in the breasts and the brushes of the immigrant artists at La Ruche was not enough to warm them on winter nights. Hunger is what lured them to Paris and hunger is what kept them there, a zealous hunger that fortified them against the physical hunger which incessantly rumbled in the bellies of the painters, the poets, and the musicians, many of them Jews, who clawed their way from their respective shtetls to the City of Light. La Ruche, which means The Beehive, was — and still is — a colony of humble artists' studios in the fifteenth arrondissement in Paris, near Montparnasse. La Ruche was among the many artist complexes in Montparnasse that together sheltered the École de Paris, which is what the French art critics christened the swarms of immigrants suddenly overflowing their academies and their galleries in the early decades of the twentieth century. The title distinguished the foreign contaminants from the École Française, which, according to street gossip as well as literary magazines, the emigres were polluting.

In a monograph on the painter André Dunoyer de Segonzac which appeared in *La Carnet de la semaine* in 1925, the art critic Louis Vauxcelles (himself a French Jew as well as a textbook *arriviste*, who was petrified that his unsavory Semitic brethren would upset his position in the art establishment) proclaimed that "a barbarian horde has rushed upon Montparnasse, descending [on the art galleries of] rue La Boétie from the cafes of the fourteenth arrondissement... these are people from 'elsewhere' who ignore and at their hearts look down on what Renoir has called the gentleness of the École Française — that is, our race's virtue of tact." (Note that anxious *our*.) The art critic Fritz Vanderpyl was a good deal nastier. In an article in 1924 entitled "Is There Such a Thing as Jewish Painting?" which appeared in the *Mercure de France,* he gnashed his teeth:

In the absence of any trace of Jewish art in the Louvre, we are nevertheless witnessing a swarming of Jewish painters in the past-war salons. The Lévys are legion, Maxime Lévy, Irene and Flore Lévy, Simon Lévy, Alkan Lévy, Isidore Lévy, Claude Lévy, etc... not to mention the Lévys who prefer to exhibit under pseudonyms, a move that would be quite in line with the ways of modern Jews, and without mentioning the Weills, the Zadoks, whose names one comes across on every page of the salon catalogues.

A year later the magazine *L'Art vivant* asked significant members of the Parisian art-sphere which ten living artists should be included in the permanent collection of a new museum of French modern art. The prominent Polish Jewish painter Moïse Kisling replied with commendable venom: "Simone Lévy, Leopold Lévy, Rudolph Lévy, Maxime Lévy, Irène Lévy, Flore Lévy, Isidore Lévy, Claude Lévy, Benoit Lévy, et Moise Kisling." The Jewish painters of Paris were a proud bunch.

Scandalous and indecorous and unconventional as they emphatically were, the School of Paris was still another of the many limbs of the French art world, and it shared vital organs with its more traditional counterparts. Like all artists in France at the time, these young rebels' careers were dependent on showing in salons. Academic *pompiers* such as William-Adolphe Bouguereau, the distinguished but kitschy painter who was president of the École des Beaux-Arts de Paris, maintained a tyrannical power over the standards of French art, imposing them most publicly by rejecting works that did not conform to the accepted canons from the official annual Salon of the Académie des Beaux-Arts. This stranglehold was momentously loosened in 1883. After having been rejected by the Salon three years earlier, the Impressionists and Post-Impressionists organized a Salon des Refusés (the second in twenty years), after which the Société des Artists Indépendants was founded. Cezanne and van Gogh were among the participants in the first Salon des Independants. Since this new salon had no jury, it lacked a wider prestige. As an alternative, the competitive Salon d'Automne was held for the first time in 1903, in the newly built Petit-Palais, which had been constructed for the World's Fair of 1900. Two years later Matisse, Derain, and their cohort famously exhibited paintings in hot violent colors, which prompted Vauxcelles, consistently averse to disruption, to call these artists *Fauves* or "wild beasts."

The painters at the Beehive, and more generally the School of Paris, plotted their progress into the establishment through their acceptance into the new salons. They were not really a "school," at least insofar as they shared no artistic theories or crusades. All the styles of their time, all the modernisms and all the traditionalisms, were represented under that octagonal roof. But they had other traits in common. While a certain degree of assimilation was inevitable for these newcomers from distant lands, their otherness never left them. Otherness was among the stimulating discomforts that all the members of the "school" shared. Many thousands of hours in Parisian cafes never drowned the aftertaste of their origins. This did not defeat them, though the history books do not honor their tenacity.

A handful from the School of Paris would carve their initials into the annals of art, but most of their names were uttered for the last time many decades ago. They made up a large part of the throng of Montparnasse in its golden years, of its tremendous artistic commotion, but they were erased and forgotten. Say a prayer for these minor artists, who consecrated themselves to art against circumstance; these men and women whose genius sputtered more often than it glowed, and did their best, which was often very good but rarely good enough; and say a prayer, too, for the open hands and hearts that welcomed and nurtured them, and could always spare a loaf or a smile for these destitute stewards of beauty.

"You left either famous or dead," Chagall said about La Ruche, into which he moved the fall of 1911. An overstatement, but barely. At the hive Chagall met Archipenko, Modigliani (a proud Sephardic Jew whose mother perpetuated the improbable origin story that her family was directly descended from Spinoza), Soutine, Kikoine, Kremegne, and Lipschitz, among the few whose names are familiar. The bohemian romance did not end well, and not only because success eluded so many. In the early 1940s history found its cruel way to the Beehive, and many of its artists were carted off to the notorious deportation center at Drancy in a northeast suburb of Paris and from there to their extinction in concentration camps in the east, mainly Auschwitz. (Chagall was long gone by then: when you could afford to get out, you got out.) The Yiddish literature about these people refers to them as "our martyred artists." But their destruction must not obscure the thrilling lives that they lived. This mélange of visionaries and dreamers made it to the nucleus of modern art in the early 1900s. They were more than extras in the high drama of the twentieth century; for a few decades they created a scrappy, infinitely exciting universe.

It is often said that La Ruche was designed by Gustave Eiffel himself. Like much of what is whispered about the School of Paris, this is a half-truth. The full tale begins with the World's Fair of 1900, held in Paris from April to October of that year, just over a decade after the international exhibition of 1889, for which Eiffel built his grand tower. (Dumas, Maupassant, Bouguereau, and Meissonier were among the many writers and artists who signed the protest against Eiffel's steel monstrosity, the "ridiculous tower dominating Paris like a gigantic black factory chimney... a dishonor to the city.") General Commissioner Alfred Picard, dubbed by the press the most important man in France, was determined that his exhibition in 1900 would exceed in brilliance and magnitude all its predecessors, and it did. Construction began eight years in advance, and included the Grand Palais, the Petit Palais, the Métro, the Gare d'Orsay, and the Pont d'Alexandre. The fairground spanned 543 acres and included pavilions representing forty-seven countries, all battling to demonstrate their technological and cultural preeminence. It was visited by fifty-one million people over the course of six months.

The world's first moving sidewalk, the first regular passenger trolleybus line, and an electrotrain ran through the exhibits. The Grande Roue de Paris ferris wheel, 96 meters high, was the tallest ferris wheel in the world at its opening. The fair also saw the first escalator which won first prize at the exposition, diesel engines, electric cars, dry cell batteries, electric fire engines, a telegraphone, and also the world's first matryoshka dolls. Thus France ushered in the new century by insisting again upon its status as the epicenter of the globe.

Reveling in the gargantuan brouhaha of the *fin de siècle,* the organizers and the attendees were of course blind to the radical political and social and cultural convulsions into which the world was about to be thrown. The boys whose blood would soon soak the Continent were mere toddlers. Einstein's theory of relativity, and its ramifications for the perception and understanding of the world, was sixteen years away. Philosophers and psychologists such as Henri Bergson and William James would soon describe human experience as essentially fractured and confused and improvisatory. Freud was poised to unleash the unconscious on European culture. The transformations that resulted from these upheavals helped to unsettle the stultifying art world as well. It created the conditions in which the creative tumult at La Ruche was possible.

When the fair was over, the city auctioned off many of the structures that had sprouted up around Paris since 1892.

Most of the others were demolished. In a remarkable stroke of magnanimity, however, the renowned (and hugely successful) sculptor Alfred Boucher, a friend of Rodin's and Camille Claudel's mentor, did the city, and the world, a favor: he bought several items from the municipal auction, including a building-sized octagonal wine rotunda that Eiffel had designed for the exposition, statues of costumed women from the Indochina pavilion, and a grand iron gate from the palace of women, all of which were dismantled and then reassembled on the Passage Dantzig in the fifteenth arrondissement. Boucher turned the hodgepodge of structures into La Ruche, which he called the Villa de Medici.

In fact there was little about the place reminiscent of the Medici. It consisted of bunks, studios, a gallery space, and large rooms into which artists could troop for weekly free life-drawing classes. The eight-sided building did indeed resemble a beehive. (Most of the people inside it certainly worked like bees.) Rent was cheap, and Boucher never made a fuss when it was late. Some of the tenants took unfair advantage — one artist managed to live on credit for twelve years, without producing a single painting or sculpture. A forty-minute walk to the storied cafes La Rotonde and Le Dôme, and an hour by foot from the École des Beaux Arts, La Ruche was well situated in the burgeoning bohemia of Montparnasse, which soon replaced Montmartre as the hotbed of the avant-garde. (The neighborhood sealed its new status when Picasso moved from Montmartre to Montparnasse in 1912.) The Beehive opened officially in 1902, and the Secretary of State for Fine Arts (a French position if ever there was one) attended the dedication ceremony, at which an orchestra played *La Marseillaise*.

The inside of La Ruche was circular, with a dim skylight

310

so weak it brightened only the top floor, which was therefore the most expensive. All the rest were cast in gloomy shadow unrelieved by the grimy windows that made up a wall of each studio. The sweaty stink of unwashed bodies — nobody mentions indoor bathrooms and the filth was infamous — mixed with the pungent scent of oils paints that filled the whole building. The misery was heaviest on the ground floor, where rats, roaches, screeching cats, and mangy dogs took shelter with the poorest tenants. The mattresses atop the iron beds were infested with bedbugs, the corridors and the staircases were dusty and stained. All were in a constant state of disorder, so much so that the whole place resembled the backstage of an abandoned theater; dirty busts, statues, vases, moldy fruit, and dead flowers cluttered the hallways, the detritus of innumerable still-life paintings. Every surface was splattered with paint. In the garden surrounding the building there were lime trees, chestnut trees, lilac bushes, and an enormous cherry tree that kept guard over the building like a potbellied gargoyle. From the neighboring slaughter-houses, where Chagall and others painted the condemned cows, bellowing cattle and grunting pigs were audible in the dorms.

In other words, if you were a penurious but determined painter, it was home. During the day sculptors and painters who did not live there would use the studio space. They had very little to do with the inhabitants who made up its ecosystem. Next to the main building, down a flight of dank mud-encrusted steps, there was a double cottage where Boucher kept his own studio and workshop. When he was not wandering the halls and peeking into the studios of the little colony that he had founded, checking on his bees, it was where he worked. Boucher liked to brag that he had influenced

Rodin, but his grateful if slightly condescending tenants wondered aloud whether the influence did not run in the opposite direction.

Word spread quickly amongst the immigrants with vivid imaginations and empty pockets, and La Ruche expanded considerably in the 1910s. Marc Chagall, Chaim Soutine, Michel Kikoine, Paul Kremegne, Fernand Léger, Alexander Archipenko, Henri Laurens, Paul-Albert Girard, and René Thomsen were among the tenants who benefited from Boucher's sanctuary. They were followed by many others of various nationalities, ideals, and dispositions, and Boucher assiduously bought up little huts, shacks, and hovels around the main edifice, into which his colony overflowed. There were nearly a hundred and forty workshops by the end. Writers such as the poet Blaise Cendrars (who wrote a poem about the place) and the art critic Maximilien Gauthier often visited. Rumors circulated that the socialist Adolph Joffé and even Lenin himself dropped by at one time. (It is certain that he and Trotsky frequented Le Dôme, one of the cafés in Montparnasse that would become a haunt for the circle of German artists from La Ruche, during his brief exile in Paris from 1909 to 1911.)

In the eternal battle between commerce and art, the shopkeepers and the restaurant owners surrounding the hive chose the losing side. Boucher knew that, more often than not, his artists ate and drank on credit. To repay this generous folly he converted a nearby house into a makeshift, dilapidated, and exceedingly romantic theater. Between two hundred and three hundred people could squeeze inside for the performances, and the entry fee was optional: everyone paid what they could. With the help of the city he organized productions, until he had the brilliant idea to invite undiscovered actors and directors to try their hand at running the show. The gambit was a wild success: renowned stars of the stage and early film such as Charles Le Bargy, Maurice de Féraudy (the father of Jacques de Féraudy), and Édouard Alexandre de Max had their start there. Marguerite Morena, Jacques Hébertot, and the heart-throb theater actor and movie star Louis Jouvet also appeared at La Ruche. Jouvet (who at that time spelled his name Jouvey) stuck around for several years. It was at La Ruche that he met Jacques Copeau, the theater director and founder of Théâtre du Vieux-Colombier, where Jouvet would go on to earn early celebrity. The next time you see *Quai des Orfèvres*, remember the Beehive.

The artists were dependent on one another for introductions to agents and buyers, and for charity (often reciprocal, since good and bad luck share a half life), and for hot tips about which restaurant owners got to work after the early morning bread had been delivered (thievery was a professional hazard). In 1914 the war deepened the mutual dependence. The art market slowed to a glacial pace, salons were postponed, art collectors' fists squeezed shut, and those who had received an allowance from relatives were suddenly on their own. The artists' stipends provided by the French government dwindled rapidly.

Yet creative solutions abounded. The Russian artist Marie Vassilieff, born in 1884, was responsible for one of them. Vassilieff was a revered figure in Montparnasse. She came to Paris in 1907, at which time, as she would tell you herself, she was unbearably beautiful. Legend has it that days after her arrival Henri Rousseau spotted her on a park bench and fell immediately in love. He proposed marriage, she declined —

bad breath, she explained. In 1908, when Matisse found an abandoned convent to use for a studio, he was stalked by a crowd of implacable groupies, most of whom were foreigners, including Vassilieff, and for two years the young master gave them grudging instruction. (This became known as "Matisse Academy.") From 1910 on, she exhibited her brightly colored cubist paintings regularly at the Salon d'Automne and the Salon des Independants. Vassilief co-founded and served as director of the Académie russe, where many of the artists of Montparnasse would go for free life-drawing classes. After she resigned owing to tensions with coworkers, she founded the Vassilieff Academy on Avenue du Maine. During the war she transformed her academy into a canteen where hungry artists could always find something to eat. A Swedish painter remembered that:

> The canteen was furnished with odds and ends from
> the flea market, chairs, and stools of different heights
> and sizes, including wicker plantation chairs with high
> backs, and a sofa against one wall where Vassilieff slept.
> On the walls were paintings by Chagall and Modigliani,
> drawings by Picasso and Léger, and a wooden sculpture
> by Zadkine in the corner. Vassilieff would put different
> colored papers around the lights to change the mood
> of the place. In one corner, behind a curtain, was the
> kitchen where the cook Aurelie made food for forty-
> five people with only a two-burner gas range and one
> alcohol burner. For sixty-five centimes, one got soup,
> meat, vegetable, and salad or dessert, everything of good
> quality and well-prepared, coffee or tea; wine was ten
> centimes extra.

Literary events, music shows, and legendary parties distracted the indigent artists from the bleak historical moment. These bashes, which bombinated with the chatter of many languages, would last until the early morning, since the police considered Vassilieff's canteen a private club and so did not impose a curfew. Matisse, Picasso, Modigliani, Soutine, Zadkine, Cendrars, Léger, the Swedish sculptor Ninnan Santesson, the Russian Marevna, and the Chilean Manuel Ortiz de Zárate were all regulars. Vassilieff, like everyone else, had a soft spot for Modigliani, which he tested regularly by wreaking havoc while grotesquely drunk. Marevna, who wrote a lively but not always reliable memoir of life at La Ruche, recalls one evening at the canteen when Modi (which is what everyone called him) stripped naked while reciting Dante to the frantic delight of giggling American girls.

When the war was finally over, and rationing ended and unemployment ebbed, the French capital reclaimed its glamorous cultural status. Woodrow Wilson became the first American president to visit Paris when he came for a six-month stay to assist in negotiating a new map of Europe. Ernest Hemingway, James Joyce, Josephine Baker, Ho Chi Minh, Leopold Senghor, and many other luminaries and eventual luminaries surged into the city. In Montparnasse especially, the revival was blinding. The streets buzzed and the wine flowed. Food was easier to come by. When Lucy, Aïcha, and KiKi — the famous artists' models of Montparnasse — stripped in studios and nightclubs across the city, they were fleshy and carefree. The great cafes had come back to life.

La Rotonde was acquired and expanded in 1911 by a man named Victor Libion, who ran it for the next nine years and was like a father to the artists of La Ruche, whom he would allow to sit all afternoon nursing the same small coffee. When they first arrived in Paris, Krémègne, Soutine, and Kikoïne, who had all studied together in Vilnius, or Vilna, as they would have called it, always sat at the same table. In fine weather, the celebrity model Aïcha would lounge on the chairs out front, and her boyfriend, the La Ruche resident Sam Granowsky, a Jewish painter known as "the cowboy" for his tall Stetson, along with the artists Mikhal Larionov, Natalia Concharova, and Adolphe Féder (another denizen of the hive), would clean the cafe to earn extra cash.

Even when the bombs stopped, the memory of horror tinctured the merriment and the swaying hips in and around La Ruche. The School of Paris was in some sense essentially melancholy. These artists from elsewhere had intimate knowledge of hardship. They remembered it from their childhoods, and at La Ruche the hard times persisted for almost all of them. At their most lighthearted they were never silly, even the ones who dabbled in Surrealism. The Soviet novelist and journalist Ilya Ehrenburg recalled that "we stayed at La Rotonde because we were attracted by each other. The scandals were not what appealed to us, and we were not even inspired by new and bold aesthetic theories. Quite simply... the feeling of our common distress united us." He was speaking specifically of the Jewish artists who had come to Paris to escape the pogroms ravaging the villages from which their families sent them anguished letters. Yiddish writers such as Sholem Asch, Oyzer Varshavksi, and Joseph Milbauer used to drop by La Rotonde, perhaps on their way from or to the Triangle Bookshop, a Yiddish bookstore and small publisher just a short walk away.

A mathematician named Kiveliovitch ran The Triangle Press and Bookstore at number 6 Rue Stanislas. In a former life he had been a student of the legendary French mathematician Jacques Hadamard. To attract the La Ruche crowd, the Triangle published a series of booklets about famous Jewish artists, short monographs with black and white reproductions. Jacques Loutchansky, Adolf Féder, Leopold Gottlieb, Moïse Kisling, Pinchus Krémègne, Jacques Lipschitz, Marc Chagall, and Abraham Mintchine came regularly to leaf through the stacks in the single narrow room. Some of the artists of the Beehive and its surroundings became subjects for the monographs, which are now bibliophilic rarities.

One day the Marxist-Zionist activist Y. Nayman sprinted into the store and breathlessly announced that the previous Sunday he had seen the Jewish sculptor Marek Szwarc kneeling in prayer at the Sacre-Coeur in Montmartre. A scandal! Szwarc had fallen "off the path," which came as a surprise to his coreligionists. Jewishness, for most of the Jews in Montparnasse, was mainly an identity imposed upon them by anti-Semitic prejudice, but Szwarc's Jewishness had been fuller. He practiced Judaism, and was an active member of the small observant cohort at La Ruche. For a few years in the early 1910s, he, Henri Epstein, Moissey Kogan, and other yarmulke-clad residents of the hive founded and ran *Makhmadim* (which means "delicacies" or "precious things" in Yiddish and Hebrew), a publication dedicated to defining Jewish art, which was funded by the influential Russian art critic Vladimir Stassov. The series had no text and featured only reproductions of drawings by Jewish artists. The issues were thematically devoted to occasions on the Jewish calendar, such as the Sabbath and the holidays. This was an attempt to give some substance to the appellation "Jewish School," so often used by the critics of the period. This series is now even more rare than the Triangle's publications.

The question of Jewish identity at the Beehive is complicated. Most of the Jews at La Ruche were not interested in

317

developing a uniquely Jewish style of art, whatever that might mean. National identity united them, just as national identity united the Russians and the Italians and the Americans, who all moved together like schools of fish. (In the Jewish case, of course, the national identity was a sense of people-hood, not a derivation from a nation-state.) On the landings of the staircases at the hive arguments would break out in all languages — Yiddish, Spanish, Russian, Japanese, Polish, German — about the merits of fauvism, about the trajectory and the limitations of cubism or surrealism, about Chardin, Corot, Cezanne, Rembrandt, and so on. It has been reported that often no one bothered to listen to what anyone else was saying, but every once in a while someone committed that fatal mistake and fist fights would follow. An artist needed a group with which to argue.

One such group, a circle of German Jews, claimed the cafe Le Dôme as their perch in 1903. Le Dôme, just across the street from La Rotonde, was founded in 1898, and was in its many years haunted by artists and writers such as Kandinsky, Henry Miller (who at one point lived in the apartment below Chaim Soutine), Cartier-Bresson, Beckett, de Beauvoir, Sartre, and many others. It was there, such a long way from "the old country," that the young Jewish painters sat and did their business. Art dealers such as Henri Bing and Alfred Flechtheim would meet them at Le Dôme for office hours. They were there so often that Apollinaire dubbed them *Les Dômiers*, despite the fact that bands of Scandinavian and Dutch painters also had their own corners in the same cafe. *Les Dômiers* were more successful in Germany than in France: in 1911 Paul Cassirer showed the group's work in Berlin and in 1914 Flechtheim held an exhibition in Dusseldorf called *Der Dome*. He described the group as "foreign artists living in Paris who met in the same cafe and who loved Paris." Pluralize "cafe" and one has as good a definition of the School of Paris as ever there was.

They also all worshiped the same women, and regurgitated the same bits of gossip, and they stumbled into and out of the same parties, delirious and semi-conscious hours later. One of the most notorious of these bacchanals began on August 12, 1917 and wound down in the wee hours of the morning four days later. It was the marriage celebration of two artists — Renée Gros and notorious Polish-Jewish wild man Moïse Kisling. Gros had spotted Kisling on the street the previous year, found out where he lived, and knocked on his studio door. The nuptial bash began at the restaurant Leduc, moved to La Rotonde, reverberated off the walls of several nearby brothels, and culminated in the Kislings' tiny apartment, into which swarms of guests poured into the ensuing debauchery. Max Jacob recited poetry, mimicking esteemed poets of the day, and Modigliani wrenched the bedsheet off the bridal bed, wrapped himself in it, and recited lines from *Julius Caesar* as Caesar's ghost. Renée shrieked and chased him from the room when she recognized his costume. Three days later Kisling reported that Modigliani had been discovered entirely naked sprawled on the Boulevard Montparnasse.

His wedding ranks among the most outrageous of Kisling's exploits, but it does not top the list. A few years earlier, on June 12, 1914, inflamed with rage regarding a mysterious "question of honor," Kisling challenged the artist Leopold Gottlieb to a duel. The Mexican cubist Diego Rivera (who years later would abandon the artist Marevna and their love child, move back to Mexico, and marry Frida Kahlo) served as Gottlieb's second. Early in the morning the small group gathered by the bicycle racetrack at the Parcs des Princes. The two men fired one shot each and then switched to swords. Tempers flared and the duel

319

lasted an hour, ending only when the large crowd that had by then accumulated forced the two men apart. Gottlieb escaped with no more than a cut on the chin, and Kisling with one on the nose, which he called "the fourth partition of Poland." Magazines and newspapers printed the story complete with pictures that very evening.

Nearly two decades later, when the clouds darkened and the black curtain fell, Kisling was one of the lucky ones. He volunteered for French army service, then fled to America when the French surrendered and the Nazis occupied France. Until 1946 the Kislings lived next door to Aldous Huxley in southern California. When peace was declared Kisling and his family moved back to France, where he died in his home in 1956. The Nazis failed to destroy his paintings, as they did those of so many of his friends. His works now hang in museums in France, America, Japan, Switzerland, and Israel.

Many of his peers, however, were murdered. These are some of their stories.

Moissey Kogan was born in Bessarabia on March 12, 1879. A precocious childhood interest in chemistry gave way to a passion for drawing and sculpture, which led him to the Academy of Fine Arts in Munich in 1903. The great art critic Julius Meier-Greafe, who was instrumental in introducing the achievements of Manet, Cézanne, van Gogh, and other painters of their time, encouraged Kogan to make a pilgrimage to Paris and visit Rodin, which he did in 1905. Rodin advised the young artist to dedicate his life to sculpture. Three years later Kogan returned to Paris and settled down at La Ruche, where he joined *Les Dômiers*. Kogan's work evinces the influence of Rodin and Maillol, both of whom admired him. Like Rodin and Maillol, Kogan's bodies are full, fleshy, sensuous, and simultaneously austere and formally pure. Most of his works depict nude female figures. In every form — drawing, woodcuts, textile and, primarily, sculpture — his line is consistently delicate without sacrificing force. Terra-cotta, bronze, plaster, and wood were his preferred mediums. Kogan eventually became one of the greatest French neoclassical sculptors. His work was admitted into the illustrious Salon d'Automne for the first time in 1907, after which he served regularly on its jury. In 1909 he exhibited at all three exhibitions of the Neue Künstlervereinigung München (NKVM) in Munich, where he became close with Jawlensky and Kandinsky. In 1925 he was elected vice president of the sculpture committee of the Salon d'Automne, a great honor for an emigre artist. He kept a studio near La Ruche at the Cité Falguière (where Modigliani and Soutine both once lived) from 1926 until his death in 1943. In 2002, art historians in Germany discovered Kogan's name on a list of deportees to Auschwitz. The official documents that would have detailed the circumstances of his death were destroyed by the Nazis during their evacuation and liquidation of the camp. It is a matter of record, however, that Kogan was on Convoy 47 from Drancy to Auschwitz. He, along with 801 others, were likely taken to the gas chambers upon arrival on February 13, 1943. Many of his works were destroyed by the Nazis in their "Degenerate Art" campaign.

George Kars was born in Kralupy, Germany in 1882. When he was eighteen years old, he left home to study art with Heinrich Knirr and Franz von Stuck in Munich. He traveled to Madrid in 1905, where he met Juan Gris and was deeply influenced by the works of Goya and Velasquez. In 1908 he settled in Montmartre. He spent the First World War on the

Galician front and in Russian captivity. At the end of the war he returned to Paris, where he renewed friendships with many residents of La Ruche, including Chagall. Kars had the refined dexterity of an academic painter, but his works are spiced with the styles that dominated Paris in his day — styles which he managed to synthesize seamlessly. Goya's and Velasquez's rich blacks darken still-lifes and portraits that also bear the influence of Cézanne. He was enriched by cubism but not overwhelmed by it. His portraits especially display his skills as a colorist. His most exciting works are his drawings; some look so energetic it is as if he just put down his pen. When the Nazis occupied Paris, Kars fled first to Lyon and then to Switzerland. In 1945 he killed himself by jumping out of the fifth-floor window of his hotel, likely after hearing that many of his relatives had been murdered by the Nazis. When his widow died in 1966, his atelier was sold at auction. Many of his paintings were acquired by the French collector Pierre Levy and the Swiss collector Oscar Ghez. When Ghez died in 1978 he bequeathed 137 works in his collection, Kars' among them, to the University of Haifa.

Rudolf Lévy was born in Germany in 1875. He enrolled in carpentry school but left to study painting with the artist Heinrich von Zügel at the School of Fine Arts in Munich in 1899. Lévy moved to Paris in 1903, where he joined *Les Dômiers*. He studied at Matisse's academy from 1908 to 1910, and then took over as head of the academy when Matisse left. Lévy would often return to Germany, where he befriended Alfred Flechtheim, who exhibited the *Dômiers* many times in his gallery. During the First World War he happened to be in Germany and was conscripted into the German army. When the war was over he returned to Paris, but traveled often to North Africa where he befriended Max Ernst and Oskar

Kokochka. In addition to painting, Lévy was a gifted writer, and wrote novels and poetry in German and French. When the Nazis came to power Lévy found himself in Germany, but moved swiftly to Majorca, and then to the United States. In 1937 he visited Naples with other German artists and remained in Italy for the next two years. He was in Florence in 1939, attempting to escape to America, when SS officers arrested him and transferred him to Milan. On April 5, 1944 he was deported to Auschwitz in Convoy 9. He was murdered five days later. Most of his paintings and writings were destroyed by the Nazis.

Roman Kramsztyk was born in Warsaw in 1885. He studied painting in Cracow for a year in 1903, where he befriended several artists including Henryk Kuna and Leopold Gottlieb. Several years later these men would together form the Society of Polish Artists, known as Rytm. Kramsztyk studied at the School of Fine Arts in Munich before moving to Paris where, in 1911, his work was accepted at the Salon d'Automne. He lived in Paris for four years at the start of the first war, after which he would spend the rest of his life traveling between Paris and Poland, where he became quite famous. His work was entered in the painting event at the art competition in the Summer Olympics in 1929. Kramsztyk was visiting family in Warsaw when the Germans invaded Poland in 1939. His fate was sealed. In October of the following year, when the Warsaw Ghetto was established, Kramsztyk, along with all other Jewish residents of the city, was imprisoned within its walls. There he assiduously documented the ugliness in a sketchbook. These sketches of the ghetto are the most haunting and lasting of all his works. In one drawing, gasping children with hollow cheeks cling to a father with dead eyes; they are delicately, achingly rendered. In another the skeletal head of a young

323

boy staring hopelessly into space is conveyed with Durer-like grace. In that hell, while doing his grim duty to document the extermination of his own people, frenzied colors and contorted perspectives, all the Parisian innovations, were of no use to Kramsztyk. He drew what he saw. Sometime between August 6, 1942 and August 10, 1942, during the liquidation of the ghetto, he was shot and killed by a Ukrainian SS officer.

Adolphe Feder was born on July 16, 1886 in Berlin. He became involved in the Bund Labor Movement in 1905, as a result of which he was forced to flee Berlin for Geneva, where he remained briefly before moving to Paris in 1908. There Feder became been one of the most active members of La Ruche. He studied at Académie Julian and then with Matisse at his academy. In the 1920s he did illustrations for *Le Monde* and *La Presse*, and for books by Rimbaud and Joseph Kessel. When the Second World War broke out, he remained in France, and joined the underground in Paris. He and his wife Sima were betrayed, and they were arrested on June 10, 1942. The two of them were interned for four months in a military prison on the rue du Cherche-Midi in Paris. Four months later Féder was transferred to Drancy. There he managed to produce many oil-pastel drawings and watercolors of life in the internment camp. Féder's landscapes and still-lifes that predate his internment at Drancy show Cezanne's influence, though Féder preferred hotter and more luscious colors. But the heat disappears in his works from the internment camp. Perhaps this was due to a lack of supplies, though there was in fact a place to buy paints inside Drancy. Féder was not an exceptional draftsman, he was an illustrator, but his rudimentary skill somehow makes his drawings from 1942 and 1943 impossibly moving. His Drancy works differ in medium, color, subject, and location, but each person depicted has the same crushed expression. There is no light in their eyes, nor is there hope, or anger, or even sadness. These are, without exception, portraits of despair. Feder was deported to Auschwitz, where he was killed on December 13, 1943. Sima Féder survived the war and donated a number of his drawings to Beit Lohamei Hagetaot, or the Ghetto Fighters Museum, in Israel.

There are many more such biographies from La Ruche. In 1942 and 1943, the École de Paris was decimated. At the Beehive, life, like art, went on, as it did in the rest of the cold world.

LEON WIESELTIER

Christianism

Under new management, Your Majesty:
Thine.
JOHN BERRYMAN

I

"And the king went up to the house of the Lord, and all the men of Judah and all the inhabitants of Jerusalem with him, and the priests, and the prophets, and all the people, both small and great; and he read in their ears all the words of the book of the covenant which was found in the house of the Lord. And the king stood by a pillar, and made a covenant before the Lord, to walk after the Lord, and to keep his commandments and his testimonies and his statutes with all their heart and all their soul, to perform the words of this covenant that were written in this book. And all the people stood to the covenant." A great awakening took place in the kingdom of Judah in the seventh century BCE, or so the king intended it to be. Josiah was the sixteenth king of the kingdom of Judah, which included Jerusalem, the rump state that remained in the wake of the secession of the ten tribes after the death of Solomon. He ruled for thirty-one years, from 640 to 609. Three centuries earlier, not long after the disintegration of the Davidic kingdom, his birth had been foretold by a strange unnamed prophet, who predicted ("O altar! O altar!") that Josiah would be a great reformer. The Bible records — there are two accounts, in 2Kings and 2Chronicles — that he came to the throne at the tender age of eight, and eight years later, "when he was still a lad," the young monarch began to "seek after the God of his forefather David." It appears that there followed four years of intense spiritual work, because it is reported that Josiah began the religious reform of his kingdom in the twelfth year of his reign.

The Josian reformation, his *rappel a l'ordre*, proceeded in stages. It is a dramatic tale. It began with a ferocious campaign against idolatry, which involved the physical destruction of pagan statues and altars not only in his realm but also beyond — a "purification" of the entire land of Israel. (The recent weakening of the Assyrian power to the north emboldened the Judean king to extend his campaign beyond his borders.) He also uprooted Israelite places of worship, with the objective of what historians like to call the centralization of the cult — the re-establishment of Jerusalem, and more specifically the Temple, as the only legitimate site of Jewish priestly rites and Jewish sacrifice. In his twenty-eighth year on the throne, in accordance with his plan, Josiah began a massive renovation of the Temple. It was during this project that lightning struck. As often happens on construction sites, an antiquity was found — in this instance, an old scroll. It was the book of Deuteronomy, which was Moses' valedictory summation of the Biblical commandments and his ethical testament to his people. When the scroll was read to the king, he rent his garments and cried out in anguish at how much had been forgotten. He then summoned the population of Judah, high and low, to the Temple and read the ancient scroll to them, and announced a new covenant, a grand restoration, which was then marked by a spectacular Passover celebration at the Temple. Judging by the scriptural accounts, which is all the evidence that we have for these events, it was an electrifying moment. Zeal was in the air.

The shocking element of this tale is that Deuteronomy, fully a fifth of the divine revelation at Sinai, the climax of the Torah, was unknown in Israel. How much more of the tradition had been lost — or more accurately, shunned and neglected and indifferently consigned to oblivion? Idolatry, and the cruelty of some of its practices, was widespread. Josiah was himself preceded and succeeded by idolatrous kings. When one reads the Hebrew verses carefully, it becomes clear that the emotion that overwhelmed Josiah when he heard Moses' farewell address for the first time was not so much guilt as panic. For if Deuteronomy was unknown to the Jews of the time, then so were many of the fundamentals of the religion, which meant that a colossal delinquency, a terrible fall, a vast collective iniquity, had taken place. The king's first feeling was fear. "Great is the wrath of the Lord that is poured out upon us, because our fathers have not kept the word of the Lord, to do after all that is written in this book." This explains the vigor, and the violence, of his correction. When Josiah reflected that God is just, he trembled for his country.

The interpretation of idolatry is one of the largest themes in the history of religion. At stake in its proper definition is the distinction between true and false faith — assuming, of course, that the veracity of belief is still a matter of consequence to believers, which is increasingly no longer the case. The term itself is pejorative: an idol, however it is construed, is *ipso facto* false. I was raised to recoil from the term, and to admire the many smashings of the many idols that recur throughout the ancient history of my religion. The smashers were my childhood heroes, Josiah included. It was not until I studied the history of art that I began to grasp the ugliness of iconoclasm, the brutality of it, its cost to culture. I remember the dissonance that I experienced two decades ago on the day that the Taliban blew up the monumental Buddhas of Bamyan, because the government had declared the statues to be idols. But this was what our righteous Jewish kings did, and the Lord was pleased! (I had a similarly disquieting experience when I first watched a video on Youtube of a public stoning by the Taliban and thought back to the punishment of *seqilah,* or stoning, mandated by Jewish law in capital crimes.) Regarded politically, the definition of an idol is: another person's object of worship. Idolatry is your religion, not mine.

There is nothing, of course, that could mitigate the practice of child sacrifice, but its moral offense is obviously bigger and more universal than the sin of following strange gods. So let us — anachronistically, to be sure, but we often interpret Scripture in the light of ideas that were developed long after it — pause to think kindly for a moment about ancient idolaters. They were not all savage killers. They were ordinary men and women, living vulnerably in the world, in families and communities, with needs and fears and sufferings, and they took their troubles — erroneously but sincerely — to sacralized carvings of wood and stone, and to religious author-ities whom — erroneously but sincerely — they believed had the power to help them. Folk religion (which the monothe-

329

isms have certainly not been spared) is one of the primary human expressions. Its coarseness represents the best that the theological imaginations of many people can accomplish: religion is not solely, or mainly, the province of intellectuals, much as it sometimes pains me to say so. I am the unlikely owner of an ancient Hittite idol from Canaan in the third millennium BCE, about three inches tall, finely made of clay — a domestic idol consisting of a single flat body with two heads, one male, one female, presumably designed as an amulet of happy conjugality. On the same shelf, to its right, as a challenge to this icon of domesticity, sits a small clay mask of Dionysus, from Paestum in the second century C.E. When I look at them, I see illusion, beauty, difference, and humanity. Pity the faith that cannot withstand the sight of them.

All this, as I say, is an anachronistic way of looking — but not completely. As Hume observed, the multiplicity of the gods in polytheistic religions inculcated a climate of tolerance, whereas the exclusiveness of the monotheisms had precisely the opposite social and political effect. The ancient world was violent, but not owing to holy wars. State power availed itself of many divinities and many cults. By contrast, the human costs of the mono in monotheism have been incalculable. (It was not until modernity that we learned of atheism's equally hideous costs. Evil has a home everywhere.) If it is appropriate to speak of religious pluralism in the ancient world, then it is also appropriate to describe Josiah's (and Asa's and Hezekiah's) extirpation of the idols as a war against pluralism. Or more pointedly, as a war against what democrats and liberals believe. Our models are not to be found in Kings and Chronicles.

Yet the post-liberals of our day find them there. A few years ago a group of Catholic post-liberals founded a website, which has expanded into books and podcasts, called *The Josias*. Josias is Latin for Josiah. (The Hebrew original, Yoshiyahu, most likely means "healed by God.") The first editor of *The Josias,* Edmund Waldstein, is a Cistercian monk in Austria who — judging by his own contributions to his journal — is a sophisticated theologian, as are some of the other contributors. I have now read a good deal of *The Josias* and I can report that, except when it surrenders to a genuinely foul invective about what it abhors — abhorrence is one of its main activities — its writings have all the rigor, and all the charm, of dogmatics. In its way it reminds me of orthodox Marxist discourse, in which fine points of doctrine are scrupulously examined without any interest in the scrupulous examination of their philosophical foundations. The difference between theology and philosophy is that philosophy inspects the foundations, whereas theology merely builds on them. How serious can thinking be when its own premises are protected from it?

As in all doctrinaire writing, the writings of these post-liberals, of all post-liberals, has a settled and self-congratulatory tone, and expresses the mutual admiration of a quasi-conspiratorial fraternity. (Are there are any women among them?) They are the club of the just. The motto of *The Josias* is *non declinavit ad dextram sive ad sinistram,* "to incline neither right nor left." This may sound like an invigorating assertion of intellectual independence, until one recalls that it is also the title of the definitive historical study of the rise of fascist ideology in France. "Neither right nor left" was the motto of a crack-up, of a philosophical desperation. The purpose of *The Josias,* its founding editor has written, is "to become a 'working manual' of Catholic political thought." But not all Catholic political thought. It is the organ of a particular school, known as integralism. Here is Father Waldstein's explication of the concept: "Catholic Integralism is a tradition of thought that, rejecting the liberal separation of politics from concern with the end of human life, holds that political rule must order man to his final goal. Since, however, man has both a temporal and an eternal end, integralism holds that there are two powers that rule him: a temporal power and a spiritual power. And since man's temporal end is subordinated to his eternal end, the temporal power must be subordinated to the spiritual power." Or in the less reflective words of an American integralist, "the state should recognize Catholicism as true and unite with the Church as body to her soul."

Premises, premises. The Catholic post-liberals are animated by a crushing sense that we, America and the West, have fallen. The feeling of fallenness is not theirs alone: it is one of the few things that unites this disunited country, though we differ in our preferred heights. For the integralists, whose very name suggests that the rest of us are disintegrated, what we have lost is the magnificent unity of church and state. That is the fissure that infuriates them, that they wish ruthlessly to repair. They are wounded holists; yet another bunch of moderns with a burning hunger for the whole. They detest "the personal-ization of religion," as if there are no religious collectivities and religious institutions and religious movements in our liberal polity, as if social domination and political control are necessary conditions of spiritual fulfillment. It is important to understand who were the authors of the abomination that the American integralists wish to repeal. Whereas some of them can live with aspects of Karl Marx — neither right nor left, remember — it is finally James Madison whom they cannot abide. He, after all, was the diabolical author of the separation, and Jefferson, and Mason, and the other founding fathers of the American dispensation. (And Roger Williams, the founding grandfather, whose banishment from the highly integrated Massachusetts Bay Colony marked the inauguration of the separation.) Integralism as an ideology originated in late nineteenth-century Europe, particularly in France, in the Action Francaise of Charles Maurras (the American integralists remind even the editor of *First Things* of Maurras, and also of the Catholic phalangists of Franco's Spain); but now Maurras has been pitted against Madison. What a villain Madison was!

I call these Christians Christianists, in the way that we call certain Muslims Islamists. Christianism is not the same as Christianity, just as Islamism is not the same as Islam. (There are Jewish parallels in Israel.) Christianism is a current of contemporary Christianity, of the political Christianity of our time, a time in which religions everywhere have been debased by their rampant politicization. The Christianists, who swan around with the somewhat comical heir of an avant-garde, are in one respect completely typical of their day: they are another group in our society that judges governments and regimes and political orders by how good they are for *them*. This selfishness, which is a common feature of identity, is as tiresome in its religious versions as it is in its secular ones; it is an early form of contempt, and extremely deleterious to the social unity that the Christianists fervently profess to desire.

I am not a Catholic. I am an ardently Pelagian Jew. I would prefer not to intervene in the disputations of a church that is not my own. The problem is that these are also the disputations of a country, and a civilization, that is my own. The ideas and the programs and the fantasies of the Christianists bear upon the lives of citizens who are not Christians, who answer to other principles. I will give an example. In an ambiguous essay on immigration that treads warily between liberalism and populism, Father Waldstein remarks: "After the horrors of the World Wars of the twentieth century, a new

333

ideal of global solidarity founded in a secular, liberal conception of human rights came to the fore. This aridly rationalistic liberalism, however, cannot provide true universal solidarity, which can only be found in the Social Kingship of Christ." Never mind, for now, that the "arid" secular liberal conception of human rights, going all the way back to Kant's sublime idea of a universal right to hospitality, has been infinitely more effective in aiding and sheltering immigrants, in taking in the poor and the weak, than the ethno-nationalist regimes that the post-liberals celebrate, which scorn them outright. The fact that the vast majority of the refugees in Europe are not Christians has dissuaded these governments from acting on the Social Kingship of Christ. Would they help my kind off the dinghy and on to their land? When I read Waldstein's words, I think: those words are not for me. They are, by implication, against me. They cast me outside the circle of universal solidarity, an insulting ban, because for me the notion of the Social Kingship of Christ is nonsense. He is not my king. Such a ground cannot compel my assent. They must give me a better reason to repudiate liberal immigration policy, especially as I hold that we must give sanctuary to more of the miserable. The Christianists can do anything they wish with their church, but they cannot do anything they wish with their country. They must respond to the objections and the anxieties of their non-Christian and non-integralist brothers and sisters. When I see them palling around with Viktor Orban and extolling Nigel Farage as "the defining mind of our era," their business becomes my business.

II

In these times it is common to hear that everything is broken. As an expression of anxiety, the slogan must be accepted. As an analysis of what ails us, it is plainly wrong. Everything is not broken. Some things are, some things are not. The last thing we need in this crisis is to surrender our sense of the particulars and the possibilities. The belief in brokenness, however, has enjoyed a long career in the history of religious and political thought. In those worldviews in which brokenness is the most salient characteristic of the cosmos and the person, the existence of the many elements, the multiplicity of the parts, the clutter of the pieces, is regarded as a problem, a catastrophe, a punishment for transgression, a fate from which we must be redeemed. There is an overwhelming presumption in favor of the one over the many. Every separation is a wound, a crack, an exile, a tear in the fabric, a setback to be overcome. Once there was unity; now it is no more; may it come again soon, amen. Among the adherents of such totalistic views of life, it never occurs to anyone that perhaps multiplicity is the natural condition of the world — that it is not the problem but the solution. They do not acknowledge that the primary fact about anything is individuation: it is this and not that, it is itself and not another thing. In religious language: my soul is mine alone. Individuation is not a writ of loneliness, though loneliness may be one of its results; it is a writ of specificity, of potential. It is how we begin and how we end; what we are before we belong, while we belong, and after we belong. In a life of joinings and partings, it remains constant and irreducible. Attempts to deny it or to flee it are usually disastrous. The scanting of individuation, the attempts to amalgamate the individual soul out of its distinctiveness and to dissolve it into an imaginary whole, all the communitarian ideologies of integration, have often brought misery into the world. Surely there are recesses of the soul that public affairs ought not to reach — or is that the "privatization of religion"? So many innocent people have been hurt by other peoples' feelings, and theories, of loneliness.

Integralism is not a post-liberal innovation, of course. Its modern origins, as noted, were in the Action Francaise of the hateful Charles Maurras, whose motto was *"politique d'abord!"* But there were also non-reactionary versions of the integralist enterprise, most notably the "integral humanism" of Jacques Maritain, who began as a supporter of Maurras but in 1926 revised his views and advocated a Christian democracy that promoted the creative forces of the person — "the holy freedom of the creature" — acting in history. Maritain's integralism called for a Christendom that would "correspond to the period into which we are entering," and in a calm tone of constructive realism he renounced the dream of a new unification of altar and throne, of the sacred and the secular. He was explicit about the pluralistic nature of his integralism: "Civil society is made up not only of individuals, but also of particular societies formed by them, and a pluralist polity allows these particular societies the greatest autonomy possible." Reading Maritain's large-hearted pages, one is struck by the meanness, the stridency, the resentment, that disfigures the pronouncements of many post-liberal integralists. Our Christianists are sometimes so unChristian.

I was first introduced to the rich and troubling intellectual universe of twentieth-century French Catholicism, to its epic struggle with the relations of the sacred and the secular, by a small and beautiful book by Jean Danielou called *Prayer as a Political Problem,* which appeared in 1965. Danielou was a Jesuit and a cardinal, and a member of the Académie Française; a towering scholar who was one of the fathers of modern Patristic studies; the interlocutor of Bataille and Hyppolite and Sartre on the subject of sin; an "expert" invited by Pope John XXIII to participate in the deliberations of Vatican II. Some

336

of the post-liberal Catholics refer occasionally to Danielou's book. *Prayer as a Political Problem* is one of the primary documents of the collision of religion with modernity. It is a deep and deliberate book: "for me, the sphere of the spiritual is as rigorous a discipline as that of any of the profane sciences." I have given Danielou's book, as a cautionary gift, to Jewish friends wrestling with similar perplexities. This little volume is a precious statement of what I do not believe, and it is an honor to argue with it.

Danielou begins by noting the "incongruity in the juxtaposition of a private religion and an irreligious society," which he regards as the lamentable norm in modern Western societies. The obvious course of action is to relieve religion's confinement to the private realm and find a way to release it into the public realm — "the extension of Christianity to an immense multitude, which is of its very essence." But Danielou, at least at first, does not seem to harbor holistic aspirations. "How are society and religion to be joined," he asks, "without either making religion a tool of the secular power or the secular power a tool of religion?" A splendid question! The frontiers are not trespassed. It has an air of patience and friendship. There is no program for transforming the sacred and the secular into one thing. The objective seems to be co-existence, with boundaries and a generous understanding of the realms.

But soon there follows a less splendid question. "What will make the existence of a Christian people possible in the civilization of tomorrow?" And he continues: "Our task is to discover what those conditions are which make a Christian people." What does Danielou mean by "a Christian people"? A people composed entirely of Christians? But there is no such people, at least none that conforms to any national borders. Though he has some skeptical things to say about the separationist arrangement, Danielou makes a resounding defense of religious liberty. Yet slowly his argument creeps disappointingly towards holism, and on strangely practical grounds. "Experience shows that it is practically impossible for any but the militant Christian to persevere in a milieu which offers him no support...Christians have need of an environment that will help them. There can be no mass Christianity outside Christendom." And more generally: "Only a few would be able to find God in a world organized without reference to him." In other words, to be a Christian somewhere there must be Christianity everywhere. Otherwise heroism would be required for faith.

Danielou makes the issue more concrete with the case of prayer. "Prayer is a personal relationship with God," he writes. "Does it not belong strictly to personal life? It is true that it does, but it is also true that the full development of this personal life is impossible unless certain conditions obtain." He concludes that "the civilization in which we find ourselves makes prayer difficult." I do not understand this complaint. Prayer *is* difficult. It is an attempted communication with occult metaphysical entities, a regular approach on transcendence. It requires that one collect oneself from one's own dispersal. Is there anything harder to do? To want prayer to be easy, to make it banal and frictionless, is to invite decadence into your faith. And if prayer is difficult, it is not because there are people of other faiths, or of no faith at all, in the society in which you live. Communal prayer is one of the pillars of traditional Judaism, and in its strict construction it requires a quorum of ten men; and I can testify that not once in my many attempts to pray in my synagogue was the presence of the church down the street an obstacle to my concentration. There were obstacles, to be sure, and sometimes they included the other nine Jews in

338

the room, but mostly they were inside myself. I would not have the audacity to blame my spiritual infirmities on others, and certainly not on my Christian neighbors.

Many years ago I got into a spat with William F. Buckley on this very point: he remarked that the social and cultural diversity of New York was making the formation of Catholic identity more difficult, and I replied that my difference from him was not the reason that he might be having trouble keeping his children in church. Anyway, all communities of faith in an open society are confronted by this challenge. (As Danielou sagely observes, "engagement in temporal affairs is at one and the same time a duty and a temptation.") Are we to conclude, then, with Danielou, that the transmission of religion is impossible in a multi-religious society? This would be perverse: it is precisely the philosophical and political framework of pluralism, of liberal indifference ("neutrality") to the fortunes of particular confessions, that makes such transmission possible, by leaving it in the hands of the believers themselves. If they fail, however, it is largely their own fault. Of course we could offer them some assistance by constricting and even closing down our society and thereby make their dream of conformity a reality. But close it down to whom, and for whom? Which faith will dominate, and why should other faiths trust it? Should the church or the mosque or the synagogue seize the government for the sake of their children? My children, or yours? These jeremiads against the separation of church and state can only have been composed by people who are confident that they would be the winners.

Religious traditions with historical memories of persecution should carefully ponder the moral consequences of undoing the separation. They might also consider whether Danielou's vision of the identification of religion with its environment does not betray one of the central tasks, and privileges, of religion, which is to be counter-cultural. When the church and the state are unified, the state will no longer hear the truth from the church. Social and political criticism will be heresy. The standpoint from which power may be criticized independently and disinterestedly, in the name of values that are supported only by their own validity, or by their supernaturalism, will have vanished. The efficacy of Martin Luther King, Jr.'s agitation was owed in large measure to the force of the religious language that he hurled against the policies of government; a stranger to the state, he came to chastise and to castigate. If there must be no established religion, it is in part because religion's role in society must be adversarial. There is an embarrassing passage in Danielou's book in which he notes that "Christianity works alongside those [institutions] which exist, purifying them of their excesses and bringing them into conformity with the demands of the spirit" — and so "it was in this way that it acted on slavery, not condemning it as such but creating a spirit which rendered its continuance impossible." But over here, in America, where no such alignment of religion with the institutions is required, there were Christians who denounced slavery directly and bitterly, and on Christian grounds. The abolitionists could say it straight; the critics were separated and free.

Here is Danielou's sentence again, except that I have altered one word: "Experience shows that it is practically impossible for any but the militant Jew to persevere in a milieu which offers him no support." I have heard that sentiment my entire life from people who were sincerely frightened by change, by their children's physical and spiritual mobility. For this reason, traditionalists like to stick together. The

340

Christianists, too, can stick together. They can also secede, in the manner of "the Benedict option," except of course that they are enjoined by the Gospels to do good in the world. Our society can become a collection of bubbles, a bubble of bubbles — not the best deployment of a multicultural society's resources, and certainly not any sort of tribute to the various traditions that are terrified of being tested by the world, but we are headed in that direction anyway. As a historical matter, the Jews in the West *did* persevere in a milieu which, to put it mildly, offered them no support. That milieu was Christianity. There were no sympathetic surroundings to buck them up and ratify their exertions. And ironically enough, it was not owing mainly to social isolation that they survived, and without possessing political power created a civilization. Even though the Jews lived in walled quarters of the city, they had many kinds of relationships with their Christian neighbors, and they were exposed, sometimes by compulsion, to Christianity regularly. (Some of them could not withstand the pressure of their otherness and converted.) But it was not a bubble that protected them and their tradition. A hostile environment permits no bubbles. What protected the Jews was their faith and their will, and perhaps also the steadfastness that is one of the rewards of minority experience. There is indeed a measure of heroism, or at least an extra measure of inner resources, required of all minority faiths, of Jews in Christian surroundings and of Christians in secular surroundings.

341

But here are the Christianists, whining that they do not run everything. How much compassion should we muster for the pain of the post-liberals? How hard is it, really, to be a Christian in America? I appreciate the constant dissonance that a religious individual experiences in our secular culture, not least because of its lunatic sexuality. Raising children in a digital society is a traditionalist's nightmare; the wayward influences get in like water under the door. So resistance must be offered, certainly, and not only by devout Christians. Resisting the world is one of the signature activities of the spiritually serious. "The greatest danger for the Christian," Danielou says, "does not come from persecution but from worldliness." But is the burden of resistance not worth the prize of freedom? The Christianists like to mock religious freedom, or as they prefer to call it, "religious freedom," as a counterfeit corollary of the separation. The First Amendment does not suffice for the apotheosis of their particular Christian ideal. There is something especially obnoxious about people who enjoy freedom and disparage it. Do they have no idea of what the world is like?

Where in America is a Christian prevented from practicing Christianity? Of course there are occasional tensions between certain interpretations of Christian fidelity and the law, such as selling a wedding cake to a gay couple, and the courts may not always rule in favor of the Christian party in a dispute, but this is not exactly being thrown to the lions. The frustration of a Christian in a non-Christian world is inevitable, but it is ahistorical and self-pitying to mistake frustration for persecution. (The American Jews who insist upon the erosion of their "religious freedom" in America are just as bratty.) There are ghastly wars against Christians taking place in many countries around the world now, but the United States is not one of them. As for the infamously naked public square, I see religious words and symbols, Christian words and symbols, wherever I wander. God is plastered all over America, and so is Jesus. I can live comfortably with the ubiquity of Christianity in my country, because my belief is not damaged by the evidence of a different belief, and because the evidence of their own belief delights many of my fellow citizens, and because other streets display other messages. The public square should illustrate the public.

And yet, all the glittering Christian iconography notwithstanding, America is not, in Danielou's phrase, "a Christendom," even if most of its inhabitants are Christian; and it is not the duty of Americans, even of Christian Americans, to make it one. This was the American innovation: to interpose rights and freedoms between the religious definition of the country and the religious persuasion of its majority. Insofar as Americans are a people, we are not a Christian people, because we have chosen to alienate no gods and no godless, to embark upon a kind of post-Humean experiment in securing a polytheistic tolerance for a monotheistic society. Perhaps, from the standpoint of justice, pluralism is a restoration of polytheism. No wonder it rubs certain true believers the wrong way. "Thou shalt have no other gods before Me": the One (or the Three-in-One, but never mind) must be the only one — this is the status anxiety of God. There is no room in the cosmos for many gods; but there is room in America.

The Christianists teach that it is the responsibility of Christians to influence the institutions of government in ways that will be favorable to the realization of their churchly goals. As Danielou writes, "Christianity ought for the sake of its own final end to influence the institutions of the earthly city." Enter the bizarre Adrian Vermeule, the man of the integralist hour. (It was he who issued that encomium about Nigel Farage.) He has a plan of influence, which he calls "integration from within." It is his retaliation against the separation. His plan is to infiltrate the government with post-liberals of his persuasion: "non-liberal actors strategically locate themselves within liberal institutions and work to undo the liberalism of the state from within. These actors possess a substantive comprehensive theory of the good, and seize opportunities to bring about its fulfillment through and by means of the very institutional machinery that the liberal state has providentially created." *Politique d'abord!* This is a program for a long march, even for a crusade; and even for the kind of organized hostile penetration, stealthy or otherwise, that provoked Sidney Hook in 1953 to lay down a splendid rule: heresy, yes; conspiracy, no.

"The state will have to be *re-integrated from within*, by the efforts of agents who occupy strategic positions in the shell of the liberal order," Vermeule explains. "Less Benedict, more Esther, Mordecai, Joseph, and Daniel." Those "agents," you see, "in various ways exploit their providential ties to political incumbents with very different views in order to protect their views and the community who shares them." Political incumbents: plainly he does not have only Nebuchadnezzar in mind. In the cases of Joseph and Esther, it is worth noting, their alleged efforts at reintegration involved deception: they were under deep cover, and we don't take kindly to that sort of thing in America. But Vermeule should read his Scripture more closely. Esther, Mordecai, Joseph, and Daniel may have performed certain services for the Egyptian, Babylonian, and Persian states, but they were not placed in their positions by the God of the Hebrew Bible for the purpose of reforming those states, or of making them over so as to achieve a Jewish purpose. They were there to protect their family and their people from eventual hardships, from famine and discrimination and slaughter. That is all. Egypt remained Egyptian and Babylon remained Babylonian and Persia remained Persian. In

344

any event Vermeule is not satisfied with the successes of the Jewish agents. "It is permissible to dream," he writes, "however fitfully, that other models may one day become relevant" — Saint Cecilia, whose "martyrdom helped to spark the explosive growth of the early church," and Saint Paul, who "preached the advent of a new order from within the very urban heart of the imperium." Vermeule is talking about the American government. Who does he expect to persuade with this sectarian rapture? Madison never looked better.

Vermeule has other bright ideas for his sacred subversion. By the grace of God, for example, the manipulative techniques of behavioral economics have been invented. "We have learned from behavioral economics that agents and administrative control over default rules may nudge whole populations in desirable directions." Are you nudging with me, Jesus? Like all revolutionaries, even reactionary ones, Vermeule is opportunistic about his methods and teleological about his history: "The vast bureaucracy created by liberalism in pursuit of a mirage of depoliticized governance may, by the invisible hand of Providence, be turned to new ends, becoming the great instrument with which to restore a substantive politics of the good." In this way, he and his gang will "find a strategic position from which to sear the liberal faith with hot irons." An American Christian, a professor at Harvard Law School, wrote those words. I seem to recall from the history of Christian painting that hot irons were what Romans did to Christians, not what Christians did to Romans. It is not, in any event, what Americans do to Americans.

Am I taking Vermeule's grisly metaphor too seriously? I don't think so. It is of a piece with the rhetorical violence of his other remarks about liberalism. For Vermeule, and for the other post-liberals, liberalism is not wrong, it is evil. It teaches depravity and tyranny. I confess that I find such an evaluation baffling, it defies what I know about history and what I perceive around me, though I have myself, from within the liberal camp, done my bit over the decades to challenge and to refute certain liberal dogmas. But here is Vermeule, warning that non-liberal or anti-liberal communities in America are in mortal danger, because they "must tremble indefinitely under the axe." At least the axe sometimes comes with a tax exemption. And here he is, in an even greater panic: "even if the liberal state lacks the time, resources, or attention span to eliminate *all* competing subcommunities collectively and simultaneously, it may still be able to eliminate any competitor at will, taken individually and one by one." This is, well, nuts. Vermeule has no reason to fear the jackboot of Nancy Pelosi in the middle of the night. But his extreme view of his position in contemporary America enables him to cast himself grandiosely. He is the lonely knight of the faith who has taken up the Cross to do battle with the Jeffersonian infidels.

For Vermeule, liberalism is not merely a political ideology, or a political party with which he disagrees — it is nothing less than a religion, "a fighting evangelistic faith," "a world religion" with "a soteriology, an eschatology, a clergy (or 'clerisy'), and sacraments." If he says so. Calling liberalism a religion no doubt makes the war against it feel more holy. Yet liberalism differs strikingly from religion, and even more strikingly from Catholic religion, in at least one fundamental way: it has a different principle of authority, intellectually and institutionally. This difference was established, prejudicially, by Cardinal Newman in an appendix to his autobiography — a text with which every honest liberal must make himself familiar. Liberalism, he propounded, is "the exercise of thought upon matters, in which, from the constitution of the mind, thought cannot be brought to any successful issue, and therefore is out of place... Liberalism is the mistake of subjecting to human judgment those revealed doctrines which are in their nature beyond and independent of it, and of claiming to determine on intrinsic grounds the truth and value of propositions which rest for their reception simply on the external authority of the Divine Word." Simply!

Premises, premises. I have always envied people who find too much reason in the world. My view of what hobbles the world is different. Whatever the limits of reason, we are a long way from reaching them. When rationalists seem to be acting imperialistically, they can be challenged rationally, on their own grounds, and a rational argument for humility or restraint can be made; but no argument can be made with anybody who dissociates reason from truth, who repudiates "intrinsic grounds," who demands of authority that it be "external." The integralist enemies of reason are Rortyans with chalices. I recall gratefully how I came by my own enthusiasm for reason: when I was a boy in yeshiva, we wondered, as we studied Genesis 1:26-27, which aspect of the human being was the one that demonstrated the divine image in which he and she were said to have been created — what attribute could we possibly have in common with God? We pored over commentators and discovered an answer: the mind. I have been grateful ever since for having a religious sanction for my critical thinking about religion. But He knew what He was doing, right?

III

The most ambitious, and the most ludicrous, attempt by the Catholic integralists to discredit the separation of church and state is a work of history. It is called *Before Church and State: A Study of the Social Order in the Sacramental Kingdom of St. Louis*

IX, which appeared in 2017, and its author is Andrew Willard Jones, a theologian and historian at Franciscan University in Steubenville, Ohio. Jones is a learned man, at least about the Latin sources that are useful to his purpose, which is to paint a portrait of a time before the separation, a period in history when wholeness existed and everything went lustrously together, a "differentiated" but fundamentally seamless society that was unified, top to bottom, in its social and political order, by a pervasive belief in Christianity and in the unity of altar and throne. A "sacramental kingdom," a golden age, a world we have lost. Jones has written five hundred pages about thirteenth-century France "to establish a vision of a social order very different from the liberal," in which "integrated players" operated in "one field of action upon which both the spiritual and temporal functioned."

Jones contends that one of the consequences of the separation of church and state has been the widespread conviction that we live in two discrete realms, the sacred and the secular, and that too much medieval history has been written with this dualist error in mind. His adopts his theology as his methodology:

> I argue that thirteenth-century France was built as
> a 'most Christian kingdom,' a term that the papacy
> frequently used in reference to it. I do not mean that the
> kingdom of France was a State with a Christian ideol-
> ogy. I mean that it *was* Christian, fundamentally. There
> was no State lurking beneath the kingdom's religious
> trappings. There was no State at all, but a Christian
> kingdom. In this kingdom, neither the 'secular' nor the
> 'religious' existed. I do not mean that the religious was
> everywhere and that the secular had not yet emerged
> from under it. I mean *they did not exist at all.*

The objectives of this pre-separated and numinously integrated kingdom were utterly unlike "the assumptions of modern politics": they were the *negotium pacis et fidei — the business of the peace and the faith.*" In Jones' account, those are the motives and the intentions of the medieval figures that he describes; they act not for the sake of interests or passions, but for the peace and the faith. "Society was organized around the notion of peace, a peace that was real, and not simply another name for submission." Jones further asserts that this is how the people of thirteenth-century France understood themselves, and that we must therefore understand them "on their own terms," because "their language is better at capturing who they were than ours is." This Christian idyll was exemplified in the figure of the king, Louis IX, the perfect Christian monarch, who reigned from 1226 to 1270, and was canonized in 1297.

These methodological cautions should not be mistaken for another warning against "presentism" in the writing of history or another exercise in the history of mentalities. Jones is writing triumphalist history, sacred history, in which the hand of God is revealed in the power of His representatives on earth. There is a tradition of such "historiography" in all the faiths. (In the Jewish case, sacred history had to be dissociated from triumphalist history, for reasons I will get to in a moment.) While this may be the way Christians do history, it is not the way historians do history. That is not because historians are the blinkered products of a secular age. Look again at Jones' claim that the distinction between sacred and secular did not exist in thirteenth century France. What can this possibly mean? It is true that Louis' France was officially and significantly a religious society, in which earth was universally believed to be subordinated to heaven. But anybody who has studied a religious society knows that the totality is never total. There are precincts of religiously untreated reality, unhallowed spots, everywhere. Consider only the culture of thirteenth-century France, its literature and its music. (Jones has no interest in such things.) It is full of — do you not like the word "secular"? — profane humane experience lived by mentally free men and women who carry desire and alienation and humor through a world in which everything is not clear. The religious polyphony of the medieval church, for example, the stupendous literature of the masses, found regular inspiration in the irreligious songs of ordinary folk. For secularity is not primarily a social or political category. It is a description of a constitutive trait of human existence: its creatureliness. We are dust and clay, even if not only dust and clay; we are animals, even if not like other animals; we live in time, even with visions of eternity; we decay. No "sacramental" interpretation or arrangement of our lives can nullify our intrinsic earthiness. It will never be fully incorporated or completely dissipated. "The secular" was not born on July 14, 1789, and neither was "the individual." The magical kingdom for which Jones yearns never existed.

For many of Louis' subjects, moreover, there was nothing magical about it. For them, it was a realm of oppression and massacre. Jones' treatment of the political history of Louis' France is outrageous. He extenuates the Inquisition, which was established during Louis' reign by Pope Gregory IX, and pokes fun at its "black legend," which he dismisses as merely another instance of "the mental furniture of the enlightened mind." He seeks to show that there was no significant difference between the inquisitors and the *enquêteurs*, or the itinerant magistrates whom the king dispatched throughout the land to settle local disputes, and that both the religious inquisitors and the civil judges were "dimensions of the same project," which was "*the business of the peace and the faith.*" Jones' apologetics continue: "The ecclesiastical and the secular [oops!] 'inquisitions' [were they not inquisitions?] were integral [abracadabra!] institutions within a complex social order that was rooted in a sacramental understanding of the cosmos that did not allow for the divorce of the spiritual from the temporal." Similarly, in the Albigensian Crusade, another glory of thirteenth-century France, a genocidal campaign that exterminated Cathar belief by exterminating Cathar believers, "the *business* was directed against what was understood as a heretical and violent society in the south." After all, "a heretic shattered the peace." Well, yes. That is his or her role. Is it presentism — or worse, liberalism — to suggest that such an acquiescent and exculpatory tone will not do? There is not a trace of horror in Jones' accounts of the crimes of his church. He is so busy making church and state disappear into each other that he is dead to the consequences of Constantinism for non-Christians. One way of describing a liberal democracy is as an order in which heresy is just another opinion. If this is what writing Christian history from the inside looks like, I invite the Christian historian to step outside.

351

The Jews are mentioned six times in Jones' history of the illiberal paradise in medieval France. They are all glancing references in which anti-Jewish ordinances are cited in passing. The subaltern status of Jews in the kingdom, and the atrocious ways in which it was enforced, is not a theme over which Jones cares to linger. Here is what you will not learn from *Before Church and State*. The reign of Louis IX was a series of monarchically supervised catastrophes for the Jewish community of France.

Christianism

"The Jews, odious to God and men," wrote one of the king's biographers, "he detested so much that he was unable to look upon them." It was Louis, according to his seneschal Jean de Joinville, the author of the most renowned biography, who declared that "no one who is not a very learned clerk should argue with [a Jew]. A layman, as soon as he hears the Christian faith maligned, should defend it only by the sword, with a good thrust in the belly as far as the sword will go." *Tant comme elle y peut entrer*: the king was monstrous.

Louis organized a devastating attack on the economic basis of Jewish life in his kingdom, which was moneylending. The throne announced that it would no longer enforce the collection of Jewish debts, and it reduced and even cancelled debts that Christians owed to Jews. Jews were forced to re-pay loans from Christians. New controls were imposed on Jewish loans and Jewish goods were confiscated. This was not only a campaign against usury, an economic policy, it was also a campaign against Jews, an ethnic policy — as, for example, in this royal edict: "The Jews must desist from usury, blasphemy, magic, and necromancy." And alongside this royal campaign the baronial classes were permitted all manner of excess in the economic oppression of the Jews on their lands. Finally Rome was offended by this despoliation, and in a papal letter in 1233 Pope Gregory noted with disapproval that "some of the Jews, unable to pay what security was considered sufficient in their case, perished miserably, it is said, through hunger, thirst, and privation of prisons, and to the moment some are still held in chains."

After the sustained royal assault on the economic sustenance of the Jews came the sustained royal assault on their religious sustenance. In 1239, under the poisonous influence of a converted Jew, one in a long line of such apostates who turned virulently against the people that they left, Pope Gregory launched a campaign against the Talmud, which was (and still is) the legal and spiritual foundation of rabbinical Judaism. He asked the vengeful convert to collect the Talmudic materials that offended Christianity and sent them out, with an accompanying invitation to take action against them, to "our dear sons the Kings of France, England, Aragon, Navarre, Castille, Leon, and Portugal." The only king who accepted his invitation was Louis IX of France. The books of the Jews were ordered to be expropriated by the beginning of Lent in 1240. They were seized as the Jews were in their synagogues. The prosecuting convert drew up a list of thirty-five charges, an inventory of Talmudic passages that allegedly slandered the Christian faith, and between June 25 and June 27, 1240 there occurred in Paris a public disputation, in which the Talmud was put on trial. There are two unofficial Latin protocols of the proceedings and one longer Hebrew account. The defenders of the Talmud included some of the giants of medieval Jewish learning. They lost, of course, and two years later, in June 1242, twenty-four wagonloads with thousands of Jewish books were publicly burned in Paris. It was a cultural disaster for French Jewry. Wrenching Hebrew poems of lamentation were composed about the holocaust of the books. And the king did not relent. In 1247 and 1248 Louis ordered further confiscations of Jewish books and then gave the campaign against the Talmud another royal endorsement in 1253. It continued until the end of his reign. In the year before he died, Louis sponsored the rabid conversionist efforts of Paul Christian, or Pablo Christiani, the converted Jew who had debated Nahmanides in the extraordinary disputation in Barcelona in 1263. He was given royal authority to "preach to the Jews the word of light and to compel the

Jews to respond fully." An anonymous Jew left this testimony of his efforts: "Know that each day we were over a thousand souls in the royal court or in the Dominican court, pelted with stones. Praise to our Creator, not one of us turned to the religion of vanity and lies."

There was still another way in which Louis IX distinguished himself in the history of anti-Semitism. He was a Crusading king, and twice went to the holy land to make war on its Muslims (he spent four years there in his first attempt and died in his second attempt); and he was so tolerant of the anti-Jewish atrocities committed by French Crusaders on their way east that in 1236 he was reprimanded by the Pope himself, who had heard reports that the Jews in France were living "as under a new Egyptian enslavement." "Force the Crusaders to restore to the Jews all that has been stolen," the pontiff scolded the king, "that you may prove yourself to be an exhibition of good works." But this papal reprimand is not the distinction to which I refer. Like many rulers in the history of Christendom, Louis sought to segregate the Jews of his realm — to this end, for example, he forbade Christians from serving as nurses to Jewish children and as servants in Jewish homes. But then he went further: he ordered the Jews to wear a badge. The royal ordinance reads: "Since we wish that the Jews be distinguishable from Christians and be recognizable, we order you that, at the order of our dear brother in Christ, Paul Christian, of the Order of Preaching Brethren, you impose signs upon each and every Jew of both sexes — a circle of felt or yellow cloth, stitched upon the outer garment in front and in back. The diameter of the circle must be four fingers wide; its area must be the size of a palm." Saint Louis!

None of this is to be found in Jones' hundreds of dense pages. Instead he has the temerity to write that in the sacramental order of Louis IX, where there was no separation of church and state, "society was organized around the notion of peace, a peace that was real, and not simply another name for submission." By giving his book the title that he gave it, he clearly implies that life was better and less sinful back then, and that this story of the Middle Ages is in some way of allegorical utility to our unsacramental country. I note in fairness that Jones' nostalgia has provoked mixed feelings among the integralists. Vermeule plainly states that "there can be no return to the integrated regime of the thirteenth century, whatever its attractions." But it is a pragmatic objection: Christians must face the sorrowful fact that those "attractions" can no longer be theirs. They were born too late for the Capetian utopia. Of course none of the integralists care to acknowledge all the people for whom the kingdom was dystopian, or that the thirteenth century was not integrated, except in theory. Father Waldstein is even more stubborn, and speaks up for the politics of nostalgia. "I am not going to let myself be bullied out of my nostalgia'" he protests. "I reject the whole notion that nostalgia is something bad." So do I, especially these days. But surely nostalgia for something bad is something bad.

355

I assume that the general picture of the anti-Jewish vehemence of Louis IX is known not only to Jones, but also to some of the admirers of his book — it is not exactly a secret, even if the repulsive details are mainly the possessions of scholars. And so, given their silence on this matter, I assume also that they can live with it. It is an acceptable price for the sacramental kingdom. That is how teleological history operates. In one of his more revealing passages, Vermeule expresses his impatience with too much ethical fussing about his eschaton. "Of course it's true — it's obvious! — that there are versions of non-liberalism that are worse than liberalism. At a certain point, however, people can no longer abide perpetually living in fear of the worst-case scenario." Vermeule would have us assess fascism probabilistically. He is right that worst-case scenario thinking is irritating and easily exploited. But there are situations involving questions of justice in which worst-case scenario thinking is also moral thinking. The moral worth of a society is not quantitatively determined, nor should its commitments to principle await an analysis of risk. Vermeule's peculiar mixture of spirituality and social science lands him in a morally dubious place. Perpetually living in fear of fascism is precisely how we should be living, now and forever, and especially in an era of fascism's return.

Vermeule relates an anecdote about a colleague's anxiety. "In a fully Catholic polity," his friend asked him, "the sort you would like to bring about, what would happen to me, a Jew?" He condescendingly admires the "passionate concreteness" of the question, its affecting concern with "the fate of an individual, a people, and the shape that a polity might take." For him it was a dialogically romantic moment. But there was nothing romantic about the moment for his friend. He was demanding to know if the realization of Vermeule's political program would require him to pack his bags. Vermeule answered him with more condescension, and recorded his answer in a coy parenthesis: "(Nothing bad, I assured him.)" His parenthetical assurance is not good enough. He might just as well have winked. The roots of his quasi-theocratic ideal are rotten with Jew-hatred, and so are some of his intellectual and political allies, as he might trouble himself to notice on his next visit to Budapest or Warsaw.

IV

The most prominent policy of Catholic integralism, its putative contribution to the resolution of our crisis, is "common good constitutionalism," whose primary author is Adrian Vermeule. The polemical energy of his religious writing disappears into a thicket of legal and philosophical abstractions in his legal writing, even though he prides himself on his aversion to theory, which he regards as another vice of the liberal elite. The idea is pretty simple: that American constitutional practice "should take as its starting point substantive moral principles that conduce to the common good, principles that officials (including, but by no means limited to, judges) should read into the majestic generalities and ambiguities of the written Constitution." This is the same "substantive comprehensive theory of the good" with which he equipped his post-liberal infiltrators of American institutions. Common good constitutionalism is presented as an exciting alternative to other doctrines of constitutional interpretation, and also as a revival of the classical tradition in law.

First, the good news. The grip of originalism upon the conservative legal mind has been loosened. Vermeule and his colleagues no longer wish to be trapped in the eighteenth century. They have recognized that the founders were themselves not originalists, and that they differed significantly among themselves, so that there were many views that could be treated as canonical, which is not helpful to scholars and judges who seek to locate a definitive old authority. While it would be an exaggeration to say that these conservatives have discovered a living Constitution, they do seem to represent a new conservative respect for contemporaneity. I guess it is easier to admit contemporaneity into your understanding if you are operating under the aspect of eternity. "For Catholic scholars in particular," Vermeule observes, "it is simply inadmissible — inconsistent with the whole tradition — to imply that law has no objective content beyond the text and original understanding of particular positive laws, or that [law] is nothing more than the interpreter's subjective and arbitrary desires." Law must refer back to an objective source of legitimacy, to some abiding principle that cannot be reduced to the wishes and the partialities of any individual or group. This belief in objectivity, an outcropping of rock in a sea of perspectives, is commendable. There remains the question of what abiding principle Vermeule has in mind.

Common good constitutionalism is a restoration of moral values to the heart of the legal enterprise. Vermeule takes pains to show that his doctrine is not simply a substitution of morality for law, or that "it reduces legal questions to all-things-considered moral decision-making from first principles." The relationship between legal rules and "a higher source of law" is more complicated, he shows; and I believe him. These complications, the serpentine methods of interpretation and argument in our schools and our courts, are presumably what rescue the common gooders from arrant "judicial activism" and all the other conservative prohibitions that conservatives anyway violate regularly. But I see no way to deny that in the end Vermeule seeks to establish a meta-historical standard of ethical value as the ground of law — a remoralization of law. (As an antidote, not least, for the demoralization of law professors.) In fact, Vermeule admits to "a candid willingness to 'legislate morality' — indeed, a recognition that all legislation is necessarily founded on some substantive conception of morality, and that the promotion of morality is a core and legitimate function of authority." Well said. I admit that I am not completely horrified by this. I believe in the grandeur of meaningful living with others and I support intellectual ambition in the courts. As far as I can tell, liberal jurisprudence of the last thirty years tried very hard to squeeze first principles, moral principles, as far out of the law as it could; this was called "judicial minimalism," and by my lights it represented a collapse in scale and an abdication of responsibility. The law was shrunk and intimidated. The liberals unilaterally disarmed, leaving the impression that they stand only for proceduralism and rule-regulated behavior. The higher dimension of law was usurped by a fetishization of text and a reading of statutes that was designed to be as unrepercussive as possible. Of course not all, or even most, of the cases that come before judges require exercises in moral reasoning, but many of them do, and more generally I do not see how you can work in the field of justice without an ever-present moral sensibility, an intense awareness of the pertinence of values. No society can function without empiricism and no society can live for empiricism.

That liberal diffidence was conceived as a retort to the moral interpretation of law ("there is inevitably a moral dimension to an action at law") promulgated influentially by Ronald Dworkin, and Vermeule's breakthrough is Dworkinism for the right. I mean methodologically, and in his larger kind of justification; but Dworkin's view of liberalism, by contrast, must be anathema to Vermeule, who is another one of those communitarian preachers for whom liberalism is nothing more than a maniacal pursuit of "individualism" and the rest be damned. (The Antichrist is Mill.) Who, really, can be against the common good? But also, *what is it?* The integralists throw the phrase around like a talisman with healing powers. Its level of generality may be emotionally edifying but it is intellectually crippling. Before it can be critically assessed, it needs to be specified. After all, there are many versions of the common

Christianism

good, and they do not all go together. (There are philosophical contradictions that are not amenable to integration.)

According to Danielou, "politics exists to secure the common good. An essential element of the common good is that man should be able to fulfill himself at all levels. The religious level cannot be excluded." An ecumenical religious humanism; fine. Father Waldstein's characterization of the common good starts out with a lovely thought: "A common good is distinguished from a private good by not being diminished when it is shared" — rather like what the old mystics said about the bounty of light. "For this reason," he continues, "common goods are better than private goods." Moving sedulously toward politics, he stipulates that "the primary intrinsic common good is peace." Still lovely, but still general. And then, the descent into specificity: "the temporal common good is subordinate to the eternal common good, and the temporal rulers are subject to the hierarchy of the Church." Until the Second Coming, that is, when everything will be celestially transfigured. It makes you miss the generalities.

And Vermeule? He is made of harsher stuff. His "substantive moral principles that conduce to the common good" include "respect for the authority of rule and rulers; respect for the hierarchies need for society to function; solidarity within and among families, social groups, workers' unions, trade associations, and professions; appropriate subsidiarity, or respect for the legitimate roles of public bodies and associations at all levels of government; and a candid willingness to 'legislate morality'...." It is only a list, and we all have our lists. Some of his list seems reasonable, but all of it awaits reasoning. Indeed, it has a catechismic quality. The problem is that it is impossible to read Vermeule's constitutional proposals without recalling his religious certitudes. Is it revealing that he begins his list with

360

a validation of political power? Even when he writes about America he refers to "the ruler"; but we do not have a ruler, we have a president. (Not surprisingly, Vermeule has espoused an almost authoritarian view of presidential power.) He endorses "soft paternalism" and remarks that "law is parental." He asserts that the common good may be legislated by rulers "if necessary even against the subjects' own perceptions of what is best for them" — an uncontroversial observation about political reality even in republics, but without a whiff of democratic deference and haunting in its evocation of Christian rulers of the past.

Vermeule has no special place in his heart for democracy, which he views mainly as an instrument of liberalism: what matters for him is that the common good, whatever it is, be achieved, and this can be done in a variety of "forms of constitutional ordering centered around robust executive government" depending on "socio-economic conditions." To attain his goals, "questions of institutional design are not settled *a priori.*" This may account for his acceptance of illiberal democracies and their authoritarian leaders. The road to heaven is paved with bad intentions. He writes chillingly that whereas the liberal virtues of "civility, tolerance, and their ilk are bad masters and tyrannous when made into idols," they may be useful "when rightly placed within a larger ordering to good substantive ends" — to wit, "civility and tolerance may be cryptic terms with which to measure the substantive bounds of the views and conduct that will be permitted in a rightly ordered society, but such a society will also value charity, forbearance, and prudence." Is it a liberal blindness to suggest that charity is not an adequate substitute for social policy, and that nobody who has ever experienced a violation of his rights and an abrogation of his freedoms should suffice with forbearance? Vermeule's imagination of power is too happy to include its abuses. And so he cheerfully announces that "the claim [in *Planned Parenthood v. Casey*] that each individual may 'define his own concept of existence, of meaning, of the universe and of the mystery of human life' should be not only rejected but stamped as abominable" — stamped by whom? And also that "the state will enjoy authority to curb the social and economic pretensions of the urban-gentry liberals who so often place their own satisfactions (financial and sexual) and the good of their class or social milieu above the common good." Why not shoot them?

Enough. I would not trust this man with the Constitution of the United States. In Vermeule's common good constitutionalism I do not see much common and I do not see much good. There is something pathetic about faith that seeks the validation of power, that needs to dominate a state to prove its truth. Such a faith is too easily rattled. It has forsaken the still small voice. Why is community not enough for the Christianists? Why must they have society? They will have to learn the art of absolutes without absolutisms. To my Christian friends, I say: neither Benedict nor Louis, please. I say also that America was not designed for integralism, because it was founded on the wisest intuition in modern political history — that conflict is an ineradicable characteristic of human existence, that a perfectly harmonious state of affairs is a sign of freedom's waning, that unanimity is the program of despots, that social consensus is not the condition of social peace. This is even more sharply so in a religiously and ethnically heterogeneous society, in which commonality cannot be complete but only sufficient to the purposes of a fair and decent polity, and differences may overlap but never coincide. The overlap is where the common good,

362

whatever it is, may be found. The overlap is where democracy flourishes. We will never rid ourselves of the tensions of our complexity, and we should be alarmed if we did. Studying the Catholic integralists, I looked back fondly to the days of John Courtney Murray, S.J. and the American integrity of his non-integralism, his profound wrestlings with the religious realities of an open society, his theology of the tensions.

There is nothing that this country needs more than a common good. In the name of liberalism, and more often of progressivism that is mistaken for liberalism, the American commonality has likewise been severely damaged. The intolerance of the godless is fully the match for the intolerance of the godful. Progressives are attempting to regulate thought and speech and behavior as if they were integralists. What unites all the varieties of contemporary American integralism is that freedom is not what moves them the most. The Christianists have nothing of interest to say about it, and neither do the secular enforcers on the other side. Yet it is this, the inalienable freedom of the mind in matters of belief, its immunity to compulsion, that will eventually defeat them all, as it defeated Josiah. His reformation failed. The people deceived him. The midrash tells that the king sent out pairs of students to survey the success of his campaign against the idols. They could not find any idols in the houses that they inspected, and the king was satisfied with their report. What they did not know was that the dwellers had painted half an idolatrous image on each of the doors to their homes, so that when they closed them upon the departure of the thought police they beheld their forbidden images. The fools, we must learn to respect them.

Christianism

CONTRIBUTORS

LAURA KIPNIS is the author, most recently, of *Love in the Time of Contagion: A Diagnosis*.

DORIAN ABBOT is a geophysicist at the University of Chicago.

BERNARD-HENRI LÉVY is the author most recently of *The Will to See: Dispatches from a World of Misery and Hope*. This essay was translated by Steven Kennedy.

BRUCE D. JONES is the author of *To Rule the Waves: How Control of the World's Oceans Shapes the Fate of the Superpowers*. He is the director of the Project on International Order and Strategy and a Senior Fellow at the Brookings Institution.

DURS GRÜNBEIN is a German poet and essayist. His most recent collection of poems in English is *Porcelain: Poem on the Downfall of My City*.

DAVID GREENBERG teaches history at Rutgers University and is completing a biography of John Lewis.

INGRID ROWLAND is the author, among many books, of *From Pompeii: The Afterlife of a Roman Town*. She teaches at Notre Dame.

DAVID A. BELL is a professor of history at Princeton University and the author most recently of *Men on Horseback: The Power of Charisma in the Age of Revolution*.

NATHANIEL MACKEY's most recent volume of poems is *Breath and Precarity*.

ROBERT COOPER is a British and European diplomat, and the author of *The Ambassadors: Thinking about Diplomacy from Machiavelli to Modern Times*.

STEVEN M. NADLER is a professor of philosophy and a member of the Center for Jewish Studies at University of Wisconsin at Madison, and the author of many books on Spinoza and the seventeenth century.

MORTEN HØI JENSEN is the author of *A Difficult Death: The Life and Work of Jans Peter Jacobsen*.

CLARA COLLIER is a writer in California.

HELEN VENDLER is the A. Kingsley Porter University Professor Emerita at Harvard University.

HARIS VLAVIANOS is a Greek poet, translator and historian. The poem "Poetic License" was originally written in English.

CELESTE MARCUS is the managing editor of *Liberties*.

LEON WIESELTIER is the editor of *Liberties*.

Liberties — A Journal of Culture and Politics is available by annual subscription and by individual purchase from bookstores and online booksellers.

Annual subscriptions provide a discount from the individual cover price and include complete digital access to current and previous issues along with the printed version. Subscriptions can be ordered from libertiesjournal.com. Professional discounts for active military; faculty, students, and education administrators; government employees; those working in the not-for-profit sector. Gift subscriptions are also available at libertiesjournal.com.

366

As a matter of principle, *Liberties Journal* does not accept advertising or other funding sources that might influence our independence. We look to our readers and those individuals and institutions that believe in our mission for contributions — large and small — to support this not-for-profit publication.

If you are interested in making a donation to *Liberties*, please contact Bill Reichblum, publisher, by email at bill@libertiesjournal.com or by phone: 2 0 2 - 8 9 1 - 7 1 5 9.

Liberties — A Journal of Culture and Politics is distributed to booksellers in the United States by Publishers Group West; in Canada by Publishers Group Canada; and, internationally by Ingram Publisher Services International.

LIBERTIES, LIBERTIES: A JOURNAL OF CULTURE AND POLITICS, is published quarterly in Fall, Winter, Spring, and Summer by Liberties Journal Foundation.

ISBN 978-1-7357187-6-7
ISSN 2692-3904

Printed in Canada.

The insignia that appears throughout *Liberties* is derived from details in Botticelli's drawings for Dante's *Divine Comedy*, which were executed between 1480 and 1495.